《国际汉语文化研究（第四辑）》

编委会

国际汉语文化研究

International Studies of Chinese Language & Culture

（第四辑）

四川大学出版社

项目策划：周　洁
责任编辑：周　洁
责任校对：宋　颖
封面设计：墨创文化
责任印制：王　炜

图书在版编目（CIP）数据

国际汉语文化研究．第四辑 / 刘荣主编．— 成都：四川大学出版社，2019.12
ISBN 978-7-5690-3197-3

Ⅰ．①国… Ⅱ．①刘… Ⅲ．①汉语－对外汉语教学－教学研究 Ⅳ．①H195.3

中国版本图书馆 CIP 数据核字（2019）第 268913 号

书名　国际汉语文化研究（第四辑）
Guoji Hanyu Wenhua Yanjiu（Di-si Ji）

主　　编	刘　荣
出　　版	四川大学出版社
地　　址	成都市一环路南一段 24 号（610065）
发　　行	四川大学出版社
书　　号	ISBN 978-7-5690-3197-3
印前制作	四川胜翔数码印务设计有限公司
印　　刷	郫县犀浦印刷厂
成品尺寸	170mm×240mm
印　　张	12.25
字　　数	220 千字
版　　次	2019 年 12 月第 1 版
印　　次	2019 年 12 月第 1 次印刷
定　　价	46.00 元

◆ 读者邮购本书，请与本社发行科联系。
电话：(028)85408408/(028)85401670/
(028)86408023　邮政编码：610065
◆ 本社图书如有印装质量问题，请寄回出版社调换。
◆ 网址：http://press.scu.edu.cn

四川大学出版社
微信公众号

目　　录

对外汉语教学

孔子学院

古代汉语

现代汉语

对外汉语教学

专门用途汉语的研究特点与趋势分析

——基于国内主要期刊2014—2017年研究内容的分析

白巧燕

北京语言大学人文社会科学学部；西南财经大学国际教育学院

摘　要：随着汉语作为第二语言教学的不断发展，对有关专门用途汉语教学的研究也日益深入。本文通过对2014—2017年国内主要期刊关于专门用途汉语研究论文的内容进行梳理，发现专门用途汉语的教学与研究主要在教材研究、专门用途汉语教学、预科教育中的教学与研究、需求分析理论相关研究等方面展开。有关专门用途汉语的研究内容越来越多样化，研究中对概念的界定更加清晰，研究方法多以内省式研究为主。本文认为，在今后的研究中应更多地运用实证研究方法，加强专门用途汉语教学资源的建设，更加注重学术汉语方面的研究。

关键词：专门用途汉语；需求分析；学术汉语

Research Characteristics and Trend Analysis of Chinese for Specific Purposes

—Based on Research Content of Major Domestic Journals from 2014 to 2017

Bai Qiaoyan

Department of Humanities and Social Sciences, Beijing Language and Culture University;
College of International Education, Southwestern University of Finance and Economics

Abstract: With the development of Chinese as second language teaching, research related to Chinese for Specific Purposes (CSP) has become increasingly widespread. This paper analyzes the content of CSP research papers of major domestic journals in 2014-2017 and finds that the research on CSP is mainly carried out in aspects bellows: research on Chinese textbooks for specific purposes, teaching and research of Chinese for specific purposes, teaching and research in preparatory education for Chinese for Specific Purposes, research on needs analysis theory and research methods. It is found that the research content of Chinese for Specific Purposes is more and more diversified. Most of the research methods are introspective researches, and there is still a lack of empirical research; and with the increase of academic learners, more attention should be paid to the study of academic Chinese.

Keywords: Chinese for Specific Purposes (CSP); Needs Analysis; Academic Chinese

一、引言

本文收集了《语言教学与研究》《世界汉语教学》《语言文字应用》《华文教学与研究》《国际汉语教学研究》《汉语学习》《海外华文教育》等期刊中2014年1月至2017年12月涵盖商务汉语、专门用途汉语、需求分析等关键词的相关文献，共19篇，并对其进行分类整理，归纳已有研究的现状与意义，发现学术研究动态，总结现有研究存在的问题，思考进一步研究的方式与方法。本文采用内容分析法（content analysis），通过对核心期刊、相关度高的普通期刊中包含“专门用途汉语”“需求分析”等关键词的内容进行搜索、整理、分析，尝试梳理以下问题：发现近三年专门用途汉语所涉及的研究内容、研究重点以及在专门用途汉语研究上发生的变化，从而发现今后专门用途汉语研究有哪些新的研究空间。

表 1　本文所选国内主要期刊

材料来源类别	时间	具体内容
核心期刊	2014 年 1 月—2017 年 12 月	《世界汉语教学》《语言教学与研究》《语言文字应用》《华文教学与研究》
普通期刊	2014 年 1 月—2017 年 12 月	《海外华文教育》《国际教育研究》《云南师范大学学报（对外汉语教学与研究版）》

本文的检索对象限定在语言学专业核心期刊及与汉语教学相关度高的普通期刊，为更好地了解学术前沿动态，时间选定在 2014—2017 年，再以关键词“专门用途汉语”并“商务汉语”并含“ESP”或“需求分析”进行二次搜索，共收集近三年间在核心期刊发表的论文 19 篇①，并按研究内容进行分类，如表 2 所示：

表 2　2014—2017 年国内主要期刊专门用途汉语研究内容统计

项目	研究内容分类	分类依据	篇目	比例
1	专门用途教材研究	教材述评类研究、专门用途国别化教材、多语种军事汉语教材	4	21%
2	专门用途教学研究	课程与教学设计目标、教学设计、特殊目的短期项目目标设计、专门用途语言教学目标定位	8	42%
3	预科教育中的专门用途汉语研究与教学	宏观指导研究、预科教育中专门用途汉语研究	3	16%
4	需求分析理论的研究与应用	学习需求、需求导向、基于需求分析理论的教学应用	3	16%
5	其他	研究方法、理论认识	1	5%

① 笔者通过题名和关键词检索了中国知网期刊数据库，搜集了目前刊登在主要期刊上的专门用途汉语教学的相关研究。虽然仅就搜集到的论文来对该领域的研究作结论尚存在一定的局限性，但也可大致反映出目前这一领域的主要研究动态。

二、研究的主要内容

（一）专门用途汉语教材研究

针对专门用途汉语教材的建设，吴中伟（2017）提出应完善相关基础理论研究与建设，加强相关的语言学理论（如语域理论和语类理论）和语言教学理论（如需求分析理论）的应用，进一步加强对学习者的目标需求和学习需求的分析，拓展对不同领域目标情境和目标任务的调查和采样，制订专门用途汉语教学的标准和大纲。刘弘、蒋内利（2015）对2003—2012年603篇对外汉语教材研究论文的内容进行分析，采用描写统计分析方法，指出对外汉语教材研究的重点及其变化情况。

汪景民（2017）从编写背景、编写思路、指导思想三个部分阐述了《中级军事汉语》的编写过程，通过与《初级军事汉语》的比较，发现《中级军事汉语》在教材编写中注意到了学习者的需求，较为清晰地界定了适用对象为军事院校的汉语专业学生，这较《初级军事汉语》有所进步，但该文中所说的“多语种”教材即为当下一本多版的教材，并没有进行国别化的改编。文章更多的是作者自身对教材编写实践的思考，并没有教材编写的实证材料。另外，关于如何界定语料的难度、词汇的难度等文中并未提起。

赖铮（2017）通过对国际汉语教育推广的大环境、学习者在二语学习中较多使用比较法以及比较法对国别化教材的开发优势的研究，提出基于比较法的国别化商务教材开发的几个原则：（1）文化领先，文化主题尽量涉及学生熟悉的母语文化；（2）课堂活动、课后练习注重交际性、难度适中；（3）提供真实的商务案例和具体操作。赖铮提出，教材语言编写应重视真实性，不能为练语言点而生编对话，同时他也提出了学界关注的一个问题：国别化教材不是同一种教材的不同注释版本，也不是针对不同国家汉语学习者而特别设计的教材。附加中外语言对比分析的“学习手册”是一种尝试。赖铮在文章中提出，教材中每个对话均应提供两个不同版本的对话做比较，如中国人打招呼的对话、带有翻译腔的打招呼对话，以及厦门人打招呼的对话等。笔者认为无此必要，因为在学习的过程中，学习者自然会与其母语进行比较，教师引导指出差异即可。

（二）专门用途汉语教学研究

针对商务汉语认识的几个误区，张黎（2015）结合专门用途语言教学指出：（1）商务汉语不一定是一种单一的语言社会变体；（2）商务汉语的特点不只体现在词汇层面；（3）商务汉语不一定只是工作或专业学习活动中使用的语言；（4）商务汉语教学不一定只能在具有一定汉语基础之后再开始；（5）商务汉语教师不一定要熟悉与商务相关的专业知识。这些问题在商务汉语教学中长期存在，张黎的研究客观清晰地解决了长期困扰研究者的几个核心问题，对零起点商务汉语教学、基于需求分析与目标情景分析进行的课程研究，以及教材编写都具有积极意义。

笔者考察发现，三年来所选期刊中关于专门用途汉语教学的研究主要集中在教学设计及教学模式方面。翟宜疆（2016）以金融汉语主干课——综合课为研究对象，从现代教学设计理论和建构主义教学理论出发，梳理了金融汉语综合课程的教学目标、教学内容及课堂环节。沈庶英（2014）结合商务汉语教学实际，就商务汉语实践教学的理论基础、参与各方的角色定位、任务的目标和实施等进行探讨。在商务汉语实践教学部分，作者从课堂实践教学、校园模拟实践教学、社会实践教学三个维度设置商务汉语实践教学的实施方案，其中不乏可取之处，如建立模拟实训实验室、开展商务活动学术月活动、进行企业实习等，这种商务汉语实践教学的理念是好的，但是在实际操作过程中可能存在一定的困难。比如，课堂教学内容是否与真实商务环境中的交际事件相符？外国学习者的课堂学习语言是否就是中国人在商务活动中所使用的地道表达？商务汉语是一个较笼统、宽泛的范畴，不同行业、领域、职位在交际场合中所使用的语言表达各有差异，这就导致了学校人才培养与岗位人才需求脱节。据笔者调查了解，很多企业之所以同意外国学习者到岗实习，是因为有一定的宣传效应，但这些外国实习者到企业后因沟通障碍难以融入，在校所学专业知识与实际岗位需要并不相符；久而久之，一些企业不愿意接受外国实习者，学习者也因学无所用失去到企业实习的兴趣。

对于中医汉语教学的目标定位，周延松（2015，2017）以高等院校中医药专业预科留学生为主体，提出教学内容具体体现在中医药专业术语、话语方式及中医文化等不同的层面，并从性质与功能、教学对象、知识与技能以及教学内容与要求等不同层面，对中医汉语课程进行定位，提出关注文化因素在中医汉语教学中的重要地位。周延松强调中医汉语教学应将通用汉语中的中医中的义项及中西医区别的语义侧重灌输给学生，笔者认为没有完全割裂的必要，如文献中所举“菊”，再如教授内容“中医学话语方式”及“中医文化的教学”等，过分割裂无疑会加重学习者的记忆负担。

郭睿（2016）对“短期特殊需要汉语项目的目标”进行了阐释，以美国学者泰勒（Tyler，1949：3—25）提出的教学目标来源为研究基础，分别从对学生的研究、对当代社会生活的研究和学科专家的建议三个来源对短期特殊项目的目标来源进行分析。学习者的学习需求是汉语项目目标的重要组成部分，短期特殊需要汉语项目目标的设计所应遵循的步骤分别是：需求分析（Needs analysis），包括谁的需求、什么需求、哪些方面的需求、确定调查对象、确定要收集的信息类别、确定收集信息的方法、收集并分析数据信息、形成分析报告；任务分析（task analysis），即目标情景分析，未来使用第二语言的需要，提出两种任务分析的方法，一是活动分析法，二是工作分析法，二者侧重点不同；起点确定（determination of starting point），即目前学习者的语言水平，关于如何确定起点，文中提到用学习者最近参加HSK的成绩、课程设计者针对学习者专门设计的试题、参照学习者“已学学时基准”和“教材基准”及口语测试的方法、环境因素分析（situations or contexts analysis）等。笔者认为文中提出的起点确定方法的准确性及客观性还有待进一步证明。

（三）预科教育中的专门用途汉语研究与教学

李泉（2016）对汉语预科教育学科建设的问题进行了探讨，对预科教育的定性与定位、学科与体系、任务与定量、理念与原则等提出了一些可参考意见。他把专门用途汉语分为专业汉语和业务汉语两大类：前者如理科、工科、中西医、文史哲、政经法等专业学习、教学和文献中所经常使用的汉语材料和表达方式；后者如涉外的外交、外贸、媒体、军事、旅游、工程、公司、航空、酒店、办公室等跨文化交际场合经常使用的汉语材料和表达方式。李泉将预科教育内容分成通用汉语、专业汉语、专业基础（数理化等）三部分，并提出这三类课程设置及学时比例可分别为70%、10%、20%，采取此种比例的主要理由是专业汉语仍应以汉语为主。

学术论文语体研究方面，高增霞、刘福英（2016）指出，按照使用场合，汉语可分为通用汉语和专门用途汉语。通用汉语是指日常生活、工作中使用的汉语；专门用途汉语指与某种特定职业、学科、目的相关的汉语。学术汉语属于专门用途汉语，主要指从事专业学习和学术研究所使用的汉语。汲传波（2016）通过自建汉语学术论文语料库，对比分析中国学者和韩国学生使用含“于”“者”“以”“而”“之”字的文言结构的异同，发现韩国学生学术汉语的语体能力存在不足。李泉（2016）指出学术用途汉语（Chinese for Academic Purposes）教材尤其值得重视。

（四）需求分析理论的应用与研究

20 世纪 80 年代，对外汉语教学界开始关注 ESP（English for Specific Purposes）理论，并将其引入对外汉语教学。专用语教学的前提是对学生进行学习需求和目标情景分析。需求分析是专门用途汉语课程设置的基础。现代专用语教学研究是在区分学习者需求和语言用途的基础上，进行系统的合成设计和资源开发的教学理念和系统方法。专用语教学重视需求分析，其目的主要是以学习者的需求作为基本的教学意识，并以其为引导进行具体的课程设计，最终解决专用语课程教什么和怎么教的问题。专用语的需求分析是专用语教学的基本组成环节，是进行语言分析和课程设计的前提（张黎，2006）。因此，以需求分析理论为框架展开的研究也越来越受到学界重视。

董杰、韩志刚（2014）在 ESP 理论框架下对来华留学生预科教育的专用汉语展开研究，提出从特定语域的语言要素分析、功能项目研究、语境分析以及专用汉语与通用汉语的关系研究等方面，对预科学生未来所学专业中使用的汉语进行研究，研究应采用定量研究、限定语域、对比分析等方法，研究内容主要涉及各专业领域所使用的汉语的具体特点，如语言要素分析、语域分析、词频分析与根字分析、固定短语分析，专用汉语的功能项目研究、专用汉语的语境分析研究等。

需求分析是专门用途汉语的重要特点，是专门用途教学的前提和基础。关于对汉语作为第二语言的学习需求，李燕（2007）认为，国内汉语作为第二语言的需求研究数量相对匮乏，平均每年的文献数量仅 4 篇左右，研究的成果也尚未形成一定的体系和影响力。由于研究基础相对薄弱，汉语学习需求研究还有待提升。张健、李莉（2017）基于需求分析理论将商务汉语划分为一般商务用途汉语和专门商务用途汉语两大类，并对这两种类型的学习者进行了需求分析，针对零基础阶段是否应当开设商务汉语课程这一问题，从理论来源、实证依据以及影响等方面对以往文献中的观点进行了总结归纳，认为从学习者需求出发，针对不同类型的学习者可以采取不同的教学策略。

（五）其他

丁安琪（2015）对汉语教学研究内容如教学主体、教学课题、教学方式、教学环境、教学载体等进行研究，归纳整理了汉语教学的各类研究方法。在国际汉语教学领域中，了解什么方法适用于哪一类的研究内容，有助于我们选择合适的研究方法。其文章中所展示的研究方法为今后一线教师在教学与研究过程中不断探索更多的研究内容提供参考。

三、专门用途教学研究的发展趋势

（一）研究对象与研究内容多样化

以专门用途汉语、需求分析为关键词进行文献检索梳理，能够对专门用途汉语研究与教学有深入的认识，了解专门用途汉语研究的热点。从研究对象来看，有专门用途教学研究、教材研究、基于 ESP 理论的应用研究，以及在预科教育中的专业汉语的研究。与以往更多集中在狭义的商务汉语研究方面相比，近年来的研究呈现出多样态势，如有关于中医汉语、军事汉语、金融汉语、学术汉语等的研究，也有针对职业发展的短期项目教学研究。但研究总量不多，而且商务汉语的研究有所减少，未来的研究中应加强跨学科、跨专业的多领域合作研究。

（二）对概念界定更为清晰准确

针对学界长期以来对商务汉语的一些认识，张黎（2014）给出了更为科学、更为实际的阐释。张黎认为，“商务汉语”概念包含多种语言变体，具体的商务汉语课程所教的只是其中一种。商务汉语课程是针对的某个行业、职业或学科专业的汉语学习者需求所设计的专门用途汉语课程。因此，应先分析教学对象正在或将要从事的具体行业、职业或专业学科领域，据此调查研究该领域语言使用特点，依此设计课程。商务汉语与通用汉语相比，不仅仅是词汇方面不同，一种专门用途语言的特点可能从语音、词汇、句法结构到语篇结构等各个层面都有所体现，而不只是一个层面的问题，应根据真实使用环境进行目标情景分析，从学习者未来需要面对的交际活动方面考虑，解决学习者最迫切需要掌握的目的语知识和技能，采取“急用先学”的策略，并且不仅仅限于专业学习或业务工作领域的学习。

（三）在研究方法和操作路径方面，仍然以内省式经验式为主，极少运用实证研究科学分析

笔者选取的19篇文章中，近十年对外汉语教材述评（刘弘、蒋内利，2016）采用了描写统计分析方法，对教材发展进行量化分析。学术汉语研究（汲传波，2016）运用个案对比开展研究，其他文章仍沿用提出问题、分析问题、解决问题的路子，但更多的是经验总结，对解决方案的适用性并没有得出具有科学实证性的研究结果。因此，我们应更多从实证研究的角度，将量化研究与质性研究相结合，使研究结果能够更好地指导教学。

（四）加强专门用途汉语教学资源的建设

结合国家战略及海外孔子学院的发展需要，专门用途汉语教学应与智能产业机构合作，拓展研究视野，改进研究方法。专门用途汉语教学及其教材建设、教学资源现代化和立体化建设问题，如教材评估、教材与课程关系、教师使用教材实证反馈都有待深入研究。随着大数据的深度影响，应在纸质教材的基础上，立体化、动态化开拓大数据教学资源。教材编写与研究还应重视语言的真实性与实用性，使用自然真实的语言。

（五）加强对学术汉语的研究

重视学术汉语教学和研究，针对高年级学习者学术汉语能力的培养，可考虑开设如汉语语体类型、口语语体分析、书面语语体分析、口语语体和书面语语体对比、典型口语和典型书面语转换例析、汉语话语结构分析、汉语语篇结构分析等基于语体的高层次语言课程，以支撑学术汉语的教学及教材编写（李泉，2004）。

参考文献：

[1] 刘弘，蒋内利. 近十年对外汉语教材研究特点及趋势分析 [J]. 国际汉语教学研究，2015（1）：55－62.

[2] 吴中伟，耿直，徐婷婷. 汉语教材建设的发展趋势和相关理论问题 [J]. 国际汉语教育（中英文），2017，2（1）：15－19.

[3] 汪景民. 多语种《中级军事汉语》教材的编写思路与指导思想 [J]. 海外华文教育，

2017（6）：753－758.
［4］赖铮. 比较法在国别化商务汉语教材中的应用［J］. 海外华文教育 2017（3）：369－373.
［5］张黎. 商务汉语教学的认识误区［J］. 国际汉语教学研究，2014（4）：31.
［6］翟宜疆. 金融汉语综合课课堂教学设计刍议［J］. 国际汉语教学研究，2014（4），37－42.
［7］沈庶英. 来华留学生商务汉语实践探索［J］. 语言教学与研究，2014（1）：45－50.
［8］周延松，陈杨国生. 专门用途汉语教学中的文化因素——基于中医汉语的考察［J］. 海外华文教育 2017（5）：677－684.
［9］周延松. 中医汉语课程与教学的目标定位［J］. 海外华文教育，2015（3）：415－420.
［10］郭睿. 论短期特殊需要汉语项目的目标设计［J］. 海外华文教育，2016（5）：689－696.
［11］李泉. 试论汉语预科教育若干问题［J］. 国际汉语教学研究，2016（3）：19－27.
［12］董杰，韩志刚. 试论面向来华留学生预科教育的专用汉语研究［J］. 语言教学与研究，2014（4）：42－48.
［13］汲传波. 韩国学生汉语学术论文中文言结构使用初探［J］. 汉语学习，2016（6）：77－85.
［14］高增霞，刘福英. 论学术汉语在对外汉语教学中的重要性［J］. 云南师范大学学报（对外汉语教学与研究版），2016，14（2）：44－51.
［15］张黎. 专门用途汉语教学［M］. 北京：北京语言大学出版社，2016：123.
［16］李燕. 汉语作为第二语言学习需求研究述评［J］. 海外华文教育，2017（6）：857－864.
［17］张健，李莉. ESP需求分析理论下零基础商务汉语教学述评［J］. 海外华文教育，2017（10）：1427－1432.
［18］丁安琪. 汉语教学的研究内容与研究方法［J］. 国际汉语教学研究，2017，1：7－13.
［19］张黎. 商务汉语教学需求分析［J］. 语言教学与研究，2006（3）：55－60.
［20］李泉. 面向对外汉语教学的语体研究的范围和内容［J］. 汉语学习，2004（1）：63.

作者简介：

白巧燕，北京语言大学博士研究生，研究方向为商务汉语教学与研究、话语分析、对外汉语教学研究。

坚持“以学生为中心”的教学理念及其他
——读《法语作为外语和第二语言的教学法研究》有感

程　文
四川大学海外教育学院

摘　要： 本文通过介绍《法语作为外语和第二语言的教学法研究》一书，指出其作为教学指南的价值，并结合笔者自身教与学的感受，强调该书中一些重要的教学理念与教学方法，以与对外汉语教学相呼应。这些教学理念主要有重视学习者的个体学习过程、重视个性化的学习指导，优化教学环节设计、加强教学材料的真实性与跨文化交际性、提高测评的效度等。

关键词： 外语教学法；学习过程；教学设计；教学测评

On Adhering to the "Student-Centered" Teaching Philosophy and Some Others
—Thoughts on Reading *Le français Langue étrangère et seconde: Enseignement et Apprentissage*

Cheng Wen
School of Overseas Education, Sichuan University

Abstract: This paper introduces *Le français langue étrangère et seconde: Enseignement et apprentissage*, and points out its value as a teaching guide. Combined with personal own feelings of teaching and learning, the author of this paper emphasizes some important teaching ideas and teaching methods in the book, in order to echo the teaching of Chinese as a foreign language. These teaching concepts mainly include attaching importance to learners' individual learning process, attaching importance to personalized learning guidance, optimizing the design of teaching links, strengthening the authenticity of teaching materials and intercultural communication, and improving the validity of the assessment.

Keywords: Foreign Language Teaching Method; Learning Process; Teaching Design; Teaching Evaluation

《法语作为外语和第二语言的教学法研究》（*Le français langue étrangère et seconde: Enseignement et apprentissage*）是比利时列日大学现代语言学院院长兼法语系主任、世界法语教师联合会主席让-马克·德法伊（Jean-Marc Defays）于2003年出版的法语教学法专著，于2004年获得比利时皇家科学院奖。作为德法伊的代表作之一，该书整合了教学法的各家观点，对外语教学理论和对外法语教学的各个环节进行了全面的介绍和分析。德法伊长期在比利时、法国、芬兰等地从事对外法语教学，对法语语言学、法语教学法、跨文化交际和语言教育政策等都有深入体会与研究。该书译者为北京外国语大学法语教学法专家傅荣和北京外国语大学资深对外汉语教师张丹。他们二人谙熟法语和汉语教学，因"国内至今未有一部系统阐释法语教学法理论的译著面世"（德法伊，2018：V）而译出此著作，译文准确而流畅。笔者曾学习过法语，并曾在法国大学的法语中心感受过对外法语教学有诸多行之有效的教学法，因此，阅读此书颇有共鸣。不同外语的教学法有诸多共性，而且对外法语教学历史悠久、方法独特，对外汉语教师可以从这本著作中得到不少教学法的启示。该书涉及的教学法相关内容很多，笔者先简单介绍该书内容，然后结合自己的教与学的经历，着重阐述阅读该书最有心得的地方，并与汉语教学法进行比较。

《法语作为外语和第二语言的教学法研究》共分为六部分，每部分针对对外法语教学的特定方面及其演变历程和现今的状态都进行了历时的梳理和共时的展示。目录极为细致，可看出本书的写作风格具体而实在。导论部分对外语教学法的用途、学科地位、命题、相关术语、复杂性等做了总体介绍。第一章是客体研究，着重于"学什么？教什么？"的问题，介绍了对外法语的教学内容，并阐述了语言、文化与交际的相互关系，强调"语言涵括文化，二者又深深地融入于交际之中”（德法伊，2018：18）。第二章是主体研究，着眼于“谁在学？谁在教？”的问题，详述了学习者和教师的各种类别以及二者的不同互动模式。第三章是环境研究，关注何时、何地教与学，对不同地域、不同机构、不同时段的对外法语教学进行了展示。第四章是教学的动机与目的研究，回答了“因什么教/学？为了什么？”的问题，梳理了学生的各种动机与期待，强调外语教学的终极目标以及评估和水平分级。第五章着眼于“如何教？怎么学？”的问题，是教学方法与策略研究，剖析了学习过程和学习策略，展示了教学法的演变与不同的教学实践活动。全书既有对语言学、教育心理学和社会语言学等相关理论的陈述，也有对很多颇具启发性的具体操作方法的说明，体现出一位资深语言教学专家的功底。该书既适用于有志于从事外语教学工作的新教师，也适用于希望对自己的教学经验进行总结、更新的资深教师（德法伊，2018：Ⅲ），是一本实用的外语教学指南。下面，笔者结合自己学法语、教汉语的经历，从该书中总结出几点最深的教学体会，与同行交流。

一、重视学习者的个体学习过程

在现代外语教学理念中，以学生为主体的观念已成为共识，这也是贯穿《法语作为外语和第二语言的教学法研究》的一条主线，并在不少章节中被强调。作者在该书简短的前言中，明确指出“教应该服务于学……教师不能只满足于教，还应该理解学习过程，促进和引导每一个学习者都参与其中”（德法伊，2018：2）。在导论部分关于外语教学法术语概念的定义中，他也鲜明地强调“教学”是“众多的学习方式之一”“教学从属于学习”（德法伊，2018：10）。坚持以学生为教学主体的理念，尤其是关注到每一位学习者，绝非易事。在实际的对外汉语或对外法语教学班中，学生水平常常参差不齐，这给教师的教学带来不少困扰。一般情况下，教师会按照班上中等水平学生的情况决定教学进度与节奏，班上水平低和水平高的学生就可能不适应。那么，怎么才能关注到每一位学生，使每一位学生都得到“量体裁衣”般的指导呢？德法伊有这样的建议：“教师通过建立学习者的个人档案，通过定期和学习者面对面地交流，……这时候，他的对话人是班上的每一个学习者。”（德法伊，2018：126）而笔者遇到的一位对外法语教师正是这样做的。具体做法是在学期开始的一两周内，在学生与教师相互熟悉后，教师与学生定下一个见面顺序表，在每次课后用 10～15 分钟时间分别与一位学生谈话。教师可询问学生的学习动机、学习难点等，并针对学生实际的学习期待和学习情况提供个性化的指导和建议。在学期中后期，师生可再做一次轮流交谈会。教师这样轮流与每位学生交流后，学生往往会感觉到自己得到了教师的特别关注而更有信心，教师也密切关注了学生的学习过程，在需要时及时调整自己的教学细节。此方法充分体现了以学生为主体的教学理念，使教师能对每位学生的学习状况有持续的了解，以更好地因材施教。另外，在具体教授语言要素时，也应贯彻个体化教学的原则，比如语音课程初期，教师一定要仔细辨听并纠正每位学习者的发音，而不只是全班齐读，这也是笔者的对外法语教师的做法。另外，作业也可以是个性化的、体现学生动机的、有难度区别的。

二、优化教学设计和教学材料

在《法语作为外语和第二语言的教学法研究》第五章中“关于教学安排”这一部分，德法伊指出：“现在，包括笔者在内的很多人都把单元（séquence）视为外语教学安排的基本单位，用以取代过去的课（leçon）。这样做的目的是打破以往课时的限制，使课堂教学活动更加协调更有意义。”（德法伊，2018：256）作者所谓的单元是指长度为一个或数个星期的教学时段，其中包括言语学习、特定主题、文化、各种语言任务等。确实，笔者所见的很多对外法语教材都是以单元为编写单位，每个单元包括语言要素的学习与运用、与课文紧密相关的文化链接以及各种交际任务，形成一个从语言到跨文化交际的小循环；各个单元之间形成大循环，以使学习者实际运用语言的能力得到循序渐进的提升。反观对外汉语教材，一些比较传统但仍广泛使用的教材仍是以“课”为编写单位的，偏重于课文的文学性与词语教学（有些主课文的难度排序不太合适），文化链接与现实生活的联系有的不太紧密，体现出语言交际性的交际任务相对不足。在这样的情况下，教师就需要对教材和教学环节做一些优化处理，比如按语言难易程度调换课文顺序，从课文中提炼出与学生实际生活紧密相关的话题并设计出比课本练习更细致的交际任务，通过鲜活的话题激发学生使用新学的汉语材料进行恰当表达，强化对外汉语教学的实用性与跨文化交际功能。也就是说，把比较单一的练习语言技能的“课”变成内容丰富、技能要求多样、文化交际突出的“单元”，并使单元间的语言渐进阶梯更合理，从而更好地提高学生的实际交际能力。

此外，对外法语教学一直非常重视教学材料的真实性、时效性。德法伊在书中列举出了真实的语言素材的类型，如图像（包括图画、漫画、海报、照片等）、歌曲（可进行歌词填空、歌词排序等练习）、实物（特别是体现学习者不同母语文化的物品）、书面材料（如报纸、旅游宣传页、广告、政府的各类通告）等（德法伊，2018：288－289）。巴黎第三大学对外法语系教授、华东师范大学法语教师毕笑（Jean-Claude Beacco）也指出，法语教学法一贯强调“真实的材料”，因为它比编写的材料更有“被信任的优势”（Beacco，2011）。根据笔者的教学经验，经过精心挑选的真实而适当的语言补充材料的教学效果很好，这就需要教师不囿于已有教材，通过各种途径寻找合适的教辅材料，以提升教学效果。

三、科学有效地进行教学测评

在《法语作为外语和第二语言的教学法研究》一书中，作者将“评估与水平等级”放在第四章的“外语教学的终极目标”一节之后，说明其对教学测评非常重视，认为评估是达成目的的重要手段。实际上，研究语言测试对教学等带来的反拨效应（Washback Effect）早已是语言教学研究的重要课题（陈颖，2009）。德法伊在书中区分了不同种类、不同内容的测评，强调了有效测试的标准，也描述了不理想的测评情况，如“测评项目重叠、测试结构失衡，有的能力漏测了，有的能力则被考察了好几次”（德法伊，2018：189）。

反观我们的教学组织，可能存在重教学、轻测试的现象，且测试的效度有待提高。曾有一位学生对笔者说：“我知道怎么通过考试，但我知道我的语言能力不好。”这说明我们有的测试可能结构不太平衡，只注重测试语言知识，而忽略了测试语言能力。这就需要教师在设计考题时尽量全面地考察学生的能力，尤其是语言的实际运用能力。相对于笔试，口试达到客观性与均衡性的难度更大。德法伊在书中建议口试最好由两位测试人员共同打分，进行“联合评估”。这其实也是笔者在法国任教时，当地进行汉语口语测试时使用的办法。

另外，测试的持续性也很重要。德法伊在书中强调了“形成性/跟踪性评估”，也就是教师在教学期间，要多次考察学习者的知识和能力，及时发现问题、解决问题并调整教学（德法伊，2018：190）。确实，学期末的测评对学生学习的引导作用不明显，更多的是一种总结，而正是学习过程中持续进行的单元测验、语言报告测试等更能让学习者及时知道自己的学习效果，使学习者的学习更有方向性和针对性。

总之，现代外语教学法都把培养学生的实际语言运用能力作为教学核心，而如何使学生真正掌握并运用技能，教学中还有很多细致的工作要做。德法伊撰写的《法语作为外语和第二语言的教学法研究》一书，对外语教学法的诸多方面进行了介绍，关于教学法的很多观点具体、实在，对外汉语教师阅读此书后也一定会有很多感悟和收获。

参考文献：

[1] 毕笑. 当今对外法语教学法 [J]. 外语教学理论与实践，2011 (4).

[2] 陈颖.《通过语言测试带动语言教学的改革：反拨效应研究》述评 [J]. 现代外语，2009 (1).

[3] 让-马克·德法伊. 法语作为外语和第二语言的教学法研究 [M]. 傅荣，张丹，译. 外语教学与研究出版社，2018.

作者简介：

程文，四川大学海外教育学院副教授，研究方向为对外汉语教学法及汉外对比。

How Do Novice-Level Learners React to Using a Web-Based Textbook to Learn Chinese?*

Han Jining

Faculty of Education, Southwest University

Abstract: Web 2.0 has largely influenced second language teaching and learning. With the continuing development of digital devices, applying web-based learning material to second language learning has drawn many researchers' attentions. This study aims to explore how learners react to using a web-based learning material as a "textbook" to learn Chinese. A quantitative is conducted in a Chinese program in a large public university in the southeastern part of the U. S. The study results reveal how scores for a writing assessment differ between students who used a traditional paper-based textbook and the students who used a web-based textbook.

Keywords: Web-Based Textbook; Teaching Chinese as a Foreign Language; Novice-level Chinese Language Learners; Computer-assisted Language Learning

摘　要：网络2.0时代对二语习得产生了很大的影响。随着数字科技的持续发展，采用基于网络的学习材料辅助二语学习已经吸引了很多研究者的注意。本研究的目的在于探讨汉语学习者对于使用网站教材学习汉语的反响。本研究在美国东南部的一所公立大学的中文项目中开展实验，实验的结果反映了使用传统纸质教材的学生与使用网站

* 本课题为2019年度西南大学教育学部青年基金项目，项目编号：2019QNZJ06。

教材的学生在中文写作测试中分数的差别。

关键词：基于网络的教材；对外汉语教学；初级汉语学者；计算机辅助语言教学

1. Literature Review

1.1 Web-based learning material as a medium in teaching foreign languages

The trends and developments of using web-based learning materials to teach foreign languages have been drawing attention by researchers and educational companies around the world (e.g., Chinnery, 2006; Godwin-Jones, 2011; Kukulska-Hulme & Shield, 2007; Song & Fox, 2008; Stockwell, 2008). Ducate and Arnold (2006) suggested that web-based tools could promote many second language learning skills: 1) video and audio materials could help learners to improve pronunciation; 2) electronic dictionaries help improve learners' reading abilities; 3) web-based tools are able to provide various types of assessments; 4) videos and films provide authentic materials for learners to improve intercultural communicative competence. Liontas (2009) provided an inventory of features that an App would need in order to teach students idioms, and he designs an anatomy of AI knowledge system for idiom learning including introduction, user-centered interface design, providing input through sources, multimedia aids, presentation modes, learning formats, producing output focusing on forms, meanings, functions, pragmatics, error correction, and so forth.

Educators of Chinese have pointed out the significance of employing technology as a scaffolding in the field of teaching Chinese as a foreign language (e.g., Jiang, Wang, & Tschudi, 2013; Jin, 2009; Walker, 2005; Yao, 2009). Yao (2009) discussed the development of utilizing computers to teach Chinese since the 1970s. He has pointed out the significance of employing technology in the field of teaching Chinese as a foreign language and further emphasized that technology-based online material provides an excellent scaffolding to activate the Zone of Proximal Development (ZPD) in teaching Chinese as a foreign language. Yao also offered some suggestions and wishes to develop websites to accompany textbooks, pointed out that learners of Chinese could benefit from websites that teach interpersonal and presentational skills, and highlighted the importance of better feedback among learners and teachers.

1.2 Empirical research for effective of Computer-Assisted Language Learning (CALL)

An important question in the field of CALL: does its use promote students' foreign language learning? As Chapelle (1997) suggested a critical question for CALL research "How good is the language experience in CALL for L2 learning". Chapelle (2001) highlighted that "most convincing way to demonstrate the language learning potential of a CALL activity is through the study of learning outcomes" (p. 74). Zhao (2005) indicated six principles for conducting research in using technology for language learning, and the first principle is "pose significant questions that can be investigated empirically" (p. 5).

Many researchers have focused on exploring the effective of CALL in the context of teaching English as a foreign language by using quantitative research (Khalid, 2005; Harless, Zier, & Duncan, 2005; Schcolnik & Kol, 2006; Kleij, Feskens, & Eggen, 2015; Takacs, Swart, & Bus, 2015). Khalid (2005) explored the effect of multimedia annotation modes on L2 vocabulary acquisition. The study examined two types of image modalities—dynamic video or still picture—is more effective for 30 ESL students in aiding vocabulary acquisition. In order to see if there was a significant difference between using the two types of image modalities, the researchers used a repeated-measures one-way ANOVA. The data result showed that dynamic video is more effective in teaching vocabulary than still picture. Harless, Zier, and Duncan (2005) evaluated an interactive multimedia method. Kleij, Feskens, and Eggen (2015) applied a meta-analysis to explore the effects of feedback in a computer-based learning environment on students' learning outcomes. The results suggested that immediate feedback was more effective for learning than delayed feedback. Takacs, Swart, and

Bus (2015) conducted a meta-analysis to discuss benefits and pitfalls of multimedia and interactive features in technology-enhanced storybooks. The results showed that multimedia features like animated pictures, music, and sound effects were beneficial for learning and interactive features were distracting. Schcolnik and Kol (2006) conducted a study on testing the effective of reading and learning from screen. Based on a *t*-test, the test results showed that students who learned from the HTML text performed significantly between than students who learned from the MS Reader text. The study also added gender as the second variable, and the result showed that no significant difference between male students and female students.

In the field of teaching Chinese as a foreign language, Jin (2009) explored Chinese language learning and instructions within a technology-rich, collaborative and participatory learning environment in terms of the effects of three different types of web tools: discussion boards, blogs, and Skype. Blogs offered participants more opportunities to generate and respond to conversation, and they gave participants more modes (spoken, written, etc.) in which to communicate. The conclusion was that blogs elicited the highest degree of interactivity and participation. Cai and Zhu (2011) conducted an empirical study to explore the motivations of first-year Chinese students toward an online learning community project. The participants are required to write reflective journals, post samples of pronunciation, and provide feedback to other participants. The research result showed that there is a significant difference in the learning experience between the online group and the offline group. Kim and Wang (2013) explored Chinese language learners' social communication in Chinese on Facebook. Based on a *t*-test, the research revealed that students using Facebook has a positive impact on their writing skills.

2. Research Questions

Web 2.0 has largely influenced foreign language teaching and learning. With continuing development of personal computers, internet services, and portable digital devices, applying web-based textbook to foreign language learning has drawn many researchers' attentions. Some researchers have focused on how effective of the CALL material and the connections between second language acquisition theories and foreign language educational website design in the teaching English as a second language (TESL) context. There is little published research exploring how effective of CALL learning material in the context of teaching Chinese as a foreign language. The research aims to fill the research gap by discovering how learners react to using a web-based textbook to learn Chinese. Two research questions will be raised in the study:

(1) How do scores for a writing assessment differ between students who used a web-based textbook and the students who used a traditional paper-based textbook?

(2) How do two different types of learning material comparatively effect male students' and female students' writing assessment grades?

3. Research Methodology

I conducted the study in a Chinese program in a World Languages Department in a large public university in the southeastern part of the U. S. Courses in Chinese level 1 include Modern Chinese 1 and Modern Chinese 2 offered in fall semester and spring semester, separately. The method of sample selection applied probability random sampling. The study randomly selected 30 students who enrolled in Modern Chinese 2 in the spring semester of 2015, and the study also randomly selected 30 students who enrolled in Modern Chinese 2 in the spring semester of 2016. The 30 students who enrolled in Modern Chinese 2 in the spring semester of 2015 and used a paper-based textbook to learn Chinese writing were in the control group: 11 are male students, and 19 are female students. The 30 students who enrolled in Modern Chinese 2 in the spring semester of 2016 and used a web-based textbook to learn Chinese writing were in the treatment group: 13 are male students and 17 are female students. All participants had no previous experiences in learning Chinese writing before taking Chinese courses at the university.

There is one writing class each week. The first section is a reading-focused class in which students are required to read the target material in new contexts during class, and the second section is writing-focused and requires students to engage in writing activities during class. The Chinese program developed learning materials called Chinese Learning in the Culture (CLIC). In the spring semester of 2015, each student had a paper-based version of the material, and the content was simply displayed in a printed textbook. In the spring semester of 2016, students began to use a web-based CLIC Chinese writing material; the CLIC reading/writing sections provide videos, animations, pictures, audio files, and interactive activities for learners to learn Chinese writing in novice level.

At the end of the semester, the writing assessment is a 30 minutes in-class quiz. The writing assessment includes three sections: dictation exercises, multiple choice questions, and writing Chinese characters based on a reading. All the Chinese characters used in the writing assessment have been introduced in the CLIC learning material and in the class. The content and instructions for the writing assessment are the same for the control and treatment groups.

The independent variable is the type of textbook. The dependent variable is students' scores in the writing assessment. The study design applied a quasi-experimental research. There is a control group and a treatment group and only one independent variable. To answer the first question, the study applied an independent-means t-test. To answer the second question, the study added a new independent variable, gender, and, because the numbers of participants in each cell are not equal, the study applied an unbalanced factorial ANOVA test.

4. Data Analysis

4.1 To answer the first question

Students who used a web-based textbook are in the treatment group, while students who used a paper-based textbook are in the control group, and participants were not assigned to groups prior to group assignment. The question is interested in the difference between two means. For these types of data, inferences about population mean differences are made using the independent-means *t*-test.

An independent-means *t*-test is used to compare how scores for a writing assessment differ between the control group and the treatment group. That is, the null hypothesis states there is no difference between the means of control group and treatment group. In this case, the null hypothesis is: the mean of the writing assessment scores for students who used a traditional paper-based textbook (control group) is the same as the mean of the writing assessment scores for students who used a web-based textbook (treatment group).

Based on the SAS output (see Appendix 1), mean and standard deviation for the control group is 8.5067 and 3.1478, and the mean and standard deviation for the treatment group is 11.9533 and 2.1660. Although the mean of the treatment group is higher than the mean of the control group, we cannot say there are statistically significant differences between these two groups.

We also need to consider some outliers, extreme scores, and other factors that may have relationships with the scores. Then, the obtained *t*-value is −4.94, and the *p*-value is 0.0001. Since the *p*-value is less than the alpha level (0.05), we can reject the null hypothesis. Therefore, we can say that there are statistical differences for writing assessment scores between students who used a paper-based textbook and students who used a web-based textbook. To be more accurate, we must acknowledge that there might be a chance that we have made a Type 1 error in this decision. A Type 1 error is the incorrect rejection of a true null hypothesis, in other words, the null hypothesis that there is no difference between the control group and the treatment group is true, and we made a mistake in rejecting the hypothesis. In order to control the Type 1 error, the study further calculates a 95% confidence interval. A 95% confidence interval for the difference in population means is between 7.3312 and 11.1445; thus, we are 95% confident that the difference in population mean writing assessment scores between control group and treatment group is roughly between 7.3312 and 11.1445. Therefore, the data shows that this confidence interval does not contain the null hypothesized value of 0, so we can still reject the null hypothesis.

The study also considers the effect size. Based on the means and standard deviations above mentioned, the study calculates that the Cohen's *d* is 1.28 and the effect-size *r* is 0.54. The large Pearson's correlation of 0.54 indicates a good positive linear relation, and we can say that there is a relationship between the control group and the treatment group in their writing assessment scores. In addition, the Cohen's *d* of 1.28 also suggests that there is a consistent difference in writing assessment scores on average between the control group and the treatment groups.

4.2 To answer the second question

The second question is interested in comparing the effect of two different types of learning material on male students' and female students' writing assessment grades. The study explores the main effect for factor A (gender), the main effect for factor B (types of textbook: paper-based and web-based), and interaction between factor A and factor B. In this case, the main effect for factor A is the effect of gender after controlling for the types of textbook. The main effect for factor B means the effect of textbook type after controlling for the gender. The interaction between factor A and factor B means the joint effect of the gender and the types of textbook. The treatment group has 13 male students and 17 female students, and the control group has 11 male students and 19 female students. Data in this research do not have equal cell size. Therefore, the study applies an unbalanced data factorial ANOVA design.

The first null hypothesis for this study is that there is no difference in mean scores of writing assessment for students of different gender. The second null hypothesis for this study is that there is no difference in mean scores of writing assessment for students' using different types of textbook. The final null hypothesis for this study is that there is no interaction effect. Based on the SAS output (see Appendix 2), the data shows that the p-value for Factor A is 0.4319, the p-value for Factor B is less than 0.0001, and the p-value for Factor A * Factor B is 0.0895. Based on the obtained p-values, we can make decisions for the unbalanced ANOVA case. We fail to reject the null hypothesis that there is no difference in means based on gender. We can reject the null hypothesis that there is no difference in means based on types of textbook. We fail to reject the null hypothesis that there is no interaction between gender and types of textbook.

The data analysis concludes that there is no significant effect of gender after controlling for the types of textbook, there is significant effect of the types of textbook after controlling for the gender, and there is no significant effect of the gender and the types of textbook. Since the interaction wasn't significant, the study uses a Tukey test to further analyze a main effect that was significant. The study compared all levels of the Factor B, web-based textbook and paper-based textbook. Based on the SAS Tukey test output, of the two types of textbook, the mean of writing assessment scores from the web-based textbook was statistically higher than the mean from the paper-based textbook.

5. Implications and Discussions

Integrating multimedia and Web 2.0 technologies into designing Chinese writing materials could have several benefits. Since Chinese characters are logograms and some of them only have minor graphic differences, learning Chinese writing is difficult for students whose native language is English. Using a web-based textbook to teach Chinese writing could insert videos and animations to illustrate the stroke orders of Chinese characters and to highlight the minor differences among Chinese characters. Pictures, videos, and animations could also help students to memorize the Chinese characters. For example, teachers could add a video clip or a picture of a mountain to help learners to memorize the Chinese character "山" (mountain).

There are six ways to form Chinese characters: 1) Shape and sound characters, 2) indicative characters, 3) confluence of meanings/jointed meaning characters, 4) transfer explanation characters, 5) resemble shape characters, and 6) borrowed characters. Understanding the six ways to form Chinese characters are important for learners to understand, read, write, and memorize Chinese characters. In a traditional paper-based textbook, teachers use several pages to explain the six ways to form Chinese characters, which makes the content too overwhelming for learners to understand and memorize. The web-based textbook could support audio and video explanations recorded by teachers of the Chinese program and could combine texts and pictures, giving students multiple ways and flexible times to access the learning material, such as connecting the audio file with vehicle's media player via Bluetooth or audio cables.

Each character, phrase, and sentence could connect with an audio file. When learners click the character/phrase/sentence, the website plays the corresponding audio file. Therefore, students are able to access the pictorial representations and audio pronunciations of the Chinese characters at the same time. The practice drills include multiple choice questions, fill-in-the-blank questions, and dictation exercises, so students could take the practice drills to test their uptakes. The website could provide feedback based on previously designed programming; as a result, students are able to check the errors and receive the feedback instantly. Students cannot find the practice answers until they complete the practice drills. The practice drills can be taken unlimited times and the scores of practice drills will not be sent to the teachers; therefore, students could practice Chinese writing without pressure. An additional section would offer writing assignments for learners to complete and submit to teachers, so that teachers could know students' uptakes and provide effective learning feedback. Most students engage seriously with this section because the grades for these assignments will be part of their daily grades.

The web-based textbook operates on Apple iPhones, Androids, Tablets, Mac computers, and PCs. Students could access reading and writing materials more flexibly, which could provide more opportunities to learn Chinese writing. Based on students' feedback and reactions, the web-based textbook can be revised and updated very quickly. A searching function could help learners to locate the Chinese characters immediately.

6. Conclusions

By answering the first question, the data reveals that there is a significant difference for the writing assessment scores between students who used a web-based textbook and the students who used a traditional paper-based textbook. Students who used web-based textbook have a higher mean score than the students who used a paper-based textbook. The obtained t-value, p-value, and confidence interval prove the conclusion. Effect-size in this study focuses on the correlation between variables and the mean difference. The resulting Cohen's d and the effect-size r indicate a strong effect size of this study. Since the study is a quasi-experimental design, the type of the study design decides the internal validity is high. In this study, we can conclude that the internal validity is high, and the study avoids confounding variables. However, since the external validity is not high, we cannot claim that the conclusion from current data set may apply to other experiments. There are several variables which may have relationships with the students' writing assessment scores, such as history (the events occurring between the writing assessment and at the beginning of the semester), content validity, and construct validity. In sum, we can conclude that there is a positive relationship between the writing assessment scores and the web-based textbook; however, we cannot say that using the web-based textbook impacts the writing assessment scores.

By answering the second question, the data indicates that if we control the type of textbook, there is no significant effect of gender. The type of textbook plays an important role in students' writing assessment scores because if we control the gender, there is significant effect of the type of textbook. Although the data does not find significant effect of the gender and the type of textbook, which means the interaction wasn't significant, after a following Tukey test, the data indicates that the mean of writing assessment scores from the web-based textbook was statistically higher than the mean from the paper-based textbook. We can conclude that there is no significant effect between gender and writing assessment scores. Male and female students can use the web-based textbook equally effectively. In addition, we can also conclude that compared to using the paper-based textbook, applying the web-based textbook provides a more efficient way for students to learn Chinese writing.

7. Limitations and Delimitations

Because of limitations on the research time, the sample size is not very large. The external validity is not very high, so other experiments may have different results. Although researchers have controlled the history (events) during the research, other events, such as students' communicating with Chinese native-speakers off-campus, occurring between the beginning of the semester and the writing assessment might have relationships with the writing assessment scores. The conclusion indicates that there is a positive effect in using a web-based textbook to learn Chinese writing. A qualitative research method is necessary to further explore students' reactions toward using the web-based textbook. A survey and an interview will supply some in-depth insights for researchers to understand how to design or revise the web-based textbook to help learners learn Chinese writing more effectively. To further develop the pilot study, the study suggests that add other variables (such as learning style), provide more detailed information about data collection and data analysis, and explore more advantages and disadvantages of applying a web-based textbook to learn Chinese writing.

References:

[1] Al-Seghayer, K. (2005). The effect of multimedia annotation modes on L2 vocabulary acquisition: A comparative study. In Y. Zhao (Ed.), Research in technology and second language learning: Developments and directions (pp. 133—164). Greenwich, CT: Information Age Publishing, Inc.

[2] Bax, S. (2003). CALL: Past, present and future. System, 31 (1). 13—28.

[3] Cai, S., & Zhu, W. (2012). The impact of an online learning community project on university Chinese as a Foreign Language students' motivation. *Foreign Language Annals*, 45 (3), 307—329.

[4] Chinnery, G. M. (2006). Going to the MALL: Mobile assisted language learning. *Language Learning & Technology*, 10 (1), 9—16.

[5] Chun, D. M. (2011). Computer-assisted language learning. In E. Hinkel (Ed.), *Handbook of research in second language teaching and learning* (pp. 663—680). New York, NY: Routledge.

[6] Ducate, L., & Arnold, N. (Eds.) (2006). *Calling on CALL: From theory and research to new directions in foreign language teaching*. San Marcos, TX: CALICO.

[7] Fabienne, M., Kleij, V., Feskens, R., & Eggen, T. (2015). Effect of Feedback in a Computer-Based Learning Environment on Students' Learning Outcomes: A Meta-Analysis. *Review of Educational Research*, 85 (4), 475—511.

[8] Fotos, S., & Browne, C. (2004). *New perspective on CALL for second language classrooms*. Mahwah, NJ: Lawrence Erlbaum Associates, Publishers.

[9] Hubbard, P. (Ed.) (2009). *Computer assisted language learning* (Vols I-IV). Critical Concepts in Linguistics series. New York: Routledge.

[10] Jiang, S., Wang, H., & Tschudi, S. (2012). Intercultural learning on the web: Reflections on practice. *National Foreign Language Resource Center Monograph Series: Culture-based exchanges*. Unpublished. Santa Barbara, CA: University of California.

[11] Jin, H. (2009). Participatory learning in internet web technology: A study of three web tools in the context of CFL learning. *Journal of the Chinese Language Teachers Association*, 44 (1), 25—50.

[12] Jones, R., Chik, A., and Hafner, A. (2015). *Discourse and digital practices: Doing analysis in the digital age*. Routledge.

[13] Levy, M., & Stockwell, G. (2006). *CALL dimensions: Options and issues in

computer-assisted language learning. Mahwah, NJ: Erlbaum.

[14] Liontas, J. I. (2002). CALL Media Digital Technology: Whither in the New Millennium? *CALICO Journal*, 19 (2), 315–330.

[15] Liontas, J. I. (2009). Artificial Intelligence and Idiomaticity. *Reading Matrix: An International Online Journal*, 6 (3), 210–247.

[16] Pennington, M. C. (2003). The impact of the computer in second language writing. In B. Kroll (Ed.), *Exploring the dynamics of second language writing* (pp. 287–310). Cambridge, UK: Cambridge University Press.

[17] Takacs, Z., Swart, E., & Bus, A. (2015). Benefits and Pitfalls of Multimedia and Interactive Features in Technology-Enhanced Storybooks: A Meta-Analysis. *Review of Educational Research*, 85 (4), 698–740.

[18] Warschauer, M. (2004). Technological change and the future of CALL. In S. Fotos & C. Browne (Eds.), *New perspectives on CALL for second and foreign language classrooms* (pp. 15–25). Mahwah, NJ: Erlbaum.

[19] Warschauer, M., & Grimes, D. (2007). Audience, authorship, and artifact: The emergent semiotics of Web 2.0. *Annual Review of Applied Linguistics*, 27, 1–23.

[20] Wang, S. (2013). Intermediate-level Chinese language learners' social communication in Chinese on Facebook: A mixed methods study. *Graduate Theses and Dissertations*. Tampa, FL: The University of South Florida.

[21] Yao, D. (2009). The current status of Chinese CALL in the United States. *Journal of the Chinese Language Teachers Association*, 44 (1), 1–24.

[22] Zhao, Y. (2005). The future of research in technology and second language education. In Y. Zhao (Ed.), *Research in technology and second language learning: Developments and directions* (pp. 445–457). Greenwich, CT: Information Age Publishing, Inc.

Appendix 1 Independent-Means *t*-test SAS output

The SAS System

The TTEST Procedure

Variable: writing

group	N	Mean	Std Dev	Std Err	Minimum	Maximum
1	30	8.5067	3.1478	0.5747	1.8000	14.0000
2	30	11.9533	2.1660	0.3955	8.3000	15.0000
Diff (1-2)		-3.4467	2.7019	0.6976		

group	Method	Mean	95% CL Mean		Std Dev	95% CL Std Dev	
1		8.5067	7.3312	9.6821	3.1478	2.5070	4.2317
2		11.9533	11.1445	12.7621	2.1660	1.7250	2.9118
Diff (1-2)	Pooled	-3.4467	-4.8431	-2.0502	2.7019	2.2872	3.3016
Diff (1-2)	Satterthwaite	-3.4467	-4.8469	-2.0464			

Method	Variances	DF	t Value	Pr > |t|
Pooled	Equal	58	-4.94	<.0001
Satterthwaite	Unequal	51.432	-4.94	<.0001

Equality of Variances				
Method	Num DF	Den DF	F Value	Pr > F
Folded F	29	29	2.11	0.0484

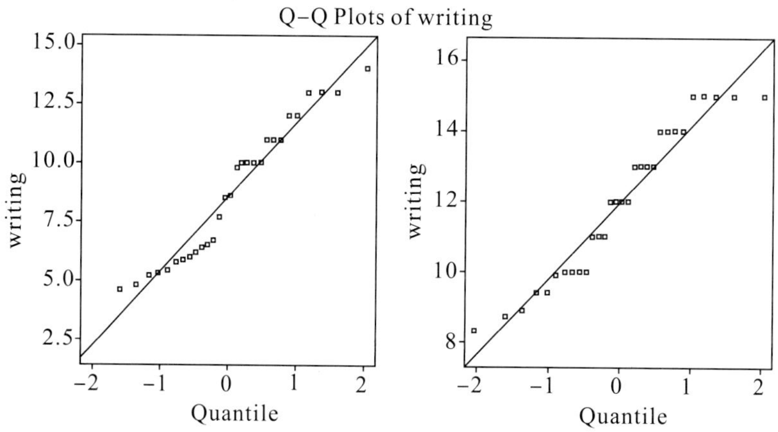
Q-Q Plots of writing
writing
Quantile
writing
Quantile

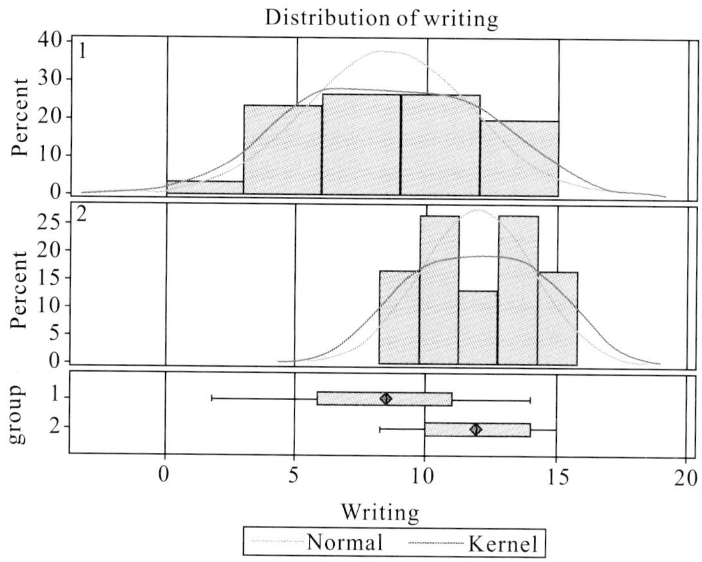
Distribution of writing
Percent
Percent
group
Writing
Normal
Kernel

Appendix 2 Unbalanced Factorial ANOVA SAS output

The SAS System

The GLM Procedure

Dependent Variable: Score

Source	DF	Sum of Squares	Mean Square	F Value	Pr > F
Model	3	232.7312341	77.5770780	9.59	<.0001
Error	56	452.9785992	8.0889036		
Corrected Total	59	685.7098333			

R-Square	Coeff Var	Root MSE	Score Mean
0.339402	27.03945	2.844100	10.51833

Source	DF	Type I SS	Mean Square	F Value	Pr > F
FactorA	1	1.6267778	1.6267778	0.20	0.6556
FactorB	1	206.9457990	206.9457990	25.58	<.0001
FactorA*FactorB	1	24.1586574	24.1586574	2.99	0.0895

Source	DF	Type II SS	Mean Square	F Value	Pr > F
FactorA	1	5.0684101	5.0684101	0.63	0.4319
FactorB	1	206.9457990	206.9457990	25.58	<.0001
FactorA*FactorB	1	24.1586574	24.1586574	2.99	0.0895

作者简介：

韩继宁，南佛罗里达大学二语习得与教育信息技术博士，西南大学教育学部讲师，主要研究方向为虚拟现实和增强现实在教育中的应用、LMS在教育中的设计与应用、科技辅助语言教学。

中国概况课程教材的时效性问题及对策

——以两个版本的《中国概况》为例*

李月炯
四川大学海外教育学院

摘　要：由于国情的不断变化，作为当代高校留学生国情教育课程的中国概况课程的教学内容也应该不断更新，以保持教学内容的时效性。而实际情况是，比起其他留学生通识教育课，中国概况课程现行的教材在时效性上的滞后现象显得尤为突出，其中的原因是多方面的。本文探讨了该教材时效性不尽如人意的两个重要表现并剖析了原因，在此基础上提出了可能的解决方案。

关键词：中国概况；国情教育；教材时效性；开放性教材

The Problem and Countermeasure of the Timeliness of Chinese Curriculum Materials

—Based on Example of the Two Editions of the Textbook

Li Yuejiong
School of Overseas Education, Sichuan University

Abstract: Due to the constant changes in China's national conditions, the general situation of China's national conditions education curriculum should be updated constantly to maintain the timeliness of teaching

---

* 本课题为2019年四川大学中央高校基本科研业务费项目“《中国概况》教材的时代性问题及对策”成果，项目编号：2019自研—海外05；亦受到四川大学教学改革项目的资助，项目编号：SCU8410。

content. Compared with other international students' general education courses, the current teaching materials of this course are relatively lagging behind in terms of timeliness, for which the reasons are various. This paper discusses the reasons for the unsatisfactory timeliness of teaching materials and puts forward possible solutions.

Keywords: General Situation of China; Education of National Conditions; Materials Timeliness ; Openness of teaching materials

一、引言

随着我国综合国力的增强以及教育水平的提高，中国教育在世界范围内的影响持续扩大，我国高校对留学生的吸引力日益增强。教育部部长陈宝生在 2017 年 10 月的讲话中指出，中国已经成为亚洲最大、世界第三的留学目的地国。立足于这一现实，他描绘了中国教育的美好愿景——到 2049 年，中国教育将引领世界教育的发展，而中国的标准也将成为世界的标准。毫无疑问，搞好来华留学生教育是中国教育在世界范围内维持良好声誉、持续扩大影响力和贡献作用的基石。面对来自不同意识形态、多元文化背景和传统习俗的留学生，中国教育必须打造向心力与普适性极强的通识课程群，才能满足中国教育走向世界并逐步在全球范围内发挥引导作用的需求。根据目前来华学生的需求，我们可以将生源划分为两类，一类是来华学习汉语言的本科生及研究生，另一类则是学习其他学科（如医学、计算机等）相关专业的本科生及研究生。对两种不同需求的学生而言，"知华""爱华"的培养目标是始终不变的，因而，使留学生了解中国国情、民情以及社会生活和人文概况等方面的情况，引导学生深入了解中国社会、正确认识中国的课程设置是必不可少的。从教学内容上看，中国概况课程是与这一目的最为吻合的课程。因此，在中国教育部、外交部和公安部联合下发的文件《学校招收和培养国际学生管理办法》中，有如下明确规定："汉语和中国概况应当作为高等学历教育的必修课。"基于以上背景的阐述和分析，不难发现：一方面，中国概况课程的开设是中国教育走向世界的要求；另一方面，中国概况课程作为一门国情教育课程，其教学内容必须包含中国的方方面面，在我国客观情况和历史文化内容之外，又要有与时俱进、体现中国变化与发展的相关内容，后者要求这门课的教学内容必须保持良好的“时效性”。其中，教材又是教学内容的主要依托，而当下的中国概况课程教材时效性较差，已经成为限制该课程实际教学质量的掣肘，给教学带来了多方面的困扰。

二、当下教材时效性的不足之处

“时效性”一词来源于管理学，指的是同一个事物在不同的时间点具有性质（或意义）的差异，而这个差异对决策有着重大影响。举例来说，一份2016年的啤酒销售市场分析对当下的啤酒销售商来说意义不大，因为当下的消费人群、竞争品牌、销售模式等相关因素已经发生了很大甚至是根本性的改变。而教材的时效性指的是教材内容与当下情形相吻合（或相关联）的程度。如果教材的内容能够准确反映当下的社会现实，与当前的社会发展联系紧密，其时效性就强；反之，其时效性就差。当前教材的时效性较差，主要表现在两个方面：一是缺乏反映当代国情变化的相关专题；二是在已有专题中，相关内容的表述与当下社会现实不相符合。本文以北京大学出版社出版、王洪顺主编的《中国概况》（2015）和北京航空航天大学出版社出版、夏自强主编的《中国概况》（1996）为例来进行分析，发现存在两个主要问题。

第一，缺乏反映当代中国国情变化的相关专题。王洪顺主编的《中国概况》初版于1994年，至2015年已经先后出版了四版。虽然编者在不同版本上进行了内容上的相关调整，“依据近10年来形势发展的新资料，做了更大幅度的更新、补充和修改……配插了许多图片，使版面显得比较活泼”（王洪顺，2015），但是该教材没有对章节结构做太大的调整。该教材主要内容涵盖以下14个专题：（1）国土，（2）历史，（3）人口，（4）民族，（5）政治制度，（6）经济，（7）科技，（8）教育，（9）传统思想，（10）文学，（11）艺术，（12）习俗，（13）旅游，（14）国际交往。而在夏自强主编的《中国概况》中，共有10个专题：（1）国土与资源，（2）人口、民族与宗教，（3）历史概况，（4）政治，（5）经济，（6）教育，（7）科学技术，（8）文化，（9）民情和风俗，（10）外交。这两种教材内容反映出了一个共性，即都回避了“事件型”专题内容，上述两种教材并没有涉及那些影响当代中国社会发展、给当代中国带来巨变的专题，比如给当代中国带来巨变的“改革开放”、改变中国地区发展不平衡的“西部大开发”以及由中国发起进而改变国际社会格局的“一带一路”倡议等。这固然是由于社会事件本身具有时效性所造成的，但是如果不对这些影响社会发展进程甚至决定社会发展方向的事件进行阐述和分析，教材中的其他专题就容易流于一种静态、孤立的阐述，各个专题之间缺乏深刻、有机的联系，学习者更多的时候就会陷入“知其然而不知其所以然”的境况。比如，在王洪顺主编的《中国概况》中，“改革开放”只在“经济发展”这一具体内容中顺带一提，对改革开放发生的背景和主要内容并无介绍，因而学生对其所产生的社会影响及给中国各个领域带来的深刻变化都无从知晓。如果说各个专门领域的知识与现状是课程内容的“经”，那么影响社会发展的重大事件就应该是“纬”，二者是有机联系的，对这些事件进行充分的阐述和分析，是使学生触类旁通、形成关于中国国情认知网络的重要途径。

第二，在已有专题中，相关内容的表述与当下社会现实不相符合，这反映了教材内容的滞后性，是国情教育课程教材长期面临的问题。这种情况又分为不同的具体情形，常见的有三种。一是数据不准确。一个典型的例子就是各教材中人口专题的相关教学内容中，人口的数量几乎是变动不居的，因此，几乎所有的教材都无法反映当下人口的实际状况。对此，不同的教材采用了不同的处理方式，夏自强的版本所采用的方法是梳理之前不同时间段的人口数量；而王洪顺的版本则是以某一年的数据（如第四版采用 2010 年的）进行说明。二是政策和制度的改变。我们仍以人口这一专题为例进行说明，迄今各版本的教材中关于中国人口政策相关内容的介绍都停留在“一胎化”时期，如王洪顺（2015）认为，中国控制人口数量的任务依然相当艰巨，“中国人口基数太大，每年全国新增人口将近 700 万人”，而实际上，我国目前的人口政策已经转变为全面实行“二胎”，与之相应的是近两年我国人口增长比例持续下滑。三是社会格局的变动。此处以“中国的疆域”这一知识点为例进行说明，在夏自强主编的教材中，中国邻国包括“锡金”，而稍晚的教材（如北京语言大学出版社 2000 年出版的《中国概况》）中也有同样的阐述，这是因为 2003 年之后中国承认原“锡金”属于印度的一部分。因此，北京大学出版社于 2015 年再版的教材中已经没有这一邻国了。而在 2003 年之后的数年间，多数高校所使用的教材相关内容仍然没有修正。

就中国概况课程而言，教材在时效性上的缺陷会给课程的教学带来两个方面的困扰。第一，加大教师的备课量，使教师无所适从。如上所言，教材是教学内容的主要依托，作为教师，如果仅仅就教材内容的具体细节进行调整是相对容易实现的，但要对内容模块的缺失进行填补则需要花费较多精力和时间，对于教学任务繁重的对外汉语教师而言，容易感到力不从心。第二，影响学习者的兴趣和信任感，不足以支撑“知华”“爱华”的培养目标。教材中关于国情的相关数据、政策等现状若与当下现实相吻合，则比较容易使学习者接受、信服，反之，会给学生带来困扰甚至产生排斥情绪。

三、时效性滞后的原因分析及相关对策

中国概况课程相关教材的时效滞后现象是由多种原因造成的，既与该课程的课程性质有关，也反映了教材编写者所面临的普遍困惑。梳理其中的因素，有助于我们发现解决问题的路径。

（一）原因探析

首先是课程性质因素。不同于社会某一领域的科学，该课程是一门综合性较强的人文通识课，虽然其在一定程度上是中国社会多个领域的科普性教学，但实际上未能触及相关领域的深度规律，这样的课程必然是在不违背相关学科规律的前提下追求综合性和简明性，这就导致该课程有相当比例的内容是关于社会表层现象的阐述（比如中国地理、中国的经济、中国的民族）或者以之为切入口进行适可而止的剖析（比如中国的人口、中国的政治制度设计），而表层现象的阐述更多地表现为孤立的数据、制度、文件以及事物。比如，夏自强主编的教材里关于人口比例的阐述是“人口性别比例基本正常”（夏自强，1996），但是实际上在该教材被使用的最后若干年，中国人口的性别比例出现了一定程度的失衡现象。

其次，本课程教材编写的周期较一般的读物而言更长。作为带有社会科普性质的读物，在理论上应该与社会发展保持高度一致，但是实际上教材又不同于其他读物或者专门手册，教材的使用范围、使用人群决定了其内容体量和编写体例必须严谨而规范，这就要求教材的编写需要花费较长时间。除了编写环节，教材的出版周期较杂志、报纸等读物中的科普文章发表周期而言更长。对大多数教材编写者而言，在可支配时间、资金支持、编写团队等方面都受到较大的限制。该课程教材的编写者多为课时较多的对外汉语教学一线教师，许多教材没有专项资金的支持，因而在组建编写团队上也显得较为困难。此外，社会发展的变化给本课程带来了比其他教材更大的困难，使

得本课程教材更容易被时代淘汰。

（二）相关对策

结合以上分析我们发现，编写周期长而使用周期短是造成中国概况课程相关教材时效性问题的根本原因，这一问题长期没有得到解决。不难发现，这一问题在传统的教材编写模式下几乎不可能得到很好的解决。为此，必须转变思路，着眼于开发新形态的教材。具体而言，应该从增强教材的开放性入手，并注重线上线下资源的融合。

第一，适应高校日渐兴起的翻转课堂，拓展教材的开放性。现行的教材多是传统的、封闭式的，主要是由编写者把相关知识点的完整叙述有条理、有层次地汇编起来，配以课后练习、少量插图与量表等素材，最终出版。这种教材的弊端在于，知识点都是既往现象，而随着人工智能在教学领域的深入使用和学生主观能动性的增强，学习者和教学人员都在努力打破这种灌输式的模式，“翻转课堂”虽不是对传统教材的弃用，但在一定程度上是对陈旧知识的规避。因此，如果能在开发教材时，就更多考虑如何打破传统教材的弊端，或许就能够设计出与“翻转课堂”相一致的教材。我们仍然以“中国人口的比例”这一知识点的教学为例，教学素材可以考虑做出如下设计：

截至去年年底，中国共有男性人口________人，女性人口________人，当前的男女比例为________。你怎么看待这一比例？

这样一来，教材编写者不用再纠结于数据的时效性，每一次教学都可以利用当下的材料，而当下社会信息获取的便捷性又给学生自主完成这一教学内容提供了可能。教材的改变又反过来要求教学者改变原有的教学模式，教学人员在设计课前预习任务、课堂教学环节，把控课堂教学，设计课程考核方式等方面都需要做出调整。当然，教学不应该为了解决教材的某一部分问题而改革，但是，实际情况是教学改革已经走在了教材改革之前，教材形态的改变只是时间问题。

第二，打破传统的教学空间，结合线上相关资源，开发线上线下相结合的教材。慕课（MOOC）的广泛开发和大量上线，突破了传统教学扁平化的局限，纸质教材形式无法传达的内容可以通过视听途径得到有效的表现。以慕课为代表的线上教学形式还有更多的好处，那就是时空的界限被打破，可视化的互动形式在多数情况下比文字更能激发学生的互动热情。因此，以后的中国概况课程教材开发，可依托已有的中国概况线上课程，开发相关配套教材，使教学材料更加立体，但是具体操作模式，仍需要教材编写者在线上线下融合的教学（SPOC）实践中不断探索。

参考文献：

[1] 韩秀梅. 谈《中国概况》课的教学思路 [J]. 云南师范大学学报，2004 (9).
[2] 郭鹏. 中国概况 [M]. 北京：高等教育出版社，2011.
[3] 王洪顺. 中国概况 [M]. 北京：北京大学出版社，2015.
[4] 夏自强. 中国概况 [M]. 北京：北京航空航天大学出版社，1996.
[5] 祖晓梅，陆平舟. 中国文化课的改革与建设——以《中国概况》为例 [J]. 世界汉语教学，2006 (7).

作者简介：

李月炯，文学博士，四川大学海外教育学院讲师，研究方向为高校留学生通识教育、汉语国际传播研究。

再谈国际汉语教学中的任务型教学法：教师认知研究

彭　越

加拿大女王大学

摘　要：在国际汉语教学领域，关于教学法的争论一直受到专家学者的高度重视。近年来，任务型教学法尤其吸引大家的注意。然而，当我们从科研人员的角度来探索任务型教学法的有效性和局限性等问题时，却几乎忽略了一线教师的声音。本文通过介绍关于第二语言教师的教师认知研究，呼吁大家更多地从教师的视角来探讨教学法，同时关注国际汉语教师的专业发展问题。

关键词：国际汉语教学；教学法；任务型教学法；教师认知；教师发展

Revisiting Task-Based Language Teaching for Teaching Chinese as a Second Language: Language Teacher Cognition

Peng Yue

Queen's University

Abstract: Pedagogy has attracted much of researchers' attention in the field of teaching Chinese as a second/foreign language. In recent years, task-based language teaching (TBLT) has been particularly much debated. However, when we approach the effectiveness and limitations of TBLT, experts' perspectives were mostly adopted while front-line teachers' voices were largely overlooked.

Through introducing language teacher cognition research, the article proposes that further understandings on pedagogy need to incorporate teachers' perspectives which will in term contribute to teachers' professional development.

Keywords: Teaching Chinese as a Second/Foreign Language; Pedagogy; TBLT; Teacher Cognition; Teacher Development

一、教学法之争及任务型教学法

“如何教”这个问题的重要性在任何形式和内容的教学中都是不言而喻的。在国际汉语教学领域，和其他的议题相比（如“如何学”“如何测评”等），“如何教”应该是专家学者们最为热衷讨论的话题之一。这一点从中文数据库中涉及汉语国际教育的教学法的论文数目可见一斑。

在二语教学领域，对“如何教”这个问题的讨论是分层次的。然而值得注意的是，汉语里常常使用的术语“××法”有时模糊了这其中的层级性。“结构法”对应着“交际法”，它们在一个较宏观的层面反映着不同的语言观、语言习得观以及语言教学观（Jack & Richards，2014）。“结构法”可以通过“语法翻译法”“直接法”“听说法”来具体实现，交际法则可以通过“任务法”“主题法”“内容法”等实现。目前，对于交际法的各种具体形式更常见的说法应该是“任务型教学法”“主题型教学法”“内容型教学法”。“××型教学法”这一说法大约对应着英文术语中的“approach”一词，区别于“method”（Jack & Richards，2014）。“approach”一词更加强调某种教学方法的灵活性，它遵循某种语言观、语言习得观和语言教学观的基本原则，但同时也灵活借鉴其他不同教学方法，并不要求统一的课堂教学步骤。而传统上使用得更多的“method”一词则更加强调某种事先固定好、教师严格执行的教学步骤。

各种教学法在20世纪直至21世纪相继出现，因此这一时期被称为“教学法的时代”（Jack & Richards，2014）。关于这些方法之间孰优孰劣的问题，学界产生了激烈的争论，且争议延续至今。结构法在20世界上半叶占据了二语教学的统治地位，其中起源于第二次世界大战时期美国军队的听说法正是其中的代表。听说法强调反复的操练、严格的纠错以及对词汇语法学习顺序的严格控制。在听说法基础上发展出来的P－P－P模式（演示—操练—成果）至今依然是全球很多语境下最主流的教学方式（Carless，2009）。在充分肯定结构法对二语教学贡献的前提下，20 世纪下半叶专家学者开始对结构法产生怀疑。这主要来自学科内部和外部两个方面的动力（Jack & Richards，2014）。学科内部的动力主要来自从结构语言学向功能语言学、社会语言学的转向。学科外部的动力在于 20 世纪六七十年代欧洲经济共同体的形成，成年人学习多门欧洲语言进行工作与交流的需求凸显，因而迫切需要找到一种培养学习者在真实语境中进行有效交际的教学方法。在内外因素共同作用下，交际法应运而生。

交际法的诞生晚于结构法，其开端本身就是对结构法过分强调语言结构的反拨。但是早期的交际法也不完美，最显著的问题是学习者在语言使用中准确度的降低。此后，衍生出了任务型教学法。早期的交际法强调意义而忽略了形式，而任务型教学法则试图平衡意义与结构（Ellis，2009）。龙（Long，2014）认为近四十年所开展的二语习得研究从理论和实证上支持了任务型教学法。与此同时，主题型教学法和内容型教学法也相继出现，并在一定范围内推广开来，与任务型教学法同属于广义的交际法（Celce-Murcia，2014）。在交际法范围内任务型教学法目前处于主导地位，比主题型教学法和内容型教学法得到更多的推广和关注。李特尔伍德（Littlewood，2004）认为任务型教学法是交际法目前最“正统”的实现形式。

以上提到的各种教学法之间的竞争不光存在于英语占主导地位的二语教学界，在汉语教学中结构法和交际法之争同样存在，对热门的任务型教学法的优劣之辩也从来没有停止过。

二、专家的声音

关于任务型教学法的教学效果的研究涉及不同语言种类，如英语（Aliakbari & Jamalvandi，2010）和西班牙语（de Ridder，Vangehuchten & Gómez，2007）；包括不同方面的教学，如词汇教学（de la Fuente's，2010）和口语教学（Aliakbari & Jamalvandi，2010）；而且不光限于一般用途的语言教学，也包括专门用途的二语教学，如商务西班牙语（de Ridder，Vangehuchten & Gómez，2007）。

国际汉语教育学界也积极介绍和引进任务型教学法。将任务型教学法应用到汉语教学的讨论基本代表的是专家学者的意见。在教学大纲方面，《高等学校外国留学生汉语教学大纲（短期强化）》于 2002 年首先引入任务型教学法，但是仅限于短期强化项目，在同时期出版的《长期进修和汉语言专业教学大纲》中则未提及。2008 年出版的《国际汉语教学通用课程大纲》则全面采用任务型教学法，并设计展示了 101 个任务作为指导。吴中伟、郭鹏（2009）认为 2008 年出版的大纲“标志着任务型教学法在汉语教学界进入了一个崭新的阶段，它不再停留在介绍、讨论阶段，而进入广泛运用、实施的阶段”。2014 年出版的《国际汉语教学通用课程大纲（修订版）》中，任务型教学法依然占据重要的地位。

除了大纲文件以外，学界发表的论文也基本代表着科研人员的观点。这其中大致分为两类。第一类是基于实证数据的探讨（如郑家平、李燕，2016），郑家平和李燕的实证研究通过对比实验发现，在初级阶段的汉语口语课方面，接受任务型教学法教学的学生比接受传统教学方法教学的学生在词汇语法的正确率、口头表达的流利度以及课堂参与度等方面都表现得更好。除了基于实证的讨论以外，更多的是第二类，即基于理论和经验的探讨。马箭飞（2000）介绍了以“交际任务”为基础的汉语短期教学新模式；马箭飞（2002）介绍了如何设计任务大纲和任务活动；吴永毅（2006）介绍了交际法和任务法之间的关系与演变；吴永毅（2016）重点区分了何为“任务”；吴中伟、郭鹏（2009）的专著从任务的设计、教材编写与使用、专门用途汉语教学等方面介绍任务型教学法。

前文所介绍的专家学者们对教学方法孰优孰劣的讨论标准主要集中在任务型教学法的有效性。这种尝试在某种教学方法和教学效果之间建立因果关系的研究在教育学中被称为“过程—产出”（process-product）模式。基于“过程—产出”模式的研究其背后的逻辑是：如果我们发现了一种有效的教学方法，那么就可以“打包”，进而在课堂教学中推广开来。“打包”在此处的意思是，在某种教学法理念的指导下，将教学大纲、教学材料、课堂流程等相对固定下来。

教育学的研究表明，“过程—产出”的思维模式背后存在着根本的“隐患”。通过实验和理论讨论，专家学者们支持或反对某种教学方法和教师在课堂上使用该方法其实是两件本质上截然不同的事情。课堂活动的主人归根结底是教师和学生。虽然受到各种因素的共同影响，但是“怎么教”这个问题根本上是由教师决定的，也就是说教师才是课堂的决策者（Borg，

2003)。然而遗憾的是，作为能动的主体，一线汉语教师们的声音在关于教学法的争论中被忽略了。

事实上，有为数众多的研究都在提醒我们，专家学者以及大纲文件想要教师采用哪种教学方法，和教师在日常的教学活动中实际上怎么教之间存在着鸿沟。以任务型教学法在英文教学中的运用为例：一方面，任务型教学法得到二语习得理论和研究的普遍支撑（Long，2014），并在世界上很多地方的中小学外语教学大纲中得以推广，比如中国香港的英文教学（Carless，2003，2004，2007，2009）、越南的英文教学（Nguyen，2014）、韩国的英文教学（Jeon & Hahn，2006），以及中国大陆的英文教学（Zheng & Borg，2014；Chen & Wright，2017）。除了英语教学以外，任务型教学法也在加拿大安大略省的法语教学、新西兰的各语种的外语教学（East，2012）的大纲中被推广。然而另一方面，任务型教学法在真正走进课堂的过程中遇到了非常明显的障碍。在亚洲的英语教学语境中开展的研究发现，传统的结构法仍然是课堂教学的主流（Butler，2017）。在大部分研究中，任务型教学法几乎都没有得以实施（Deng & Carless，2009；Nguyen，2014；Lin & Wu，2012）；在少部分研究中，任务型教学法被有限地使用，主要是作为传统教学法的辅助（Hu，2013；Carless，2009；Chen & Wright's，2017；Zheng & Borg，2014）。至于是什么因素限制了教师在课堂上使用任务型教学法，以往的研究表明原因主要来自两个方面：其一是教师对任务型教学法的了解比较有限，甚至有一些“偏见”；其二是环境因素，如大规模标准化考试主导的教育体系以及外语（而非二语）的课堂外环境等。实际上，这两个因素并非孤立存在，二者有着双向互动的关系。教师对任务型教学法的了解到何种程度？他们对实施该教学法的态度如何？教师所处的环境是如何塑造了他们的认知？这些问题正是“教师认知”这一研究领域关注和探讨的话题。

三、教师认知研究

克拉克和皮特森（Clark & Peterson，1986）将教师的教学过程归纳为两部分，一部分是教师的思维过程，另一部分是可直接观察到的教学行为及其效果。随着认知心理学的发展，对前者的研究，即教师的思维过程从20世纪80年代开始逐渐受到重视。在第二语言教学领域，对教师思维的研究开始得稍晚，大约始于20世纪90年代（Borg，2003）。时至今日，教师的认知研究已经在第二语言教学领域占据了重要地位，成为科研论文、专著和学术会议的议题。

孙德坤（2008）率先在国际汉语教育学界介绍了教师认知这一概念，并对教师认知的缘起、议题以及对国际汉语教育的重要意义进行了较为详尽的阐述。孙德坤对教师认知的介绍主要基于伯格（Borg，2003）早期的定义，即教师教学中所不能直接观察到的范畴，主要是“他们的信念、思想、知识结构及其对教学实践的影响等”。伯格的思路在于将教师认知作为一个上级概念，包含了教育学中广泛研究的教师“知识”和“信念”，而不对其进行进一步细分。这不同于以舒尔曼（Shulman，1986，1987）为代表的其他学者将教师的知识进一步细分为其中不同的类型的做法。因为在伯格看来，这样的细分虽然具有理论意义，然而在实践中我们却很难真正区分出各种细分类型之间的差异。如今的教师认知研究范围比孙德坤文中介绍的范围更广，已经超出了伯格（2003）的早期定义，包括了教师身份认同和情感等更新的概念（Borg，2019）。

近年来，教师认知开始受到国际汉语学界一些学者的重视。张黎、李泉、吴勇毅等相继通过讲座的形式介绍了教师认知研究。虽然教师认知这一概念在国际汉语教学领域日益受到关注，但是针对汉语教师的教师认知的实证研究还非常有限，少数例子包括汲传波、刘芳芳（2012），汲传波（2016），丁安琪（2013），江新、郝丽霞（2010），巴拉特、巴拉沃（Baralt & Bravo，2016），孙德坤（Sun，2012），王丹萍（Wang，2016），杨娟（Yang，2018），彭越（Peng，2019）等。其中几篇中文的文章采用的是定量的研究方法，对国际汉语教师（包括华裔和非华裔教师、职前和在职教师）的实践性知识和语法教学信念等进行了统计分析。而几篇英文的文章则采用质性研究方法，数据来源主要为课堂观察和访谈。两种研究方法性质不同、各有长短，对我们理解教师的“内心世界”起到了互补的作用。

从教师认知角度来研究国际汉语教学中的任务型教学法的文献还很有限，主要包括巴拉特、巴拉沃（2016），张玉梅、罗少茜（2018）和彭越（2019）。张玉梅和罗少茜采用定量和质性研究相结合的研究方法，研究对象为北京某高校的35名汉语教师。该研究发现，汉语教师相信任务型教学法有好的教学效果，然而对其可行性持怀疑态度。巴拉特和巴拉沃的研究对象是美国高校的汉语教师。该研究采用个案研究的方式，关注一位教师对任务型教学法中语法教学的有效时间的信念问题。该教师与研究人员配合，实施事先准备好的两套任务型教学法教案：分别将语法教学放在前任务和后任务两个不同阶段。课堂录像的分析结果显示，当语法教学发生在后任务阶段时，学习者有更多的语言产出、更高的准确度，可以更好地更正自己的语言，更多地进行互动对话。然而，开放性问卷表明，在前任务阶段进行语法教学更符合教师对语法教学的信念。该教师相信前任务阶段的语法规则的教学能够保证学生在执行任务期间的语言准确度，而后任务阶段的语法教学则不能规范学生的语言结构。

彭越（2019）的研究关注的是中国高校的汉语教师对任务型教学法的教学实践，也涉及教学实践背后的教师认知。与巴拉特和巴拉沃（2016）不同的是，彭越的研究中并不要求教师刻意进行任务型教学，而是在日常教学中关注他们对任务型教学法的自然接受或排斥情况。通过对八名教师的访谈和课堂观察，她发现传统的结构法仍然占课堂教学的主导地位，同时任务型教学法也被普遍运用到教学实践，但是处于补充辅助的地位。该研究认为，教师们决定采用任务型教学法多是一种自发性的尝试，目的在于尝试解决运用结构法时所面临的几重困境。比如，在传统的结构法主导的课堂上教师普遍遇到了难以调动学生课堂积极性的问题，而学生的积极参与对教师来说是达到好的学习效果这一目标的前提条件。在这种情况下，任务型教学法作为调动学生参与积极性的工具得到教师的认同和使用。

彭越（2019）的研究中发现教师表示自己对任务型教学法了解但又存在疑惑，因此常常表现出不自信的状态。她认为这一现象和教师教育关系密切。一方面，从教师专业学习内容上看，资历比较老的教师表示在他们进行职前教育的时候，国际汉语教育师资培训才刚刚起步，而专业训练的内容中关于课堂教学的方面很少，更多的是汉语本体研究。另一方面，从教师专业学习的方式来看，大多数教师都表示在职前教育中涉及过任务型教学法。然而，授课的方式被教师描述为“照本宣科、太理论、太抽象”，因而教师们对于如何在实践中使用该教学方法还是感到困惑。

四、结语

理论和实证方面的证据都向我们传递了一个信息：在“怎么教”这个问题上，教师才是课堂真正的主人。以上提到的从教师认知角度考察任务型教学法的研究向我们揭示了一些教师真正的想法，探讨了这些观念的形成和知识的来源。教师认知研究的直接意义在于服务于教师的职业教育和发展：一个教师教育项目能否真正影响教师，很大程度上取决于我们对教师已有的知识、态度和观念了解的程度，找到教师们的需求点，进而采用有效的教学方法对教师的认知和教学行为起到积极作用。教师认知研究也是我们推行任何一种教学改革的基础，否则教学改革很可能沦为专家学者在科研论文、大纲文件上的一纸空谈。综上所述，在国际汉语教师培训蓬勃发展的今天，学术界需要更多关注教师的研究，从而指导我们更好地进行教师教育和教学改革。

参考文献：

[1] 丁安琪. 非华裔汉语教师语法教学观念分析 [J]. 国际汉语教育，2013 (2).
[2] 国家汉办. 高等学校外国留学生汉语教学大纲（短期强化）[S]. 北京：北京语言大学出版社，2002.
[3] 国家汉办. 国际汉语教学通用课程大纲 [S]. 北京：外语教学与研究出版社，2008.
[4] 国家汉办. 国际汉语教学通用课程大纲（修订版） [S]. 北京：北京语言大学出版社，2014.
[6] 汲传波. 职前汉语教师语法教学信念变化初探 [J]. 语言教学与研究，2016 (5).
[5] 汲传波，刘芳芳. 教师认知视角下的职前汉语教师语法教学信念研究 [J]. 语言教学与研究，2006 (6).
[7] 江新，郝丽霞. 对外汉语教师实践性知识的个案研究 [J]. 世界汉语教学，2010 (3).
[8] 孙德坤. 教师认知研究与教师发展 [J]. 世界汉语教学，2008 (3).
[9] 马箭飞. 以“交际任务”为基础的汉语短期教学新模式 [J]. 世界汉语教学，2000 (4).
[10] 马箭飞. 任务型大纲与汉语交际任务 [J]. 语言教学与研究，2004 (4).
[11] 吴勇毅. 从交际语言教学到任务型语言教学 [J]. 对外汉语研究，2006 (2).
[12] 吴勇毅. 再论任务型教学中的“任务”[J]. 国际汉语教学研究，2016 (1).
[13] 吴中伟，郭鹏. 对外汉语任务型教学 [M]. 北京：北京大学出版社，2009.
[14] 郑家萍，李燕. 任务型初级汉语教学：从理论到实践 [M]. 北京：世界图书出版公司，2017.
[15] Aliakbari, M., Jamalvandi, B. The Impact of “Role Play” on Fostering EFL Learners' Speaking Ability: A Task-Based Approach [J]. Journal of Pan-Pacific Association of Applied Linguistics, 2010 (1).
[16] Baralt, M., Bravo, M. L. Teaching Chinese as a foreign language: A classroom

study on the timing of grammar around a task [J]. CASLAR, 2016 (1).

[17] Borg, S. Teacher cognition in language teaching: A review of research on what language teachers think, know, believe, and do [J]. Language Teaching, 2003 (3).

[18] Borg, S. Language teacher cognition: Perspectives and debates [A]. X. Gao. Second handbook of English language teaching [M]. Cham, CH: Springer.

[19] Butler, Y. G. Communicative and task-based language teaching in the Asia-Pacific region [A]. N. Van Deusen-Scholl, S. May. Second and foreign language education: Encyclopedia of language and education [C]. New York, NY: Springer, 2017.

[20] Carless, D. Factors in the implementation of task-based teaching in primary schools [J]. System, 2003, 31 (4).

[21] Carless, D. Issues in teachers' reinterpretation of a task-based innovation in primary schools [J]. TESOL Quarterly, 2004 (4).

[22] Carless, D. The suitability of task-based approaches for secondary schools: Perspectives from Hong Kong. System, 2007 (4).

[23] Carless, D. Revisiting the TBLT versus P-P-P debate: Voices from Hong Kong [J]. Asian Journal of English Language Teaching, 2009.

[24] Celce-Murcia, M. An overview of language teaching methods and approaches [A]. M. Celce-Murcia, D. M. Brinton, M. A. Snow. Teaching English as a second or foreign language (3rd ed.) [C]. Boston, MA: National Geographic Learning.

[25] Chen, Q., Wright, C. Contextualization and authenticity in TBLT: Voices from Chinese classrooms [J]. Language Teaching Research, 2017 (4).

[26] Clark, C., Peterson, P. Teachers' thought processes [A]. M. C. Wittrock. Handbook of research on teaching (3rd ed.) [C]. New York, NY: Macmillan, 1986.

[27] de la Fuente, M. J. Classroom L2 vocabulary acquisition: Investigating the role of pedagogical tasks and form-focused instruction [J]. Language Teaching Research, 2006 (3).

[28] de Ridder, I., Vangehuchten, L., Gómez, M. S. Enhancing automaticity through task-based language learning [J]. Applied Linguistics, 2007 (2).

[29] Deng, C., Carless, D. The communicativeness of activities in a task-based innovation in Guangdong China [J]. Asian Journal of English Language Teaching, 2009.

[30] East, M. Task-based language teaching from teachers' perspective: Insights from New Zealand [M]. Amsterdam, NL: John Benjamin Publishing, 2012.

[31] Ellis, R. Task-based language teaching: sorting out the misunderstandings [J]. International Journal of Applied Linguistics, 2009 (3).

[32] Hu, R. Task-Based Language Teaching: Responses from Chinese English teachers [J]. TESOL-EJ, 2013 (4).

[33] Lin, T. B., Wu, C. W. Teachers' perceptions of Task-Based Language Teaching in English classrooms in Taiwanese junior high schools [J]. TESOL Journal, 2012 (4).

[33] Littlewood, W. The task-based approach: some questions and suggestions [J]. ELT Journal, 2004 (4).

[34] Long, M. H. Second language acquisition and Task-Based Language Teaching [M]. Oxford, UK: Wiley-Blackwell, 2015.

[35] Nguyen, V. G. Forms or meaning? Teachers' beliefs and practices regarding Task-based Language Teaching: A Vietnamese case study [J]. The Journal of Asia TEFL, 2014 (1).

[36] Peng, Y. Finding success with pedagogical innovation: A case from CSL teachers' experiences with TBLT [J]. Language Teaching Research, 2019.

[37] Richards, J., Rogers, T. Approaches and methods in language teaching (3rd ed.) [M]. Cambridge, UK: Cambridge University Press, 2014.

[38] Shulman, L. S. Paradigms and research programmes in the study of teaching: A contemporary perspective [A]. M. C. Wittrock. Handbook of research on teaching (3rd ed.) [C]. New York, NY: Macmillan, 1986.

[39] Sun, D. "Everything goes smoothly": A case study of an immigrant Chinese language teacher's personal practical knowledge. Teaching and Teacher Education, 2012 (5).

[40] Zhang, Y., Luo, S. Teachers' beliefs and practices of Task-based Language Teachingin Chinese as a second language classrooms [J]. Chinese Journal of Applied Linguistics, 2018 (3).

[41] Zheng, X., Borg, S. Task-based learning and teaching in China: Secondary school teachers' beliefs and practices [J]. Language Teaching Research, 2014 (1).

作者简介：

彭越，哲学（教育学）博士，研究方向为汉语国际教育的教学法、语言测试及教师发展。

基于"互联网+"的在线少儿汉语教学现状研究

魏海平
西南民族大学文学与新闻传播学院

摘　要："互联网+"模式的发展和"汉语热"的持续使得在线少儿汉语教学呈现高速发展的态势。调查在线少儿汉语教学机构，分析其现状及特点，发现这个领域的优势与不足，为一线教学提供一定的专业建议和展望，是具有一定实践价值的研究。本文调查了30所在线少儿汉语教学平台，分别从情况调查、现状分析、反思与展望三个主要方面进行阐述和分析，通过数据分析对教学现状进行全面考察。

关键词："互联网+"；在线教学；少儿汉语

The Present Situation of Online Chinese Teaching for Children under "Internet Plus"

Wei Haiping
School of Literature and Journalism, Southwest Minzu University

Abstract: The great development of Internet and the heat of Chinese learning make online Chinese teaching for kids improved fast. It is valuable to investigate and analyze the present situation of this area, and to make constructive suggestion. This paper investigated 30 online teaching service organizations, analyzed their entire situation and make some solid suggestions about how to improve the online Chinese teaching for children.

Keywords："Internet Plus"；Online teaching；Chinese for Children

一、研究背景综述

随着21世纪"互联网+"趋势的到来，包括语言教学在内的各类教育产业都面临着前所未有的挑战和机遇。新型的信息技术与教学开发成果的结合"使得当前的课堂教学发生了结构性变革，大大促进了课堂教学的网络化、智慧化发展，互联网在线教学已经进入4.0时代：即'互联网+'课堂的智慧教学新阶段"（孙曙辉，2016）。

教育部及国家语言文字工作委员会发布的《中国语言文字事业发展报告（2017）》指出，截至2017年，全球已有67个国家和地区将汉语纳入国民教育体系。随着"汉语热"的不断发展，学习汉语的人群呈现从过去以成年人为主到目前越来越低龄化的趋势，多个国家在中小学开设汉语作为第二语言的课程。海外华人子女的华文教育也持续升温。这两者形成了海外汉语教学的两大主要阵营。

国家汉办把新研制的YCT考试的主要对象定为第一语言非汉语的15岁以下的汉语学习者。目前全球各地开设汉语课程的机构和平台也多采用3～12岁、6～15岁的区间来划定"少儿汉语"这类教学对象。目前国内对少儿汉语教学的研究大多将目光投向儿童心理认知对汉语教学的影响、沉浸式少儿汉语教学模式、少儿汉语教学的具体方法、少儿汉语教材建设以及少儿汉语教师培养等方面，其研究多建立在传统的面授课堂基础之上。

专门针对技术变革新形势下的汉语教学的讨论虽然也取得了一定的成果，但还有很大的拓展空间。目前关于对外汉语在线教学的研究需要的是宏观讨论整个对外汉语在线教学的现状及趋势（吕军伟，2017；张会、陈晨，2109），有的着重从信息技术层面讨论在线汉语教学平台的建设与技术开发（郑艳群，2015），或者从微观层面讨论在线汉语教学中关于教学模式、教师培训（章欣、李晓琪，2017）等问题。而专门针对在线少儿汉语教学的研究则十分稀少。

当前的现实状况是，全球学习汉语的15岁以下人群数量不断增长，国外开设汉语课程的公立及私立学校对教学资源尤其是师资需求得不到满足，海外华裔对子女华文教育的重视程度越来越高。为了打破地域和空间的限制，让更多学习者能够高效地获得汉语教学服务，近几年来，全球各地不断涌现出专门针对 15 岁以下汉语学习者的互联网在线教学机构。市场需求带动了这类汉语教学模式的发展。我们认为，对目前较为活跃的在线少儿汉语教学平台的现状进行调查分析，了解这个教学类型的特征、优势和不足，对其提出有效的发展构想，对全面发展和推进汉语国际教育事业具有重要的价值。

二、基于信息技术的汉语教学

互联网、大数据、区块链、云计算、人工智能、语音识别、虚拟现实及增强现实等信息技术高速发展，伴随着即将进入 5G 通信时代的大趋势，汉语国际教育和推广面临着前所未有的机遇与挑战。在不远的将来，传统的语言教学模式将会出现颠覆性的变革。目前已经建立且在不断发展完善的一部分基于信息技术的新型汉语教学模式已经初步打开了变革与创新的局面。

信息技术给汉语国际教育带来了新的教学模式，如具有规模大、开放性、网络化、自主化（张会、陈晨，2109）特点的慕课（Massive Open Online Course，MOOC），将传统教学模式结合信息技术辅助的混合式新型学习方式“翻转课堂”，在移动信息网络技术支持下为学生打破时空限制实现碎片化学习的移动终端 App 等。

对第二语言学习来说，其学科本身有着不同于其他知识类课程的独特性，语言的学习需要在交互式的互动和即时反馈中才能取得较好的效果。在基于信息技术的语言教学模式中，只有远程在线课程和互动直播课程能够完成语言学习的即时双向互动。慕课、网络学习资源平台、网络学习软件，甚至带有语音识别的自主学习软件只能做到单向或者准单向的语言教学。

在双向互动的互联网在线学习模式中，远程在线课程一般是一对一或者小班的实时互动模式，师生通过远程视频通话，借助视频聊天工具或者专门的直播教学平台进行教学。直播课程则是一名教师面对数量较多的学生群体，利用直播教学平台工具进行集体教学，互动方式一般采取在线文字聊天答疑的形式。对第二语言学习来说，第一种模式能够更精准和即时地给予学生互动和反馈，尤其是针对语言技能的操练更直接和高效。在线直播课对语法讲解、阅读写作等教学项目可以起到较好的作用，尤其利于教学服务机构在单位时间内服务更多的学习者，但是对听说技能的操练则不如一对一或小班教学模式效果好。

本文调查了30个当前较为活跃的线上少儿汉语教学服务平台机构，归纳出四类主要的教学模式：（1）开发提供网络教学资源，学生利用电子书、动画片、字帖、在线字典、教学视频网页等电子学习资源进行自主学习；（2）提供制作好的慕课、公开课、微课、网络录播课等，学生灵活安排时间进行自主学习；（3）开发提供少儿汉语学习软件，包括在线学习软件和下载到本地使用的学习软件，学生可随时随地利用碎片时间进行学习，但是互动性不足，语言学习纠错功能较弱；（4）提供真人教师远程实时互动教学，学生需要按照约定时间参与互动课程，通过具有远程视频通话功能的平台与母语教师进行教学活动，这是一种将现代信息技术与传统线下师生互动模式结合起来的新型教学模式。

正如上文所说，远程互动教学对第二语言学习来说是一种效率更高的网络教学模式。因此我们将考察的主要对象确立为第四种类型的“互联网+”汉语教学平台。这些平台当中有的专注于远程实时教学，有的兼顾多种类型的教学模式，有的保留了较多的传统语言学校课程设置模式，只是将教学搬到了线上，有的则吸收了互联网时代的主流模式，为教师和学生提供自主信息交换平台（与“跟谁学”“赶集网”类似），或者采用互联网社交模式（自主匹配语伴）进行语言教学。

就目前的发展现状来看，以一对一和小班教学为主的在线远程互动教学是最具市场潜力的模式。它充分调动了教师和学生的双向资源，利用互联网打破地域的阻隔，高效地为师资匮乏的海外汉语市场提供大量的专业母语背景师资，利用互联网构架了汉语“走出去”的桥梁，在平台机构的统一品控下，提供比自由信息交换平台更有保障的教学质量，还为国内汉语教师提供了可观的就业渠道。

我们调查到的30个“互联网+”在线汉语教学平台中，有10个是提供信息平台和社交功能的网站或软件，包括多语种的学习网站和专门针对汉语学习的网站。多语种教学平台如Italki、Verbling、Preply、Wyzant、MenRise等，这几个是在美国创立的，汉语只是其中一个语种。平台提供教师信息列表，学生根据自己的需求自由预约老师上课，课时费由平台中转，并抽取10%～30%不等的手续费。这种模式下参与学习的成年学习者远远多于少儿学习者，因为未成年学习者必须在家长的监管之下安排学习，这种模式对家长的监管精力要求比较高。HelloTalk、ChineseBond都是社交性语言学习网站，由于学生的自主性要求很高，且需要自由组合语伴，不太适合未成年学习者。另外还有提供学习资源的 App，其中影响比较大的有多语种的学习软件 Duolingo，比较适合初中级学习者，成人和少儿学习内容均有，但更多倾向于成年学习者。专门针对汉语学习的 Chinese Pod，提供音视频课程、一对一真人教学以及大量汉语学习电子资源，主要面向成年学习者。还有专门针对少儿汉语学习的软件 WaWaYaYa，主要提供在线少儿汉语分级阅读资源和汉语绘本。学习者可以在软件上阅读和进行打卡积分，并获取全网排名，孩子们可以在软件中看到自己在所有使用者当中的学习进度排名，具有一定网络社交的功能特点。

我们调查的另外 20 个“互联网+”在线汉语教学平台大多提供实时在线教学，并有相对系统的教学体系，与自由预约老师和结交语伴的模式存在较大的区别。这类平台的操作方式是线上教学，而教学内容依然沿革了线下传统教学机构的专业性和系统性。我们将这些平台的各项特点进行归纳，整理成数据，从中分析出当前在线少儿汉语教学的主要现状，具体的数据将在下部分进行说明。

三、当前在线少儿汉语教学的情况调查

对调查的 20 个提供在线少儿汉语教学的平台，我们从教学内容和形式、教学班级设置、教学对象、师资背景、学术背景等方面进行了分析，试图勾勒出当前在线少儿汉语教学的主要现状版图。下面就每个参项的数据进行说明。

我们首先考察的是这些机构成立和运营的地区，一般创始地区也是之后平台运营的主要地区，当然客户是面向全球范围内的汉语学习者。

从图 1 可以看出，创始基地设在国内的占一半以上，也有一部分是海外华人或中外合作的机构，国内外都有基地或者只在国外设立办公室。比如“考拉知道”平台就只在美国洛杉矶设立了办公室，主要面向美国地区的华裔儿童招生。“唐 Kid”在北京和加拿大均设有办公室，“阳阳中文”的总部在贵阳，分部在美国。“哈兔中文”的创始人是西班牙华裔，因此在杭州和西班牙都有办公室。这个现象主要与机构创始人以及合作模式有关。这些都说明目前在线教学还是以国内机构为主。调查的机构当中成都、武汉、贵阳、杭州各有一家，上海有四家，其余的机构国内创始地或办公室都设立在

北京。国外的机构除了加拿大一家、新加坡两家，其余创始地均设在美国。

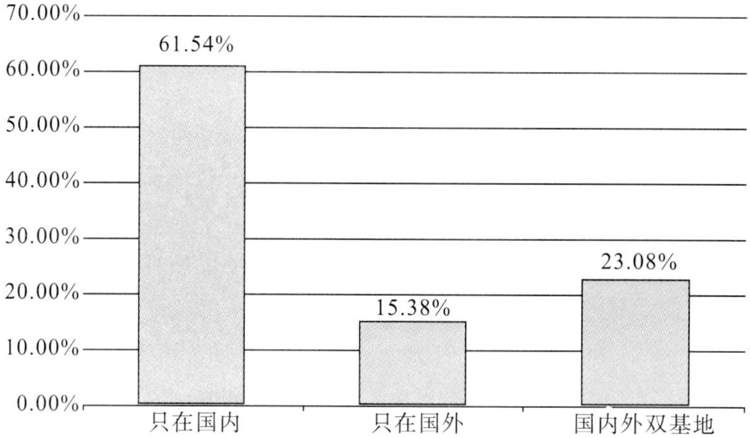

图 1　机构创始基地

第二，我们考察了不同平台的教学模式分布，统计出纯线上模式和线上线下结合两个类型，分布百分比如下：在采取纯线上教学模式的机构中，80%是只在国内有基地的。而开展线上教学和线下活动相结合的机构，大都在国外设有基地，有的甚至直接同生源地的中小学或国际学校开展教学和文化活动。

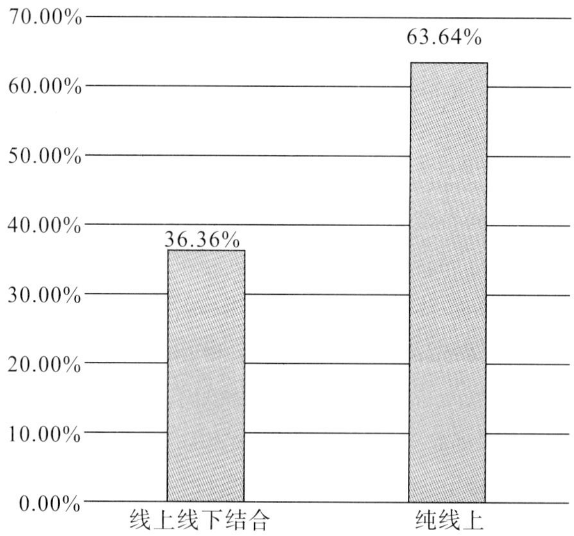

图 2　教学模式

第三，我们考察了各个平台招收生源的方向，这个部分决定了平台的教学对象，而教学对象直接决定了整个教学的内容、课程设置、大纲编写和教材选择。从这部分数据开始，不同的平台开始走向不同的类型，占据了不同的汉语教学市场板块。

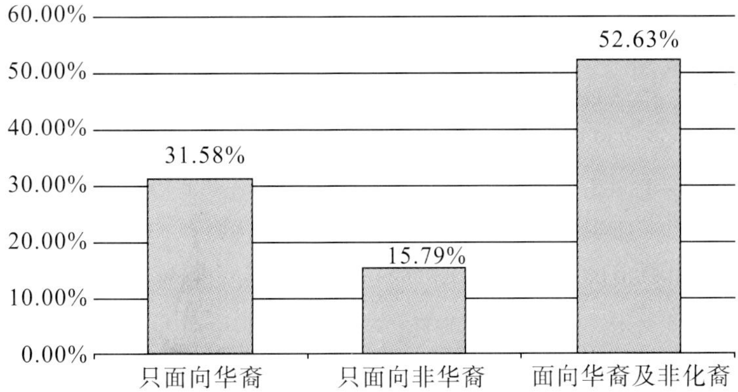

图 3　教学对象国别背景

从图 3 可以看出，当前在线少儿汉语教学服务市场上，华裔是主要的生源群体。将汉语作为第二语言学习的外籍儿童的主要学习动机源自全球化进程的推进、中国经济政治的发展以及“汉语热”的影响，兴趣和文化好奇心也是占较大比重的学习动机。对华裔儿童而言，出于母国文化的传承、家庭语言代际传承等原因，他们的学习动机更加强烈。

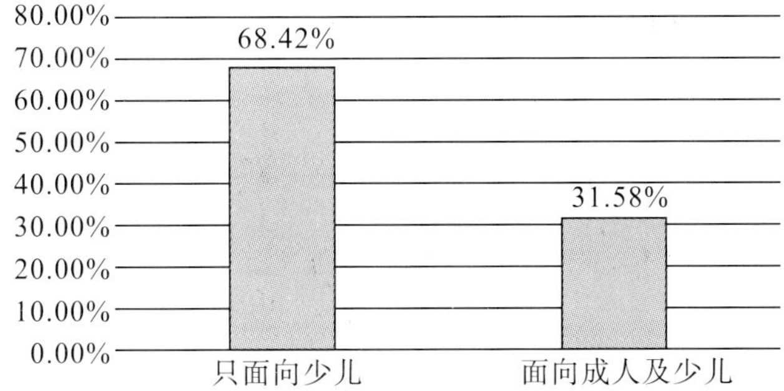

图 4　机构面向的教学对象年龄

第四，我们考察了机构面向的客户群体在年龄上的分布，由此可以筛选出专门从事少儿汉语教学的平台，以区别于随着市场需求而增加少儿汉语板块的综合性汉语培训机构。

汉办网络孔子学院这样的官方机构，所涉及的范围较广，面向成人和儿童的资源都比较丰富，但不提供实时在线教学，一般以公开课、慕课为主，也是唯一一个提供师资培训网络资源的平台。"儒森汉语 Mandarin Garden" "思道睿汉语 That's Mandarin" "美和语言进修学校 Mandarin House" 这三所机构都是发展较早、较为成熟的线下汉语培训学校，随着业务的发展而拓展出线上教学课程，但主营业务依然是传统的线下汉语教学，且成人生源多于少儿生源。而 "Lingobus" "考拉知道" "瞧瞧中文" "51KiD" "Speaking Duck" 等 16 个平台都是专门针对 15 岁以下少儿学习者开发的。

第五，我们考察的是平台提供的教学内容形式。由于在调研之初我们就把研究对象锁定在提供远程实时互动教学的平台，因此除了网络孔子学院和米诺在线中文两个平台，其余的全部提供实时在线教学，图中我们称为 "live 教学" 模式，如图 5 所示：

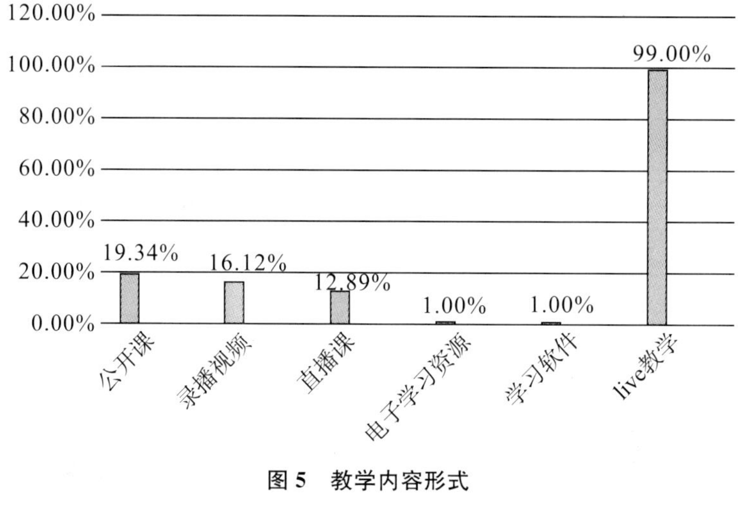

图 5　教学内容形式

由图 5 可以看出，在实时在线教学的基础之上，不少平台也自主开发或者购买第三方资源提供给自己的学员，包括公开课（以慕课形式）、录播视频（平台自己的精选课程录像）、一对多的直播课等形式。而电子学习资源和学习软件的开发耗费的技术成本较高，只有 1%的平台开设这类业务。

第六，我们对班级模式的分布做了统计。目前在线教学的班级大致分为一对一和三到五人的小班。不同的平台根据自身的情况对班级设置进行选择，分布如图 6 所示。

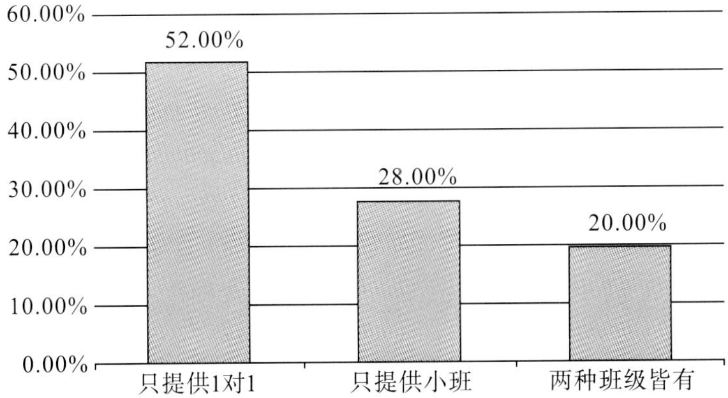

图 6　教学班级模式

第七，语言培训最大的问题之一就是师资流动性较强，不利于学生学习的系统性和连续性。许多线下机构一直在尽力解决这个问题，线上教学在这方面又有其特点。我们对师资是否固定做了统计，如图 7 所示：

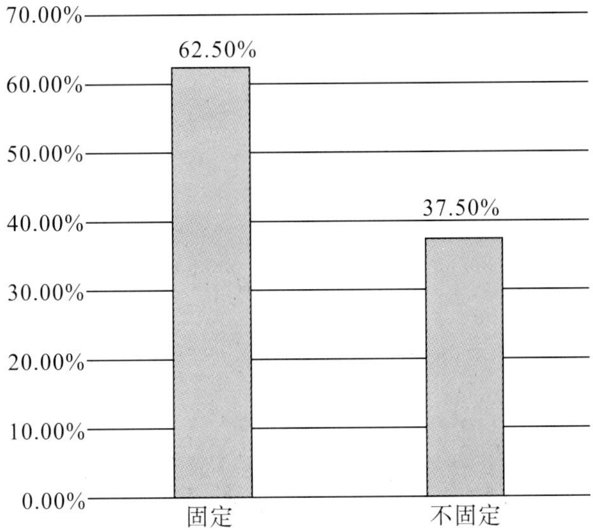

图 7　任课教师是否固定

由图 7 可以看出，过半数的机构还是尽可能尊重语言学习的连续性需求，尽量为学生安排固定老师授课。比较特殊的是国内最大的在线少儿英语培训机构 VIPKid 旗下的少儿中文培训网站 Lingobus。该平台延续了母公司一贯的“抢课”制度，系统提供老师的授课表，学生需要在每次课前预约心仪的老师，如果预约失败则安排到其他班级，这个模式在互联网教育服务中也是一个新的思路。

第八，在线汉语教学不同于传统线下教学，一个先进高效的教学平台是必不可少的工具。一些资金实力雄厚的平台都自主研发专门为在线教学使用的多媒体、多功能教学平台。如主打科技产品开发的“唐 Kid”和拿到多轮投资的 Lingobus。而另一些规模相对较小的平台则将重心放在课程研发和师资培训上，选择使用第三方专业科技公司开发的产品。如进入市场在线教育 13 年的老牌在线汉语机构 e-chineselearning 依然选择使用传统在线视频聊天工具 Skype 进行教学。成立时间较短的新加坡 Speaking Duck 平台使用的是第三方“布卡”网络教学工具。

另外一个至关重要的教学资源就是教材。一部分平台选择自己组织团队进行教材开发，一部分平台选择经典权威性教材并综合各类辅助教学材料用于教学。具体的数据分布见图 8 和图 9：

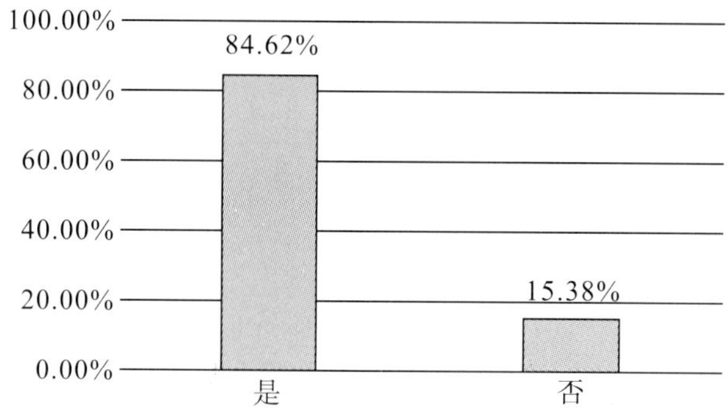

图 8　是否自主开发平台

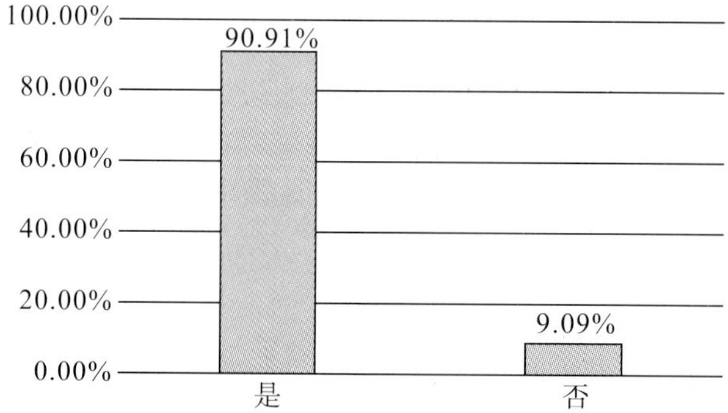

图 9　是否自主开发教材

图 8 体现的差异主要是由不同机构的规模和资金实力所决定的。一些刚刚成立不久的新平台，还没有能力独立开发多媒体在线教学工具。而图 9 体现的内容是语言教学中十分重要的一个因素，即教材的质量。并不是说没有自主开发教材的机构其教学质量就一定不能提供专业的教学服务，目前市面上有很多高质量的权威教材，使用得当是能够获得较好的教学效果的。然而专门针对在线教学尤其是符合儿童学习特征的电子教材十分稀少。将经典教材转换为在线教材，也会面临内容转换和技术嫁接等问题，这也是很多有能力的机构选择自主开发教材的原因。

最后，上一个问题其实反映出目前在线少儿汉语教学的一个紧迫需求。我们调查了这些线上教学机构的学术背景，发现拥有正规学术支持的机构占比很少，不利于这个行业的专业性提升和良性发展，如图 10 所示：

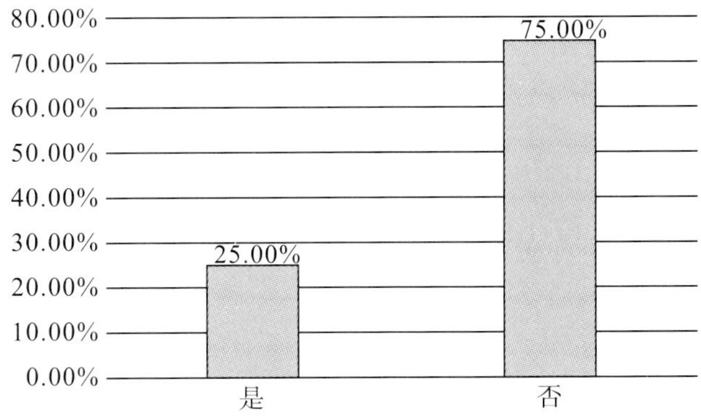

图 10　是否有学术支持背景

只有 25％的机构拥有来自高校或科研机构的学术支持。其中科研背景实力最强的当属汉办开设的网络孔子学院，该平台主要提供各类学习资源。而提供在线实时教学的机构中，学术背景较强的有北京“锦灵中文”，由中央民族大学吴应辉教授带领团队，依托国家社科基金“汉语国际传播动态数据库建设及发展监测研究”与该机构合作开发汉语课程。此外“汉声中文”长期与华东师范大学的科研团队合作开发课程。

四、当前在线少儿汉语教学的现状分析

通过对现有“互联网＋”汉语教学机构及平台进行调查分析，我们初步

了解到目前这个领域的基本现状和特点。结合第二语言教学的学科特征，我们对在线少儿汉语教学有了一定的认识，分别从优势与不足两个方面来讨论。

（一）在线少儿汉语教学的优势

第一，打破时空局限，降低教学成本。同其他学科的在线教学一样，在线少儿汉语教学最大的突破就是利用新技术的支持，打破了传统课堂在时间和空间上的限制。学生可以根据自身的需要，在任何时间段预约来自中国本土的母语背景教师。过去要通过线下课堂、游学、留学得到的教育服务，今天足不出户，在家就能完成。

少儿必须在家长或监护人的监管和帮助下才能参与学习，因此少儿学习者比成年学习者所需的人力成本要多一倍。在线教学省去了线下教学所需的通勤时间，为家长节省了大量的时间和人力成本。从教学服务方面来说，线上教学也省去了场地、设备、通勤、纸质印刷材料等多方面成本，正因如此，未来会有更多的学习者参与汉语学习，从而大力推进汉语国际教育“走出去”的步伐。

第二，学习内容的丰富性和可重复性。过去的线下传统语言教学局限于一位教师、一本教材，学生与教师面对面进行知识学习和操练。在线汉语教学尤其是远程实时教学完全可以在保留传统线下教学已有的内容之上，利用大数据的储存、网络线上传播等优势，丰富和拓展学习内容。大量的在线学习资源，配合移动终端的学习软件，可以让学生在教师真人教学的基础上吸收更多的学习资讯。语言学习的课后操练也可以利用网络电子资源和互动学习软件来完成，多方位立体化地配合教学。

此外，大多数在线互动教学都可以将实时的教学过程通过录制保存下来，学生可以通过视频反复观看、复习教师在课上讲授的内容。其他录播课、慕课、直播课形式的教学，其设计就是将制作好的优质课程提供给学生，学习没有时间限制，并可以反复观看，体现出在线汉语教学的可重复性。

第三，语言学习的个性化与交互性。“互联网＋”是一个广泛的概念，所有利用计算机网络设备提供教学信息服务的行为都可以算作“互联网＋”视域下的新型教学。前文也说到，语言学习比其他学科的技能操练要求更高，对实时互动的要求更高，因此远程实时教学是当前在线汉语教学的重要部分。目前看来，一对一模式和低于五人的小班教学模式占据了在线少儿汉语教学的主流。这种模式虽然将教学场地搬到了线上，却依然保留了真人互动的教学，即保留了语言教学必不可少的交互性特征。相比传统中小学、培训机构的线下教学，线上教学的班级更加精简。线下课堂一个班十几甚至几十个人的大班，不可能做到个性化、定制化的教学。而要在线下课堂选择个性化小班教学，场地和师资的成本都比线上要高，学费也会相应增加。这也是近年来线上教学越来越受欢迎的原因之一。

（二）在线少儿汉语教学的不足

第一，发展时间短，缺乏学术研究支持。相对于传统的线下汉语教学而言，在线教学发展时间较短，是伴随着近年来互联网发展的浪潮在短时间内涌现出来的。对于专门针对在线教学的课程系统、经典教材、大纲体系、教学方法等多个方面的研究还很匮乏。上文的数据也显示出具有专业的学术研究支持的在线教学平台很少，大多数是依靠互联网公司和教育培训公司在做产品打造。缺少科学研究的支持，教学产品和教学服务的质量都面临一定的挑战。

第二，在线师资培养不足。除了教学系统的开发，在线教师的培养也是这个行业亟待解决和开发的领域。从 20 世纪 50 年代对外汉语教学事业起步以来，我国已经培养出大量的对外汉语专业技术人才，也通过各种渠道向世界各地输送了大量的专业教师。然而传统师资培训能否适应新技术形势下的教学需求？在线汉语教师需要哪些新的技能培养？这些问题随着在线汉语教学的兴起和发展摆在了我们面前。从目前调查到的情况来看，在线汉语教师以兼职为主，大多没有接受过专门针对线上教学的技能培训，在新的教学媒介遇到的新问题大多由教师们自己“摸着石头过河”。各大高校汉语国际教育专业也没有开设专门培养线上教学技能的专业课程。

五、反思与展望

随着全球学习汉语的儿童的持续增加和互联网技术的不断发展，“互联网+”模式下的在线少儿汉语教学无疑会成为下一个热门教学领域，我们对此抱有乐观的预测。要实现在线少儿汉语教学的新一轮良性发展，需要从三个方面做出思考和努力。

第一，建立规范的市场监管，促进良性发展。目前依靠互联网公司和教育培训公司打造起来的在线少儿汉语教学市场依然存在一些不够规范的方面。办学资质、师资水平、学术支持、互联网安全等方面的问题还没有引起足够的重视。新事物的兴起总会需要一段时间的积累，这个阶段正是建立行业规范、创建良性竞争机制和发展模式的关键时期。

第二，大力培养专门化师资。教师是教学行为的重要主体，师资的质量直接决定了教学的效果。在线少儿汉语教学有两个关键词："在线"和"少儿"。专门化的师资培养必须考虑到这两方面的特殊性。建议各培训机构、各高校的汉语国际教育专业以及汉办的师资培养工作都能够考虑这方面的需求。针对在线汉语教师开设多媒体平台操作、交互式课件制作、网络教学互动方法、网络教学仪态仪表等专门性培训。针对教学对象，开设儿童心理学、儿童语言习得等相关课程及培训，从而也促进汉语师资培训走上更加专门化、精细化的路子。

第三，大力开发高质量的少儿汉语在线互动教材。目前各大机构和平台使用的在线教材主要分三种情况：自主研发的电子教材、将主流纸质教材电子化、教师根据机构内部大纲自制互动式课件。这三种类型的教材都存在这样或那样的问题。机构自主开发的教材可能由于缺少强大的学术研究背景支持，不能保证较高的教学质量，且自主开发多媒体在线教学平台人力成本和技术成本较高，许多机构不得已削减教师的人力成本从而导致课堂互动教学质量降低。简单地将已经经历了时间考验的权威主流教材电子化的方法虽然方便，但是传统教材并非为在线教学设计，许多互动模式、操练方法都不适合线上教学，且互动性不足。第三种模式更是严重依赖个体教师的专业素质和水平，教材质量难以保障。因此，组织对外汉语学科专家、在线教学一线机构和教师、软件开发技术人才、美工动画专门人才共同参与开发少儿汉语在线互动教材的工作势在必行。

六、结论

当前"互联网+"浪潮下的少儿在线汉语教学呈现出蓬勃发展的势头，为汉语国际推广事业增添了一块宝贵的阵地。随着市场需求的增加和教学水平的提升，在线少儿汉语教学将会迎来一个又一个全面推进的发展时期。把握住时代的机遇，从市场需求、技术开发、师资培养、教材建设等多个方面进行研究，在线少儿汉语教学将会成为我国汉语国际教育与推广事业的一个新的增长点。

参考文献：

[1] 吕军伟，张丽维. 基于“互联网+”的汉语国际教育在线互动教学平台建设现状研究 [J]. 前沿，2017（8）.

[2] 孙曙辉. 在线教学4.0：“互联网+”课堂教学 [J]. 中国教育信息化，2016（14）.

[3] 张会，陈晨.“互联网+”背景下的汉语国际教育与文化传播 [J]. 语言文字应用，2019（2）.

[4] 张晓燕. 试谈少儿汉语教学在整个对外汉语教学中的定位 [J]. 海外华文教育，2010.（1）.

[5] 章欣，李晓琪. 汉语网络教学教师培训研究 [J]. 语言教学与研究，2017（3）.

[6] 郑艳群. 课堂上的网络和网络上的课堂——从现代教育技术看对外汉语教学的发展 [J]. 世界汉语教学，2001（4）.

[7] 郑艳群. 新时期信息技术背景下汉语国际教育新思路 [J]. 国际汉语教学研究，2015（2）.

作者简介：

魏海平，文学博士，西南民族大学文学与新闻传播学院讲师，研究方向为对外汉语教学。

基于实践社区的商务汉语教学设想[①]

杨 恬

四川大学海外教育学院

摘 要：实践性是商务汉语的重要特征。本文借鉴温格等学者提出的“实践社区”理论，针对现有商务汉语教学中存在的问题，提出基于实践社区理念的商务汉语教学设想。本文认为，应在商务汉语学习的初级、中级、高级阶段循序渐进地引入多形态的实践社区，以供学习者操练与实践，帮助学习者获得学习的主体性地位，在人与实践社区的关系建构中真正习得语言与商务知识，提高跨文化商务交际能力。

关键词：商务汉语；实践社区；教学模式

Instructional Ideas on Business Chinese Based on the Concept of "Community of Practice"

Yang Tian

School of Overseas Education, Sichuan University

Abstract: Practice is an important feature of Business Chinese. This paper draws on the concept of "community of practice" and proposes instructional ideas on Business Chinese, aiming at solving the problems existing in the current Business Chinese teaching. This paper believes that multi-form communities of practice should be

---

① 本文为2018年四川大学中央高校基本科研业务费项目“基于实践社区的商务汉语教学”成果，项目编号：2018soe-06。

introduced step by step in the primary, intermediate and advanced Business Chinese learning stages for learners to practice, to help learners gain the subjective status of learning, and lead them to learn language as well as business knowledge by constructing the relationship between people and community, and thus eventually gain the intercultural business communication skills.

Keywords: Business Chinese; Community of Practice; Teaching Model

一、研究缘起

伴随经济的飞速发展和信息技术行业、旅游文化产业等领域的壮大，成都的国际化程度不断提高，吸引越来越多来自五湖四海的外国人前来学习、工作和定居。对于在蓉外国人这一重要的跨文化交流群体，学好汉语是他们进行跨文化交际的基础；而掌握与中国以及成都本土相关的商务知识，得体地运用基于不同情境的商务汉语，是促进在蓉外国人与中国人顺利进行跨文化合作，建构外国人对中国商务文化理解与认同的重要前提。

商务汉语课程正是以培养国际化、复合型、应用型商务汉语人才为目标的专门用途汉语课程。在这门课程中，商务汉语的核心内涵包括汉语语言知识和能力、商务专业知识和技能、商务文化知识和跨文化交际能力三个维度（沈庶英，2014）。国内多所高校早已面向留学生开设商务汉语课，或将其设置为本科专业，可见该门课程在汉语国际教育中扮演着重要角色。

与之相应，商务汉语逐渐成为国内学界研究的一个热点课题。根据对已有文献的分析，本文发现以下研究特点：第一，早期的研究主要从宏观层面探讨商务汉语的定位问题（刘丽瑛，1999；沈庶英，2006；张黎，2006等）；第二，近年来，研究逐渐呈现出细化特征，例如一些学者对商务汉语教材、教学大纲的词汇选择与分级进行了专门研究（辛平，2007；周小兵，干红梅，2008；沈庶英，2011；安娜，史中琦，2012；等），一些学者对商务汉语教学模式进行了探讨（丁存越，2010；张黎，2011；等）。但是，本文发现，对商务汉语实践教学的研究尚未引起学界足够的重视。

实践性是商务汉语的重要特征，商务实践能力是商务汉语教学“最高级别的教学目标”[①]，但关于商务汉语实践教学的探讨却较少。相比之下，国内商务英语的实践教学研究已较为成熟，并设计与建构了不同类型的教学模式（沈庶英，2014）。商务汉语教学能否借鉴其经验，设计与开发符合自身课程特征、满足学习者需求的教学新路径，是值得研究的。综上所述，基于“实践性”对商务汉语教学的重要性，本文借鉴温格等学者提出的“实践社区”概念、社会建构主义情境学习理论相关观点，对基于实践社区的商务汉语教学模式进行讨论，并提出教学设想。

二、“实践社区”的理论支持与现实基础

在理论层面，“实践社区”（Community of Practice，Jean Lave & Etienne Wenger，1991）这一概念是由温格（Wenger）等学者提出的，该概念来源于学界对于“人类学习的社会性”的探讨，而这些探讨深受人类学、社会学理论的影响。温格指出，可以将“实践社区”视作一种社会学习系统（a social learning system），其系统性体现为具有“复杂关系”（complex relationships）、“自组织”（self-organization）、“动态界限”（dynamic boundaries）以及“关于身份和文化意义的谈判”（ongoing negotiation of identity and cultural meaning）等特征。“实践社区”观点从社会维度出发思考学习的问题，认为“学习”处于人和世界的关系之中，在这种参与关系中，社会和个体相互建构。总之，“实践社区”自身可被视为一种简单的社会系统，而复杂的社会系统则是由互相关联的实践社区所构成的（Wenger，2010）。

温格等人关于“实践社区”的观点体现出了鲜明的社会建构主义理论特色。总体而言，建构主义强调知识是个人经验的统合，不是通过教师传授得到的，而是学习者在与情景的交互作用过程中自行建构的，学习过程更强调学生认知主体的作用。在语言和商务沟通领域，基于西方社会建构主义情境学习理论的课程与教学模式，如案例教学、逼真的商务环境情境教学、项目调研（PBL）等，都备受关注。其中，PBL 作为一种小组形式调研，主要通过小组讨论、调研、收集与分析数据来得出调研结论，在国外商学院的教

① 此处原文引自对外经济贸易大学国际商务汉语教学与资源开发基地编撰的《2011 国际商务汉语年度报告》，北京：高等教育出版社，2012 年。

学中备受推崇（Danford，2006）；亦有国内学者借鉴 PBL 教学模式，提出“以项目调研为主线，内嵌各种情境沟通项目的 ESP 教学环境，结合‘以评促学’的多种评估手段来实施教学”的设想（赵珂、王志军，2015）。

在现实维度上，作为中国西部最具经济活力的城市之一，成都不断吸引着来自国内外的企业前来创业，参与投资和发展。例如，仅 2018 年，新批准的外商投资项目就达到 494 个，其中 1000 万美元以上的项目 87 个，世界 500 强企业落户成都的有 285 家。为了促进城市产业发展的更新换代，成都市于 2017 年还颁布了“产业新政 50 条”，鼓励青年大学生在蓉创新创业；尤其值得一提的是，该政策同时鼓励在华高校外国留学生在成都创新创业，支持境外高校外籍毕业生来成都工作实习，并提供签证方面的支持。[①] 与此同时，国内互联网金融发达，各种类型的互联网经济形式为外国留学生全方位沉浸式体验与理解中国的商务环境提供了很好的机会。

基于对“实践社区”理论与现实基础的梳理分析，结合商务汉语课程特征，本研究中的“实践社区”主要分为线上与线下两种形态。在线上，“实践社区”分布于主要的电商平台（如淘宝、京东）与新零售平台（如盒马鲜生）、求职网站与交流社群、企业网站之中；在线下，“实践社区”则在课堂、学校、社区、企业中均有不同形式的具体呈现。需要说明的是，这里的“社区”不仅包括物理意义上的空间或者互联网技术支持的社会交往空间，也包括真实或者虚拟空间中参与信息交换、社会交往的人群。重要的是，学习在人与社会空间之间的关系中发生。处于不同水平、不同学习阶段的人群，通过实践社区学习和习得的效果各异，但在这一过程中，学习者始终是知识建构过程的重要主体。

三、教学模式设想

（一）个案分析

笔者长期负责四川大学海外教育学院高年级商务汉语课程的教学工作，在美国工作期间，也曾面向美国公司的中高层业务骨干教授商务汉语课程，

① 数据来自成都市政府官方网站：http://www.chengdu.gov.cn/chengdu/rscd/gmjjhshfzgk.shtml.

因此积累了一定的教学经验，也在反思其中存在的一些问题，现从教学内容与教学形式两个方面来对现有教学情况进行分析。

第一，在教学内容方面，笔者在教学过程中，主要参考的教材是外语教学与研究出版社出版的《卓越汉语 商务致胜》，选取了其中贴近留学生日常生活的主题，如“求职与面试”“商务谈判”“跨国公司”“企业管理”“创业”等，但由于教材内容时效性较弱，所以笔者需要通过互联网收集与主题相关的新闻材料，再根据学生水平重新编写阅读材料，并设计语言、知识重点和课后练习。经过反复调整与整合的教学内容更具有时效性与针对性，但存在内容主观性较强、重信息而轻语言的问题，学生可以了解到最新的经贸新闻、本土化的商务知识，但对其中涉及的知识点，存在了解片面、难以运用的问题。

第二，在教学形式方面，主要采用课堂授课方式。课堂授课分为知识讲授与小组讨论两个部分，一般情况下，学生能够在教师的引导下展开讨论，但是学生对语言点的掌握程度不一，拥有工作经验的学生对商务汉语的专门词汇以及相关知识的习得情况较一般全日制留学生更好，这也导致教学节奏较难控制。

（二）基于实践社区的商务汉语教学设想

实践性是商务汉语的重要特征。在跨文化交际能力的“CAB”模式（Kim，2001）中，实践性对应的是“行为”（behavior），而行为能力正是在实践的“做中学”里获得的。根据笔者自身的教学经验以及与同行的交流，已知目前的商务汉语课程大都局限在教室之内，实行一种静态偏向的教学模式。考虑到实践性对语言学习的重要性，本文认为应该以“实践社区”为切入点，对商务汉语的教学模式进行调整。

针对不同汉语水平的商务汉语学习者，“实践社区”理念的具体操作形式也各不相同。下面，本文以初级阶段（HSK3 级水平）、中级阶段（HSK4 级水平）、高级阶段（HSK5 级及以上水平）为划分标准，对各个阶段的商务汉语教学模式提出设想。

1. 初级阶段

对于刚刚进入汉语学习初级阶段的留学生而言，初步认识、了解与自己的生活密切相关的商务环境是进入实践社区的第一步。这里的商务环境既包括实体的超市、购物中心、宾馆、餐厅等，也包括基于互联网技术的旅行网站、共享类 App 等。课堂上，教师需要循序渐进地向学生介绍有关这些商务环境的背景知识，模拟真实环境，设置情境引导学生操练。在学生熟练掌握语言点的前提下，教师可以设计有关实践社区的体验任务，例如让学生调查学校内外咖啡馆消费情况、共享单车的使用体验等，引导学生从日常生活出发了解成都本土化的经济、商务文化特征，培养学生初步参与实践社区、与中国人就专门问题进行交流的能力。

2. 中级阶段

如果说初级阶段商务汉语教学的目标是培养学生的语言知识和交际能力，引导他们从生活中积累相应的商务知识，那么进入中级阶段以后，更重要的是带领学生逐渐深入真正的商务实践社区。从日常生活到专门的商务社区，这里有一个重要的前提，即通过海外教育学院建立与经济学院、商学院的合作关系，为留学生创造商务实践社区的环境，同时促进中国学生与留学生开展跨文化商务交流。

通过学院间的合作，中级阶段的留学生可以从三个方面参与实践社区。第一，请经贸、商务专业的师生走进留学生课堂。笔者曾邀请商学院教师为留学生讲授“中国的楼市”“人民币汇率”“中美贸易战”等热点议题，取得了良好的课堂效果。第二，带领留学生走进中国学生的课堂。考虑到留学生的语言水平，这里的课堂主要指一些商务类的双语课程、校内的公益讲座等。需要说明的是，教师在引导学生参加这两类实践社区时，要注意为学生提供适当的背景知识讲解，尽量保证内容的“本土化”与“针对性”，唯有如此，才能让学生学有所得。此外，除课堂交流以外，可以建立留学生与中国师生的网上交流社群，定期就某一经济话题展开讨论，确立长效的跨文化交流机制。第三，开展学生主导的小范围调研活动。不同于初级阶段由教师主导的社区调研，在中级阶段，教师主要在选题与评估方面做好把关，而调研活动的具体环节设计（如调研方式、调查问题）都由学生决定与组织。本文认为，通过这样的半开放型调研活动，一方面，教师可以从总体上掌握留学生对实践任务的理解与执行能力，通过学生的调研报告发现可能存在的问题以做总结；另一方面，留学生能够主动通过实践来检验自己所学的知识，并更深入地了解经济现象背后的发生原因与运行规律。

3. 高级阶段

经过初级、中级阶段的学习，学生大都积累了关于本地及国内的相关经济常识，具有了一定的实践活动经验，这时便可以开展商务专门业务的实践。开展实践活动之前，需要做好如下准备：向学生详细介绍实践任务目标、内容与相应的知识点、语言点；制定与明确实践活动的汇报形式、评估标准；邀请从事过商务工作的留学生，结合自己的工作实践，向同学介绍自己的工作情况，交流工作中最急需的语言知识与商务技能。

相比初级与中级阶段，高级阶段的实践社区形态更加多元，通常是实体与虚拟形式相结合；学生参与实践社区的方式也是多样的，既可以是到本地商务社区中参观考察，也可以是到本地企业中实习。本文认为，根据学生水平，可以适当开展以下几类商务实践活动。

第一，组织学生进行商务考察。具体而言，可以考察成都高新区、成都的老字号品牌、成都本土企业、外资企业、中外合资企业等具有代表性的经济环境，为学生提供近距离了解当地经济发展的机会。

第二，引导学生在真实的商务环境中做社会调查。社会调查建议采用项目调研（PBL）方式，即让学生通过小组讨论、调研、收集与分析数据来得出调研结论。调研的对象可以是当地企业，也可以是创新创业者，还可以是当地的某个经贸活动。通过调研，学生可以检验已学知识，熟悉调查方法，并通过实践更好地了解当地经济。

第三，与本地企业、外资企业合作，建立留学生商务实践基地。以成都市为例，伴随对外开放程度的不断提高，城市经济发展对国际化人才的需求也在不断提升，因此，有必要在高校课堂与当地企业之间搭建桥梁，让学生走进企业，了解真正的公司发展情况。同时，高校教师应联合企业培训师，培养学生在真实商务环境中的交际能力与业务能力，使学生在做中学，为日后在中国工作积累经验。

第四，指导学生设计商务方案。在商务考察、社会调查与实习的基础上，鼓励与引导学生参与项目策划。方案的设计从选题、市场调研、结果分析到撰写调研报告等，都由学生完成。商务方案的评估由教师、企业管理人员、具有创新创业经验的留学生未完成。

本文基于实践社区的教学理念，结合商务汉语课程特征，对初级、中级、高级阶段的商务汉语教学模式提出了一些设想。在初级、中级、高级三个学习阶段中，教师与留学生的角色发生了变化，即伴随语言与知识水平的提升，留学生的“主角”色彩日渐鲜明，其主动性在整个教与学的过程中是不断得到鼓励与推动的，而教师则慢慢从课堂的主导“退居”到引导、辅导的位置，这正体现了社会建构主义教育思想的主张。此外，初级、中级、高级三个学习阶段的实践社区形式并不是截然隔断的，而是互融互通的，即留学生课堂知识的讲解、留学生与中国学生课堂的交流、社会调研等形式在三个阶段中同时存在，只是根据学生水平体现出难度上的阶梯形递增趋势。应该说，该教学设想的提出是对目前商务汉语课程教学模式的一次突破性尝试，一方面增加了教学内容的丰富度，另一方面拓展了课堂的外延，为学生的商务汉语学习提供了各种形态、各具特色的实践社区环境。正如前文所说，根据实践社区的教育理念，“学习”处于人和世界的关系之中，在这种参与关系的过程中，社会和个体相互建构。本文关于商务汉语教学的设想正是基于人与环境的这种“互构”关系，希望留学生能在不同形态的实践社区中，通过与不同个体、社群的相互学习与交流，习得“接地气”的商务知识与交往技能，更加了解自己生活、学习的当地社会经济文化环境，为日后在中国工作积累经验。当然，如何将本文关于商务汉语教学模式的设想变为现实，需要在微观层面上做好教学内容的设计，制定合理的教学策略，同时也需要学院建立与外界合作交流的有效机制，为实践社区的构建奠定基础。

参考文献：

[1] 安娜，史中琦. 商务汉语教材选词率及核心词表研究 [J]. 语言文字应用，2012 (2).

[2] 丁存越. 商务汉语立体化教学模式的探讨 [J]. 学术界，2010 (8).

[3] 鹿士义. 商务汉语考试 (BCT) 阅读能力与欧盟框架的匹配研究 [J]. 语言文字应用，2011 (1).

[4] 沈庶英. 经贸汉语综合课的定位 [J]. 语言教学与研究，2006 (5).

[5] 沈庶英.《经贸汉语本科教学词汇大纲》理念及特色分析 [J]. 民族教育研究，2011, 22 (6).

[6] 沈庶英. 来华留学生商务汉语实践教学探索 [J]. 语言教学与研究，2014 (1).

[7] 辛平. 面向商务汉语教材的商务领域词语等级参数研究 [J]. 语言文字应用，2007 (3).

[8] 张黎. 商务汉语教学需求分析 [J]. 语言教学与研究，2006 (3).

[9] 张黎. 交际策略教学法研究——以“商务汉语口语交际”课为例 [J]. 语言教学与研究，2011 (2).

[10] 张黎. 汉语在国际商务领域使用状况调查与分析 [J]. 语言教学与研究，2012 (1).

[11] 周小兵，干红梅. 商务汉语教材选词考察与商务词汇大纲编写 [J]. 世界汉语教学，2008 (1).

［12］赵珂，王志军. 大学英语转型专门用途英语的课程设计与实践研究［J］. 外语教学理论与实践，2015（2）.

［13］Ellis，R. The Study of Second Language Acquisition［M］. Oxford：Oxford University Press，1994.

［14］Kim，Y. Y. Becoming Intercultural：An Integrative Theory of Communication and Cross-Cultural Adaptation［M］. Thousand Oaks，CA：Sage，2001.

［15］Lave，J. K. & Wenger，E. Situated Learning：Legitimate Peripheral Participation［M］. New York：Cambridge University Press，1991.

［16］Vygotsky，Lev S. Mind in Society：The development of Higher Psychological Processes［M］. Cambridge，MA：Harvard University Press，1978.

［17］Wenger，E. Cultivating Communities of Practice［M］. Boston：Harvard University Press，2002.

作者简介：

杨恬，文学博士，四川大学海外教育学院讲师，研究方向为对外汉语教学、新媒体与跨文化传播。

孔子学院

美国太平洋路德大学汉语教学现状*

何 婉

四川大学海外教育学院

摘 要：本文介绍了美国太平洋路德大学的基本情况，重点介绍了语言专业现状、汉语教学现状以及存在的问题，最后针对该校的情况，就发掘汉语教学的优势提出了相关建议。

关键词：太平洋路德大学；汉语教学；现状；优势和建议

Current Situation of Chinese Language Teaching at Pacific Lutheran University

He Wan

School of Overseas Education, Sichuan University

Abstract: Firstly, this paper introduces the basic situation of Pacific Lutheran University. Secondly, it focuses on the current situation of language major, the current situation of Chinese language teaching and the existing problems. Finally, in view of the existing situation of the school, we explore the advantages of Chinese language teaching, and put forward relevant suggestions.

Keywords: Pacific Lutheran University; Chinese Language Teaching; Current Situation; Advantages and Suggestions

---

* 本课题为2019年四川大学中央高校基本科研业务费项目“2008—2018年美国西雅图汉语教学概况与思考”成果，项目编号：2019自研—海外04。

美国太平洋路德大学是位于美国华盛顿州帕克兰的一所私立大学，2016年9月开始和华盛顿州孔子学院合作，华盛顿州孔子学院向太平洋路德大学派出汉语教师，为其汉语教学工作提供师资支持。2018年至今笔者参加国家汉办孔子学院项目，在美国华盛顿州塔科玛市太平洋路德大学教授汉语，参与了太平洋路德大学几乎全部的汉语教学工作，对该校汉语教学的情况比较了解。本文介绍并分析该校汉语教学的情况，以期能在以后的汉语教学工作中扬长避短。

一、美国太平洋路德大学概况

美国太平洋路德大学（Pacific Lutheran University，以下简称PLU）位于华盛顿州，1890年由挪威路德教会的先驱们创立，并由美国福音路德教会一区580个教会赞助。截至2017年，PLU约有3100名学生注册。学校占地63万平方米，约有220名全职教授。PLU由文理学院（包括人文科学、自然科学和社会科学部）、文理与传播学院、商学院、教育与运动学院和护理学院组成。

2012年美国新闻学院和大学排名将PLU列为西部地区第6大价值大学。根据U. S. News & World Report评选，该校是唯一每年名列西部最好大学前15名的学校。2014—2015年的学生构成如下：女性62%，男性38%；有色人种23%；76%来自华盛顿州；19%来自路德教；5%为来自26个国家的国际学生。

PLU有秋季和春季两个学期，一月份的学期称为“J-term”，还提供暑期班。在“J-term”期间，学生在一个月内修完一门课，这门课可以获得一个学期内正常的4个学分。所有的新生都要求至少参加一次“J-term”。PLU提供44个专业（major）和54个辅修专业（minor），涉及广泛的学科领域。

二、美国太平洋路德大学的语言专业

（一）美国太平洋路德大学语言专业概况

PLU的语言课程主要由人文学院开设，以最近两年为例，开设的语言专业有英语专业（English）、法语专业（French）、德语专业（German）、西班牙语研究（Hispanic Studies）、北欧研究（Nordic Studies）。除北欧研究仅开设辅修专业课程以外，英语、法语、德语、西班牙语均同时开设专业课程和辅修专业课程。

从 PLU 的官网可以看到[①]，中文研究（Chinese Studies）并未开设在人文学院下面，而是在跨学科课程（Interdisciplinary Programs）下面开设，与其并列的专业还有环境研究（Environmental Studies）、全球研究（Global Studies）、大屠杀与种族灭绝研究（Holocaust & Genocide Studies）、创新研究（Innovation Studies）、美洲原住民和土著研究（Native American & Indigenous Studies）、妇女与性别研究（Women's and Gender Studies），其中大屠杀与种族灭绝研究、创新研究、美洲原住民和土著研究仅提供辅修专业选择。

（二）美国太平洋路德大学各语言专业比较

从上文可以看到，PLU 一共开设了 6 门语言专业，我们将每门专业的教授人数、开设课程、选课人数等方面进行比较分析。

英语专业一共有 14 位专职教授，1 位访问教授，开设了两个辅修专业：儿童文学和文化（Children's Literature & Culture）、出版与印刷艺术（Publishing & Printing Arts）。2019 年秋季一共开设了 17 门课程，提供了 331 个可选名额，截至 2019 年 7 月底[②]，空余 67 个名额可选，其中有 4 门课程选课人数达到上限。

法语专业一共有两位专职教授，2019 年秋季一共开设了 4 门课程，提供了 82 个可选名额，空余 20 个名额可选。

德语专业一共有两位专职教授，开设一个辅修专业：大屠杀与种族灭绝研究（Holocaust & Genocide Studies）。2019 年秋季一共开设了 5 门课程，提供了 95 个可选名额，空余 47 个名额可选。

西班牙语专业一共有 5 位专职教授，1 位访问教授，2019 年秋季一共开设了 9 门课程，提供了 165 个可选名额，空余 32 个名额可选，其中 3 门课选课人数达到上限关闭。

---

① 参见“太平洋路德大学”官网地址：https：//www. plu. edu/

② 以下所有数据统计时间均截至 2019 年 7 月底。

挪威语专业一共有 3 位专职教授，没有主修专业，仅开设一个辅修专业挪威语（Norwegian Language），2019 年秋季一共开设了两门课程，一共提供了 40 个可选名额，空余 25 个名额可选。

汉语专业一共有 1 位专职教授，3 位其他专业教授，1 位访问教授（笔者本人），开设一个辅修专业：汉语（Chinese Language）。2019 年秋季一共开设了 3 门课程，提供了 50 个可选名额，空余 35 个名额可选，其中一门课“Intermediate Chinese C”仅有 1 人选择。

以上 6 门语言课程的师资、选课情况如图 1 所示：

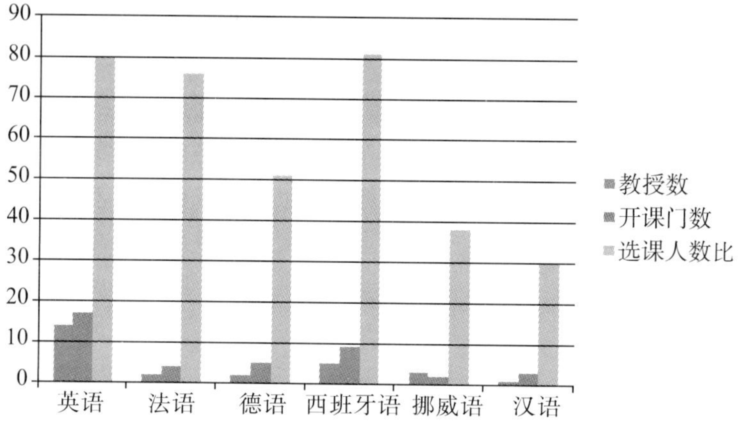

图 1　PLU 语言专业概况比较

从图 1 可以看到，我们从高到低将各个数据进行排列，教授数[1]：英语>西班牙语>挪威语>法语和德语>汉语；开课门数：英语>西班牙语>德语>法语>汉语>挪威语；选课人数比：西班牙语>英语>法语>德语>挪威语>汉语。在该校，英语作为母语在各方面均具有巨大优势，可比性不强，在外语中西班牙语优势明显，法语和德语不相上下，挪威语和汉语较弱。

三、美国太平洋路德大学汉语教学的现状

（一）汉语班级

PLU 一个学期有 14 周，汉语课每周 3 次，每次一节，65 分钟，教师提

① 此图的教授人数指专业教授人数，访问讲授不在其中。

供每周 3 次的“office hour”，每次两个小时，每周一次“Chinese table”，学生自愿参加，“J-term” 4 周，周一到周五每天上课，每次两节，共 140 分钟，每周一次“Chinese table”，至少参加 3 次。所有课程都为综合课，没有匹配的技能课。

汉语分三个年级授课，每个年级分两个学期完成，一共 6 个班。笔者自 2018 年 8 月起在 PLU 教授汉语课程，共教授了 5 个汉语班级：“汉语 101”“汉语 102”“汉语 201”“汉语 202”和“J-term”①，其中“汉语 101”和“J-term”针对零起点的学生，“汉语 102”针对学习过一个学期汉语，大概掌握了 200 个词汇的学生，“汉语 201”针对学习过汉语一年，大概掌握了 400 至 500 个词汇的学生，“汉语 202”针对学习汉语一年半及以上的学生，汉语水平大致相当于 HSK3－4 级的水平。这 5 个班级几乎囊括了 PLU 所有的汉语班级。三年级的学生人数极少，“汉语 301”学生人数是两人，“汉语 302”学生人数是 3 人。

（二）汉语教师

从近 3 年的情况来看，PLU 汉语教学工作一直由保罗（Paul）负责。保罗，博士，教授，早年求学于浙江大学，2016—2018 年负责一年级中文课，中文授课。2018 年讲授“中国历史”（Chinse History）等课程，英文授课。现任 PLU 语言系主任。

缇姆（Tim），历史学博士，曾在台湾求学，2017 年春季进入 PLU，讲授“中国历史”，英语授课。授课期间，选课人数均在 30 人以上，由于 PLU 经济问题，2018 年被辞退。

王川，孔子学院教师，2016－2018 年任教于 PLU，2016—2017 年讲授一年级和二年级汉语课，2017—2018 年讲授二年级和三年级汉语课，中文授课，现已回四川大学继续任教。

何婉，孔子学院教师，2018—2020 年任教于 PLU，2018—2019 年讲授一年级和二年级汉语课，2019—2020 年讲授二年级和三年级汉语课，中文授课。

艾瑞克（Erik J. Hammerstrom），东亚和比较宗教系副教授；格雷格

① 这是 PLU 每年 1 月的一个短学期，只有 4 个星期，要求教师上完一个学期的课程，学分与正常学期相同，每天上课两个半小时，每位毕业生必须参加一次，大一新生必须选择一门语言课程。

(Greg Youtz)，音乐和作曲家、教授，这两位教授不直接讲授中文系的任何课程，但是参加中文系的重要活动，比如讲座、毕业答辩等。

（三）汉语学习者

中文课是PLU中文专业每个年级学生的必修课，同时允许其他专业的学生选修，所以中文课的学生通常来自各个专业，中文专业的学生数量极少。2016年秋季学期，大一新生9人（同期在校生共3225人）；2017年秋季学期，大一新生15人（同期在校生共3100人）；2018年秋季学期，大一新生9人（同期在校生共3110人）；2019年秋季学期，大一新生8人（同期在校生共3107人）。从近4年的数据来看，汉语大一新生数量除2017年以外，均未超过10人，查询历史数据亦是如此。

PLU除了春秋两个学期以外，每年一月还有一个学期“J-term”，“J-term”深受学生喜欢，选课率极高，原因在于：首先，短时间修同等学分，虽然只有一个月的时间，但是学分和正常学期相同。其次，不额外收取学费。最后，PLU要求每位PLU学生至少参加一次“J-term”的课程。2019年“J-term”开设了两门和汉语相关的课程：（1）中文课，由笔者中文授课，选课人数15人；（2）中国文学课，由保罗英文授课，选课人数超过额定25人，最终选课人数确定为30人。

由此可见，PLU正常学期中选择汉语课的学生人数偏少，而且80％学生来自非汉语专业，汉语作为选修课常常为学生本专业课程让步，上课时间和学习时间得不到保障，学习效果自然不理想。相对而言“J-term”的学生无论是学习态度还是学习效果都要好很多，究其原因，一方面，“J-term”只能选择一门课，所以学生没有其他课程干扰，能够全心全意学习该门课程；另一方面，“J-term”的学生95％都是大一新生，学习热情很高。

（四）汉语课程及教材

汉语专业要求32学时（24学时必修，8学时选修），学生必须至少修一门中国历史课程。必修课包括“东亚文化”(East Asian Culture)、“中级汉语”(Intermediate Chinese)、“革命中国”(Revolutionary China)、“中国的宗教”(Religions of China)。除了中级汉语以外其他全部是英文授课。选修课包括“当代中国”(Contemporary China)、“全球管理”(Global Management)、“中国电影”(China Through Film)、“汉语研究选题”

(Selected Topics in Chinese Studies)、“中国城市文化”(Urban Culture in China)、“中国文化与社会”(Chinese Culture and Society)、“作文与对话”(Composition and Conversation)、“中国文学翻译”(Chinese Literature in Translation)、“事实与小说中的西藏”(Tibet in Fact and Fiction)、“现代中国”(Modern China)、“中国艺术”(The Arts of China)、“比较法律制度”(Comparative Legal Systems)。

汉语辅修专业(minor)要求20学时(8学时必修,12学时选修),必修课是“初级汉语”(Elementary Chinese),选修课是汉语专业选修课的部分课程。

以上课程主要分成两类。一类是汉语课程,中文授课。此类课程分为三个级别101,201以及301,其中101,201为必修,301为选修,主要使用系列教材《中文听说读写》(刘月华等著)。另一类是汉语相关课程,英文授课,教材由授课老师自己选定。

四、美国太平洋路德大学汉语教学的问题

(一)经济危机严重影响PLU汉语课程

高等教育的发展在很大程度上受到经济发展的影响,经济发展水平决定着高等教育事业的发展状态。全球经济危机引发经济衰退,美国财政收入锐减,高等教育系统的公共拨款削减,社会捐赠减少。

PLU全美排名181名,属于二流高校,经济危机对这类学校影响更加明显,特别是文科类专业,尤其是语言类课程。美国高校有个“惯例”,每遇经济危机需要削减课程和教师时,首当其冲的一定是文科类课程,其中更容易被削减的是语言类课程,而在语言类课程中最容易被削减的是汉语,不仅是PLU这样的非汉语强项的高校,汉语教学发展极好的高校也是如此,如普林斯顿大学、哥伦比亚大学等。

2016年开始PLU遭遇了一次比较严重的经济危机,连续两年没能募集到足够的资金,校长也因此辞职。经济危机引发一系列不良后果,学校为了节省支出选择削减教师,2016年至2018年从250多名教师中辞掉30余人。以中文系为例,中文系在这次经济危机之前有3名教授,他们负责讲授全部课程,保罗以中文讲授“汉语101”“汉语201”等,另外两名教授以英文讲

授中文相关课程，经济危机以后中文系授课教授只剩下保罗一人，从2016年9月开始中文课程主要由孔子学院教师承担，保罗用英文讲授相关课程。教师数量减少导致能开的课程量骤减，很多课程无法开设，因此，中文系在2017年9月招收新生以后停止了招生。

（二）汉语不具优势

美国国会1958年8月23日制定颁布的《国防教育法》，将汉语列为7种最迫切需要的外国语之一，随后美国汉语教学在曲折波动中继续前行。2004年第一所美国孔子学院建立，促进了汉语在美国的推广，十几年来汉语学习者越来越多。尽管如此，汉语推广在起步时间、推广广度深度方面并不具优势。在美国高校，学生选择外语时首选西班牙语，大约30%的学生都会选择西班牙语，其次是德语、法语，然后是其他外语，比如日语、挪威语、汉语等。

从图1可以看到，PLU最强的外语专业是西班牙语，选课率极高，其次是法语和德语，然后是挪威语，最后是汉语，汉语的选课率最低，选择的学生最少。其原因主要有两方面：一是汉语对于就业的帮助小，现阶段美国对于汉语的需求量有所增加，但是就整体需求而言，依然较低；二是汉语本身学习难度大，存在学习时间长、学习效果差的现状。

（三）教师与学生来源不稳定

由于经济危机的影响，PLU近两年没有长期固定的汉语教师，近3年汉语课程主要由孔子学院教师承担，按照惯例孔子学院教师任期都是两年，每两年要换一次教师，教师缺乏连续性。笔者2018年9月教“汉语101”和“汉语102”时，从侧面打听到一些学生因为不是以前的汉语教师授课而放弃继续选择这门课程，每次笔者完成一个学期的教学以后都有学生询问我下学期是否会继续授课，并表示如果笔者继续授课将继续选择汉语课。学生和教师总有一个磨合适应的过程，当学生适应并认可某位教师以后更容易选择该教师的课程继续学习，同时也会把这门课程推荐给其他同学，长此以往，选课人数应会稳中有升。

汉语课的学生由汉语专业和其他专业组成，比例大概是2∶8，其他专业学生远远超过汉语专业的学生，汉语课仅对汉语专业学生来说是必修课，其他专业学生均为选修，故很多学生抱着对汉语的好奇和试一试的心态选择了汉语课，但是每学期班级中继续学习的比例都不超过50%，每个班级每学期都会来一半以上的新生，学生流动性极大，生源的不稳定十分不利于汉语课的教学与发展。

四、美国太平洋路德大学汉语教学优势与建议

PLU现阶段汉语教学虽然处于不利阶段，也存在诸多问题，但是也有很多自身特有的优势，主要体现在两个方面。

第一，和四川大学的长期合作。PLU和四川大学合作由来已久，从2008年开始PLU每年都送学生前往四川大学留学，在海外教育学院学习汉语，在四川大学美国中心学习其他课程，如中国历史、中国文学等，均为英文授课。笔者2008年9月起任教于四川大学海外教育学院，其间多次教授PLU来校学生，从教学成果和学生反馈来看，PLU学生对于在四川大学留学的经历十分满意，很多学生表示愿意继续留在四川大学学习。由于语言环境的优势，四川大学留学回PLU继续学习的学生汉语水平提高较快，对汉语的兴趣增加，回校后有利于继续汉语学习。

第二，强有力的汉语学科领导者。PLU的汉语课程一直是由保罗负责，保罗是汉学家，精通汉语，知华爱华，妻子是中国人，从他与前任同事的合作来看，保罗一直致力于PLU的汉语教学，担任从汉语授课的汉语课程到英语授课的汉语相关课程的教师，深受学生喜爱，虽然由于经济危机的影响，保罗教授的有些课程无法开展，但他一直没有停止过培养汉语学生的努力，领导笔者和两位助教进行汉语教学，组织相关汉语活动。2019年3月保罗教授被任命为PLU语言系系主任，这对PLU的汉语教学十分有利。

基于以上两点优势，一方面，我们建议PLU不断加强完善和四川大学的合作，针对PLU的现状，和四川大学共同制订出更加符合PLU学生的培养计划，因为四川大学学费相对PLU便宜，有学习汉语的大环境，无论是学生自己还是对于PLU本校而言，来四川大学学习汉语都会更加省时省力，因此可以让更多的PLU学生前往四川大学学习汉语，同时增加PLU学生在四川大学留学的时间。如此一来会减轻PLU培养汉语专业学生的压力，学生学习也会更加轻松，学习者会逐渐增多。另一方面，保罗教授也能凭借自身魅力吸引更多的学生选择汉语课程学习，促进PLU的汉语教学。

五、小结

本文介绍了PLU语言教学特别是汉语教学的现状，从现阶段的汉语教学情况来看并不尽如人意，汉语和其他外语相比，无论是教授数量还是选课人数都存在较大差距，但是PLU可以借助和四川大学合作的优势，将汉语专业发展壮大。同时深化PLU和孔子学院的合作，孔子学院教师虽然每两年一换，但是教师与教师之间可以加强沟通，比如笔者的前任同事和笔者均是四川大学海外教育学院教师，在笔者赴任之前便大概了解了PLU学生的情况，这对笔者日后的教学有很大帮助，以后这种交流应该固化并形成书面文字，让每一位孔子学院老师都站在前人的肩上继续前行。我们相信今天PLU汉语教学的困境只是暂时的，在大家的共同努力下，PLU的汉语教学会越来越好。

参考文献：

[1] 毕彦华. 美国汉语教学特点及教师教学策略调整研究［J］. 大学语文建设，2019（10）.

[2] 陈鸿瑶，朱云翠. 美国俄亥俄州立大学汉语教学模式探析［J］. 东北师大学报（哲学社会科学版），2018（6）.

[3] 董学峰. 国家语言战略背景下的汉语国际推广研究［D］. 吉林：东北师范大学，2016.

[4] 李柏. 美国怀俄明大学汉语教学调查报告［D］. 吉林：东北师范大学，2013

[5] 吕蒙蒙. 英美高等教育应对财政危机的异同与启示［J］. 浙江工贸职业技术学院学报，2015（4）.

[6] 温晓芳，修玉霞. 浅谈美国汉语课堂教学模式［J］. 剑南文学（经典教苑），2012（10）.

[7] 央青. 美国犹他州汉语沉浸式教学模式［J］. 民族教育研究，2016（4）.

作者简介：

何婉，文学博士，四川大学海外教育学院讲师，研究方向为四川方言及对外汉语教学。

孔子学院对中华传统体育跨文化传播路径优化研究[①]

李　韵
四川大学海外教育学院

摘　要： 中华传统体育在孔子学院跨文化传播中具有重要价值。当前，孔子学院对中华传统体育的跨文化传播面临困难与机遇并存的环境，传播内容以武术项目为主，传播方式多为直接的人际传播。为提高传统体育的传播力，孔子学院应从加强内容建设、完善传播机制和改进传播方法三个方面不断优化传播路径。

关键词： 传统体育；孔子学院；传播路径；跨文化传播

Study on the Optimization of the Cross-Cultural Communication Path of Chinese Traditional Sports by Confucius Institute

Li Yun
School of Overseas Education, Sichuan University

Abstract: Traditional Chinese sports have important value in the cross-cultural communication of Confucius Institute. At present, the barriers and opportunities coexist in the communication environment of traditional Chinese sports in the cross-cultural communication of Confucius Institute, the dissemination content

① 本课题为2019年四川大学中央高校基本科研业务费项目“以孔子学院为载体的中国传统体育跨文化传播策略研究”成果，项目编号：2019自研—海外02。

is mainly based on martial arts projects, and the mode of communication is direct interpersonal communication. In order to improve the communication power of traditional sports, Confucius Institute should continuously optimize the communication path from the aspects of strengthening content construction, perfecting communication mechanism and improving communication methods.

Keywords：Traditional Sports；Confucius Institute；The Path of Communication；Cross-Cultural Communication

历经 14 年的发展，孔子学院在规模和内涵建设方面均取得了可喜的成就。截至 2018 年，我国共在 158 个国家和地区开办了 535 所孔子学院和 1134 所孔子课堂。① 经过多年的内涵式发展，孔子学院早已不只是海外汉语教学的机构，还成为中华文化传播的优质平台。14 年来，孔子学院在世界各国共举办文化活动 20 万场，吸引了 1300 万人参加。② 然而，伴随国际形势的起伏，孔子学院也在一些国家遭遇到了批评，甚至出现了抵制的声音。当前，如何跨越不同国家在政治制度、意识形态、价值观念等方面存在的固有差异，持续有效地推动中国与世界的文化交流，是孔子学院发展亟须探讨的重要问题。

我国传统体育既包括传统体育项目，也包括传统体育文化。作为中华民族独有的身体文化，中华传统体育是在中华民族长期的融合发展中形成的，集中体现了中华民族的创造力、哲学内涵和人文精神，是中华优秀传统文化的重要组成部分。同时，体育是世界公认的“人类的共通语言”，“这种语言能够有效克服不同人民、不同民族和不同国家之间的隔阂，具有跨越意识形态的国际属性”（钟秉枢，2019）。因此，在孔子学院跨文化传播中加大传统体育内容比重，增强传统体育传播效果，能够有效地克服语言障碍和意识形态争论、国家利益纷争等敏感问题，达成孔子学院建设之“初心”：促进世界多元文化发展，构建和谐世界。③

---

① 参见“孔子学院总部/国家汉办”官方网站：http：//www. hanban. org/

② 参见“孔子学院总部/国家汉办”官方网站：http：//www. hanban. org/

③ 参见“孔子学院总部/国家汉办”官方网站：http：//www. hanban. org/

一、相关研究综述

体育自古以来便是人类跨文化传播活动的重要内容。21世纪初，国内学界开始对中国传统体育的跨文化传播展开研究。早期成果集中在武术的对外传播方面。在十几年的发展中，研究对象、理论和方法逐渐丰富。在整体传播策略方面，学者们借鉴传播学的理论，提出应加强传播主体多元化，提高对外传播的针对性等（邓星华，宋宗佩，2017）；在具体传播过程方面，学者们对我国传统体育在中亚、北欧等地区的传播模式进行了调研（刘小学，2016），其中提到应该发挥孔子学院在我国传统体育跨文化传播中的重要作用。近年来，为适应新型全球传播范式、符合中国国家诉求，学界越来越多地关注传统体育的跨文化传播在国家形象塑造、民族文化认同中的价值与实践（葛耀君等，2017），认为我国传统体育文化内涵与国家形象具有一致性，加强其跨文化传播对塑造积极正面的中国形象、提升国家“软实力”具有重要价值。

随着在全球的蓬勃发展，孔子学院在中国传统体育跨文化传播中的价值也逐渐受到学界的关注。近年来，以武术为代表的中国传统体育成为孔子学院跨文化传播中的重要内容，围绕其传播实践的研究成果也日益丰富（张广鹏，2016）。这些成果以硕士学位论文为主，作者多具有在孔子学院任教的实践经验，对传统体育在课程设置、师资建设、教材拟定等各个环节中存在的问题等进行了研究。

可见，传统体育的跨文化传播对我国软实力构建、国家形象塑造等具有重要价值，因此在孔子学院的建设中具有不容小觑的意义。基于孔子学院的传统体育教学研究为本文提供了文献和数据基础，但由于多从教学环节着手，关于孔子学院对传统体育跨文化传播的内容、途径等方面尚未涉及。因此，本文试从传播学的角度，立足孔子学院发展，对上述问题展开分析。

二、孔子学院对中华传统体育跨文化传播的现状

（一）传播环境困难与机遇并存

全球化进程是我国传统体育跨文化传播的宏观背景。当前，以奥林匹克

为代表的西方竞技体育在体育全球化中占有绝对强势的地位。奥林匹克运动被称为“物理体育”，充分体现了西方主流文化中的竞争精神。其体育项目多以激烈的竞争、整体的协作以及强烈的感官刺激，让参与者，包括运动员和观众，得到人本力量的感受，因此具有全球传播的强劲动力。但更重要的是，奥林匹克文化借助西方世界在全球传播格局中占有的压倒性优势不断向其他国家渗透，并使接收方在生活方式和生活哲学方面不断与之趋同。这时，奥林匹克文化不可避免地显示出文化帝国主义的特征，即不断要求人们分辨什么是先进文化，从而在一定程度上忽视了其他国家传统体育的发展，甚至拒绝其他文化的广泛参与。当然，这一传播背景也明显压缩了我国传统体育跨文化传播的空间。

当前，随着世界经济中心开始由西向东转移，政治多极化、经济全球化、文化多元化和社会信息化正在成为当今世界发展的主题。背靠我国高速发展的国民经济和日益增强的综合国力，特别是在习近平总书记向世界发出的“构建人类命运共同体”的呼吁下，伴随“一带一路”倡议的不断推进，“一种新型全球传播范式正逐渐成型”（贾文山、纪之文，2018）。在这样的时代背景下，我国传统体育的跨文化传播将迎来新的历史机遇。另外，在体育全球化的过程中，西方竞技体育所存在的一些弊端也越来越清晰地为人们所认识。“当人体文化被锦标主义异化后，竞技体育自身似乎没有更好的良方对此进行修正。能够克服这方面弊端的恰好是东方人体文化的优势所在。”（周之华，2016）因此，当代体育全球化亦需要中华传统体育贡献出中国智慧。

（二）传播内容以武术项目为主

孔子学院对传统体育的跨文化传播内容以武术项目为主，具体来说就是教授或者表演武术套路。例如，美国阿尔弗莱德大学孔子学院从 2011 年成立至今，常年开设太极拳班。又如，2019 年 4 月，在孔子学院总部的支持下，由北京体育大学武术表演团打造的大型舞台剧《太极功夫传奇》，在哈萨克斯坦和乌兹别克斯坦的 5 个城市的 5 所孔子学院进行了巡演。[①] 但这类活动囿于时间有限、语言不通等，均以展示武术动作为主，未能深入揭示武术文化的丰富内涵。

---

① 参见孔子学院总部官方网站：http：//www. hanban. org/

从层次上看，文化可以分为浅层文化和深层文化。武术套路是人体文化产品，属于浅层文化范畴；武术文化内涵则属于深层文化范畴。“武术”一词最早是一个军事概念，但在漫长的历史发展中，植根于中华传统哲学、道德思想的土壤，逐渐发展出丰富的文化内涵，其中健身养生的社会功能和礼数仁爱的文化品质成为武术在当代社会中的价值核心。当前，社会竞争加剧，生活节奏加快，身心健康、和谐相处逐渐成为人们社会生活的重要话题。由此，习练武术作为提高生活质量的重要途径日益受到各国人们的注意。但事实上，习练者只有不断加深对“天人合一”、仁爱、和谐等武术文化要义的领悟，才能真正享受到武术运动的愉悦，并且通过武术文化，体会到中华传统文化的博大精深。

（三）传播途径以人际传播为主

目前，孔子学院对传统体育的跨文化传播主要有两种途径：教学和表演。如上文提到的开设传统体育的课程、组织表演团体访问表演等。从传播学的角度看，这两条途径都属于直接人际传播的范畴，即不使用传播中介的面对面传播。直接人际传播具有方法灵活、交互性强、信息丰富等优势，但由于时间、空间的限制，受众往往有限。孔子学院多与国外高校合作，不管是开设的课程，还是组织的表演，受众多限于学院或学校内部，这进一步影响了传统体育传播的范围。

孔子学院目前还较少利用海外大众媒体、社交媒体等途径来传播传统体育。海外大众媒体虽然受众广泛，但毕竟资源有限，孔子学院的活动要想得到关注，具有很大难度。相反，社交媒体平台上既有丰富的资源，又有广泛的受众，是不容忽视的一条传播途径。社交媒体这一概念最早出现在《什么是社会化媒体》（*What Is Social Media*）这本书中，作者将社交媒体定义为一种给予用户极大参与空间的新型在线媒体，具有参与、公开、交流、对话等特征（曹博林，2016），常见的例子包括微博、Facebook。随着社会信息化程度的不断加深，社交媒体的影响力越来越大，在跨文化传播中能够有效扩大受众范围，提升传播力。

三、孔子学院对传统体育跨文化传播路径优化对策

（一）加强内容建设，讲好“中国体育故事”

面对新的历史机遇，孔子学院对传统体育的跨文化传播应紧跟构建人类命运共同体的时代步伐，提出植根中华传统文化、对接全球一体化的传统体育话语议题，形成适于跨文化传播的中国传统体育文化和价值元素。具体来讲，第一，与中华传统思想、民俗文化等中华优秀传统文化紧密结合，结合对象国家不同的文化背景，加强对武术、龙舟竞渡、舞龙舞狮等传统体育项目人文元素的建设。例如，将龙舟竞渡与端午节庆文化、华夏民俗文化、强调合作的民族精神等内容相结合，将传统体育作为中国人日常生活的一部分进行介绍。第二，对少数民族传统体育项目所承载的民风民俗进行阐发，充分发挥体育在跨国民族同源文化与民族感情中的积极纽带作用。例如，“中亚各国与我国新疆在赛马、刁羊、姑娘追、摔跤、国际象棋、刀郎舞等体育项目上有一定的相似性”（张志新等，2011）。在跨文化传播过程中，应充分发挥这些项目在中外“民心相通”方面的价值和作用。第三，加强中华传统体育文化与奥林匹克文化的交流互鉴。中华传统体育文化中人体康寿的养生观念、形神兼备的和谐思想与奥林匹克运动文化中的“更高、更快、更强”追求绝非互相否定，而是具有各取所长、互有裨益的融合可能。在与奥林匹克运动的对照下讲述“中国体育故事”，更有助于目标国受众理解与认同。

（二）完善传播机制，提高传播力

当前，孔子学院已经从一个单纯的教育机构发展成为能够协调不同官方与非官方传播主体的平台。例如，“一带一路”倡议中的一些人文交流项目借助孔子学院得以落地；再如，中外很多高校、社团也因为孔子学院而建立起合作关系。因此，要提高传统体育的传播力，应该致力于不断完善传播机制，更好地发挥出孔子学院的平台作用。第一，完善协同机制，以孔子学院为平台，探索中外政府、高校、社团、非政府组织等机构协同开展中华传统体育国际传播的机制。例如，举行区域性业余武术比赛，加强各武术社团的联系与交流；再如，促进对本土体育教师的培养，追求传统体育跨文化传播的长期效果。第二，发挥渗透机制，遵循传播学基本规律，在社交媒体上主

动进行议程设置，发挥日常生活的"甜化效应"，利用中国传统体育在身心合一、强身健体等多方面的文化元素，提高议题在目标国受众中的吸引力和影响力。第三，加强对接机制，即对接传播主体和传播对象的融合度，根据不同国家，特别是"一带一路"沿线各国的特点设计相应的传播渠道、传播内容，提高传播的针对性。

（三）利用信息技术，创新传播方法

孔子学院对传统体育的教学以面对面的人际传播为主。一方面，这种传播方法符合体育教学的规律，但是容易受到时间和空间的局限，受众有限。另一方面，这种方法的传播效果受教师个人因素影响较大。相关研究指出，有的志愿者教师没有相关体育专业的教育背景，仅接受过短期培训，专业技术水平不高；有的教师在目标语的使用上存在困难，交流不易（张广鹏，2016），这一现状在短期内很难通过师资培训来改善。因此，孔子学院应充分利用信息技术，辅助教师教学，扩大受众面，保证教学效果。具体措施包括三个方面。第一，依靠网上孔子学院等平台，大力发展在线课程。设计多语种的从入门到高阶的各级课程，满足不同受众群体需求。第二，利用 VR 技术，为学员提供多维度学习体验。VR（Virtual Reality），又称"虚拟现实"，是一种综合利用计算机图形系统和各种现实及控制等接口设备，在计算机上生成的、可交互的三维环境中提供沉浸感觉的技术。当前，VR 技术在体育培训领域已经被广泛应用。孔子学院背靠中外高校资源，应致力于开发和应用 VR 精品体育课程，支持教师和学生高效地完成教学任务。第三，开发多语种体育文化读本，为不同文化背景的受众提供了解中华传统体育文化的窗口，帮助他们以此为切入口，进一步了解相关的传统思想、传统礼仪和中国人的日常生活等。

（四）增设效果评估，完善传播体系

孔子学院应基于精细化管理思路，建立一套相对完备的跨文化传播效果评价指标体系，为科学运作、专业化传播提供有针对性、可操作的规范和依据。第一，通过对孔子学院师生进行访谈与问卷调查，以年龄、国别、性别等因素作为变量对数据进行分析，充分了解不同受众群体的个性化需求，并以此为依据，设置传统体育课程。第二，使用大数据统计等方法，对孔子学院在社交媒体上的传播现状、国外大众媒体对于孔子学院对传统体育跨文化

传播的报道进行分析，总结具有关注度的议题。第三，增加年度传播效果评价环节，对不同地域孔子学院的传播状况进行及时评估和反馈，并在此基础上确定传播对象的“基本盘”和“重点盘”。孔子学院现有的传统体育传播活动多根据本地资源，因地制宜展开，依靠大数据，孔子学院总部应加强管理顶层设计，加强各孔子学院工作的指导。例如，在非洲孔子学院，武术课程很受欢迎，如坦桑尼亚的多多马大学孔子学院开设的25门课程中就有3门武术相关课程：武术基础、武术养生、武术教练培训（郭晶、吴应辉，2018），这样的孔子学院应该得到持续性的集中支持。

四、结论

当前，中华传统体育在孔子学院跨文化传播中的定位尚不够清晰，多作为语言教学的补充，因此，传播内容集中在对武术套路等文化产品的展示上，未能对深层的文化内涵进行很好的探索。事实上，作为一种独具特色的身体文化，中华传统体育能够有效跨越语言、政治、观念等障碍，成为中外民心相通的桥梁，因此在孔子学院跨文化传播中占有不可小觑的地位和价值。基于此，孔子学院应进一步建设传播内容、完善传播途径、注重效果评估，不断提高对传统体育的传播力。

参考文献：

[1] 钟秉枢. 人类命运共同体引领下的中国体育外交战略构建［J］. 体育文化导刊，2019（2）.

[2] 邓星华，宋宗佩. 中国体育对外传播的反思与超越［J］. 体育学刊，2017（2）.

[3] 刘小学. 中国民族传统体育在北欧的传播［D］. 北京：北京体育大学，2016.

[4] 葛耀君，张业安，李海. 媒介生态视阈下我国民族传统体育文化传播问题研究［J］. 北京：北京体育大学，2018（10）.

[5] 张广鹏. 冰岛北极光孔子学院武术特色活动课程的实施与评价［D］. 北京：北京体育大学，2016.

[6] 贾文山，纪之文. 人类命运共同体与全球传播［J］. 全球传媒学刊，2018（3）.

[7] 周之华. 中华民族传统体育文化概论［M］. 北京：北京体育大学出版社，2016.

[8] 曹博林. 社交媒体：概念、发展历程、特征与未来——兼谈当下对社交媒体认识的模糊之处［J］. 湖南广播电视大学学报，2016.

[9] 张志新，张少杰，武杰，庞辉，臧留鸿. 中亚地区的体育文化交流［J］. 体育学刊，

2011 (5).
[10] 郭晶，吴应辉. 孔子学院发展量化研究（2015～2017）[J]. 云南师范大学学报，2018 (5).

作者简介：

李韵，文学博士，四川大学海外教育学院讲师，研究方向为汉语国际传播研究。

美国孔子学院社交媒体传播力研究①

张　杰
四川大学海外教育学院

摘　要：美国孔子学院在促进中美两国人民交流与理解中发挥了积极的作用，但随着网络技术的发展和社交媒体时代的到来，孔子学院的社交媒体传播力还有待进一步提高，目前在信息发布频率、内容时效性和贴近性以及与粉丝的互动等方面还存在一些问题。提升美国孔子学院社交媒体传播力需要转变传播思路、培育多元主体，整合信息资源、优化传播方式，提升内容黏性、升级关系网络，关注信息反馈、增强双向互动。

关键词：美国；孔子学院；社交媒体；传播力

Research on the Communication Power of Social Media in Confucius Institutes in the United States

Zhang Jie
School of Overseas Education, Sichuan University

Abstract: Confucius Institutes in the United States have played an active role in promoting exchanges and understanding between Chinese and American people. However, with the development of network technology and the advent of the era of social media, the communication power of social media of Confucius institutes still

① 本文系四川大学海外教育学院中央高校基本科研业务费项目“基于社交媒体的美国孔子学院传播影响力研究”成果，项目编号：2019自研—海外01。

needs to be further improved. At present, there are still some problems in the frequency of information release, timeliness and relevance of content and interaction with fans. To improve the social media communication power of Confucius Institutes in the United States, it is necessary to change the communication thinking, cultivate diverse subjects, integrate information resources, optimize the communication mode, improve the stickiness of content, upgrade the relationship network, pay attention to information feedback, and enhance two-way interaction.

Keywords: The United States; Confucius Institutes; Social media; The Communication Power

一、研究缘起与背景

美国是中国重要的战略合作与文化交流伙伴，2004 年在美国建立的第一所孔子学院——马里兰大学孔子学院正式挂牌，十多年来，在美孔子学院得到了迅速发展。截至 2018 年底，美国已有孔子学院 97 所①，是全球拥有孔子学院数量最多的国家。作为中美语言文化交流的窗口和桥梁，孔子学院在美国本土为民众搭建了学习中文的平台，增进了对中国的认知，对促进两国人民相互沟通与理解发挥了积极的作用。

孔子学院作为推广汉语和传播中国文化的交流机构，是中国文化“走出去”的重要举措，也是文化领域具有代表性的“中国符号”（周亭等，2018）。美国孔子学院的建设与发展一方面深受中美两国关系的影响，另一方面，其传播力和影响力也受制于信息技术的发展和运用。以数字和网络技术为代表的新一轮科技革命，正在使包括传媒业在内的全球社会经历一场前所未有的大变革。人类在信息技术的助推下已进入社交媒体时代（强月新、夏忠敏，2018）。鉴于社交媒体在国际信息传播中的重要性日增，不少国内学者已将其视为提升媒体国际传播力的一项有力武器（胡智锋、刘俊，2018）。孔子学院积极利用社交媒体不仅可以有效拓宽信息发布渠道，加强

① 统计数据截止时间为 2018 年 12 月。

与网民沟通交流，进一步提高社交媒体传播力，而且可以树立良好的学院形象，从而为“讲述好中国故事，传播好中国声音”营造有利的舆论环境。

二、孔子学院社交媒体传播力与传播新变局

传播力的概念是21世纪初进入中国新闻传播学界的，刘建明在2003年出版的《新闻学概论》一书中提出，传播力是媒介传播力的简称。喻国明认为，传播力是影响社会的一种最为重要的软力量，是影响人们情感认同、身份认同、社会价值认同的最为重要的力量。可见，传播力的主体是一个包含各种社会机构的较为宽泛的主体的集合。丁柏铨明确提出，不能把传播力简单理解为新闻媒体的传播力，政府机构部门及其有关单位在相当程度上同样是主体（张春华、温卢，2018）。因此，本文认为孔子学院作为中华文化海外传播的一个重要平台和窗口，其信息传播行为需要基于社交媒体这一新的社会情境，以更开阔的视野重新审视孔子学院机构本身、网民个体以及社交媒体平台等多个层面上复杂多变的传播关系，不断提升美国孔子学院的社交媒体传播力。

网络与信息技术的飞速发展，使得人类传播方式从过去长时间依赖报刊、广播电视发布信息的大众传播时代进入社交媒体时代，社交媒体开创了由用户生产内容、由用户消费内容的新局面，其传播力日趋提升。身处社交媒体时代的人们，真正能够无缝地共享知识、表达意见、影响社会（强月新、夏忠敏，2018）。这种新技术不仅直接导致了传统媒介机构新闻生产和报道领域的颠覆性变革，而且使得政府、企业以及其他社会机构利用社交媒体进行自我宣传和信息传播成为一种较为普遍的现象。在这样一种全新的传播生态格局下，孔子学院的社交媒体传播也面临着一系列新情况。

（一）传播主体的变化与传播思维的变革

社交媒体是“具有天然亲民、去政治色彩，以自由、分享、平等为核心传播精神的新媒体”（朱鸿军、刘向华，2017）的代表，在社交媒体平台上，传播的主体变得更为分散、多元，规制的解除使传播话语权发生了某种程度的“漂移”，权威的组织和霸权式话语叙事未必会成为网民关注的焦点，而社交媒体上通过点击、评论、转发等表达个体意见的方式，反而易于形成声势浩大的围观力量，引发热议。

孔子学院是中国文化对外传播的重要项目之一，但是目前这一项目的传播效果还有待提升。有研究指出，孔子学院去政治化的教材反而被美国学生家长视为精心设计的，从而引起他们对教材内容的不信任（朱鸿军、刘向华，2017）。这与中美两国在社会制度、意识形态、文化观念等方面根深蒂固的差异，以及中国早期对外传播所形成的"外宣"式刻板印象有很大关系。社交媒体时代，孔子学院的信息传播必须更新观念、变革思维，在逐渐淡化官方色彩、凸显民间性的同时，依托地缘优势，通过组织机构、网络社群、网民个人等多元化的传播主体，努力融入美国本土社交圈，提升社交媒体传播力。

（二）传播客体的变化与传播场域的变革

以社交媒体为代表的新媒体迅速崛起后，为传统媒介时代几乎是有口难言、无所作为的"受众"进行了普遍性的"赋权"，传播客体发生了颠覆性的变化。一方面，技术赋权为每一个网民都提供自由发声、表达意见的平台和渠道；另一方面，社会赋权使更多的普通网民不再受制于"沉默的螺旋"，"人微"却不一定"言轻"。网民变为主动"参与生产的消费者"，在传统上由政商精英主宰的公共政治领域内产生"众声喧哗"的效应。这种以关系为导向的信息流动还能产生联结效应，从而将线上的交锋运动转变为线下的集体行动。无论是"占领华尔街"运动还是"阿拉伯之春"，都体现了社交媒体对中下层和边缘弱势群体的强大动员力量（史安斌，2014）。

传播客体的被赋权深刻地影响了传播场域的变革。场域理论是法国社会学家皮埃尔·布尔迪厄（Pierre Bourdieu）用来分析传媒的利器，他认为"一个场就是一个有结构的社会空间，一个实力场有统治者和被统治者，有在此空间起作用的恒定、持久的不平等的关系，同时也是一个为改变或保存这一实力场而进行斗争的战场"（布尔迪厄，2000）。社交媒体因其大众性、民主性、个体性、分散性和聚集性的特性，使得这一"战场"中的权力博弈更为凸显。在这一全新的场域中，孔子学院社交媒体传播面对的是一个个具体鲜活的网民，他们可能没有很高的文化水平，没有接受过高级而又系统的教育，但是他们可能对中国文化和汉语语言抱有兴趣，或者只是对生活在地球另一端这个古老而又年轻的国家有一点点好奇心。他们一般不会去主动登录中国的各级政府网站，不会去浏览中国的新闻网站，但是他们会在Facebook、Twitter等社交媒体上乐此不疲地与其他网友互动，孔子学院的信息传播就在这一次次的互动中悄无声息地完成了，其巧妙之处在于，受众的点赞、评论和自主分享避免了空洞的说教模式，降低了官方宣传所易产生的警惕和不信任，无形中改变了传播场域中的权力较量。

（三）传播渠道的变化与话语方式的变革

习近平总书记在欧美同学会成立100周年庆祝大会上曾提出："多用外国民众听得到、听得懂、听得进的途径和方式，讲述好中国故事，传播好中国声音，让世界对中国多一分理解、多一分支持。"（习近平，2013）社交媒体是当前大多普通美国民众能够"听得到"的渠道，而孔子学院的信息传播要真正利用好这一平台，还必须用他们"愿意听""听得懂"并且"听得进"的话语方式，来讲述发生在孔子学院的事情和关于中国的故事。这就意味着要提高传播内容的趣味性，使其更生活化，借助具体文化资源讲述历史与现代有机结合、丰富且立体的中国故事（薛可，2017）。同时，要从以物为主的思维向以人为主的思维转变，从呆板的说教式话语转向灵活的交流式话语，以美国民众喜闻乐见的方式，拉近与不同传播对象之间的情感距离，这也是孔子学院对外传播的民意基础。

三、美国孔子学院社交媒体传播存在的问题

作为世界上拥有孔子学院数量最多的国家，美国孔子学院已经走过了15年的发展历程。然而在孔子学院蓬勃发展的同时，美国政界、学界和新闻媒体对孔子学院的质疑声也此起彼伏。这固然是由于中美两国在政治制度、意识形态、价值观念等方面存在着差异，但与孔子学院自身的信息传播不到位、沟通交流不顺畅也有一定关系。特别是在社交媒体运用上还存在不同程度的缺位、错位等情况，未能在消除广大普通民众对孔子学院的误解和偏见方面发挥应有的作用。本文综合考察了美国仍在运行的97所孔子学院在主要社交媒体平台（包括Facebook、Twitter、YouTube以及Instagram等）账号的开通与运营情况[①]，发现存在一些问题。

① 对在多于一个平台开通账号的孔子学院，以其建设运行最好的平台为代表。

（一）账号开通数量多，信息发布频率低

据调查，97 所孔子学院中，有 78 所在主要社交媒体平台上至少开通了一个账号，其中尤以 Facebook 平台居多（71 所）。乔治华盛顿大学、西密歇根大学等 11 所大学的孔子学院同时在上述 4 个社交平台开通了账号。但与孔子学院社交媒体账号“遍地开花”不相匹配的状况是，这些账号的日常运营情况较差，内容质量欠佳。从数量上看，以 2018 年为例，全年发稿量上百条的孔子学院只有 13 家，其中华美协进社孔子学院最多，达到了 565 条（Facebook），排名第二的北卡莱罗纳大学孔子学院的发稿量是 358 条（Twitter）。而绝大多数孔子学院的账号，无论是在哪一个社交媒体平台，其发稿量总体都较少，更新频率较低，以周更居多。

（二）信息发布时效性差，内容贴近性不强

美国孔子学院社交媒体账号发布的信息动态，多数是对孔子学院本身的课程、师资以及中国文化的介绍性内容，兼有少量讲座或活动的新闻类信息，还有一些只是标题导语附上网页链接，总体而言，这些内容的时效性比较差，信息发布略显随意。同时，这类“硬”新闻与美国网民的信息接收习惯还有一定的差距，他们更愿意通过具体的人物和故事等“软”内容来增强对孔子学院和中国文化的了解，因此内容的贴近性也不强。

（三）与粉丝互动较少，用户流动性大

社交媒体区别于传统媒体的重要特点在于它能够实现与网民的即时互动，其最直接的体现就是点赞、评论、转发以及回复等功能。但从目前统计情况来看，这几项指标的数值都不甚理想，孔子学院社交媒体账号的粉丝量少，流动性大，与粉丝之间的沟通交流不多，这客观上表明社交媒体的互动功能未能得到充分开发，孔子学院的传播力和影响力都有待进一步提升。

四、提升孔子学院社交媒体传播力的策略

社交媒体兼具分散与聚合、个体与集体、大众化与去中心化等特性，使得整个社会传播体系日益关系化和网络化。提升孔子学院社交媒体传播力必须在把握其特性、遵循其规律的基础上，综合考量孔子学院本身的传播能

力、美国民众的信息接收习惯和接受心理等因素，才能生产出适销对路的信息产品。

（一）转变传播思路，培育多元主体

在“人人都有麦克风”的时代，普通网民是生产、发布新闻与信息的重要来源之一。孔子学院的社交媒体传播不能只将传播主体局限于机构本身，而应该努力开拓渠道，培育多元化的主体。一方面“向内挖掘”，鼓励孔子学院的教职员工，特别是中外双方的院长，以私人身份开通社交媒体平台账号，并积极发布有关孔子学院、中国文化、汉语知识以及个人感悟等方面的内容。另一方面“向外拓展”，加强与当地社区和民众的互动，发现并邀请那些较为活跃且对中华文化有了解、有好感的民众，在个人社交媒体账号上发布相关信息。同时，做好孔子学院学生及“院友”毕业后的联络工作，鼓励他们在不同社交媒体上分享自己学习的心得体会等。当然，更为重要的是，多元的传播主体之间还应该保持互动和交流，强化双向链接关系。简言之，就是要采用“众包”的形式，顺应社交媒体时代“全媒、全民”的传播格局，不断淡化孔子学院的官方色彩，从而提高信息传播的公信力和亲和力。

（二）整合信息资源，优化传播方式

孔子学院天然具有内容资源的优势，无论是汉语教学的课程安排，中华文化的活动推广，还是日常的信息咨询与报名服务，都是孔子学院独一无二的信息资源。但这样的信息如果没有进行很好的整合和优化传播，只能是“藏在深闺人未识”。社交媒体的技术发展兼容了文字、图片、音频、视频等表现形式，多数孔子学院在上述平台上的信息发布也是以“文字+图片”的形式完成的，偶有一些音视频类信息。事实上，在智能手机和移动互联网的普及下，视觉化信息逐渐成为社交媒体的重要组成部分，一种以图像信息为基础传播信息模式的新型社交形式——图像社交媒体应运而生（周翔、韩为政，2017），其中尤以 Instagram 为代表。但目前美国孔子学院中仅有得克萨斯南方大学孔子学院、南佛罗里达大学孔子学院等少数几家对图像社交媒体运用得较好。因此，未来可视化信息传播和图像社交媒体的运用应是提升孔子学院社交媒体传播力的方向之一。

（三）提升内容黏性，升级关系网络

这首先意味着孔子学院发布的信息内容要更具吸引力和感染力。美国学者奇普·希思和丹·希思（Chip Heath & Dan Heath）兄弟在合著的《让创意更有黏性》（*Made to Stick*）一书中提出了黏性创意的“SUCCESs法则”，他们认为信息只有遵循了如下原则——S（Simple 简洁的）、U（Unexpected 出乎意料的）、C（Concrete 具体的）、C（Credible 可信的）、E（Emotional 富有感情的）、S（Story 故事），才能更吸引人（奇普·希思、丹·希思，2007）。具体而言，就是在日常动态信息中多发布一些真实的人和事——美国人通过学习汉语在工作、生活乃至人生的体验、经历方面发生了怎样的变化。要善于用人性化、个性化的网络语言和多媒体的形式把上述内容体现出来。年轻人是社交媒体的主要用户，因此社交媒体上的内容需要根据年轻一代的语言习惯进行设计，摒弃生硬直白的宣传化语言，采用生动自然的表达方式，体现亲切、人性化的话语特色。

孔子学院具有很大的内容资源优势，这一点固然重要，但就社交媒体的传播效果而言，关系优势有时更为重要。一条信息被社交媒体上某个“流量名人”转发后，可能会产生几何数量级人群的围观，其传播效果也不可同日而语。一个最具代表性的例子是2015年习近平主席访美。时年，中国的外宣团队在Facebook上创建了一个名为“XI's US VISIT”的主页，向海外受众提供习近平访美期间的新闻、图片及视频。这个主页减少了传统大而空的叙事框架，采用了美国本土化的传播符号，符合美国人使用社交媒体的习惯，特别是经过Facebook的创始人扎克伯格的转发而受到广泛关注，该主页获得超过58万个点赞和28万条评论，在美国形成了一股中国热，激发了美国受众了解中国的热情，增进了中美之间的沟通了解（强月新、夏忠敏，2018）。由此可见，孔子学院社交媒体传播应该通过多种方式和渠道推广社交账号，广泛合作提升知名度。比如有选择性地关注社交媒体上的大学教授、媒体精英以及一些知华爱华的知名人士，有选择地转发他们的言论，与其加强互动和交流，提高账号的活跃度和知名度。

（四）关注信息反馈，增强双向互动

社交媒体的技术特性决定了这一平台不仅仅是孔子学院进行信息发布的简单渠道，更是一个需要及时做出反馈、与网友加强沟通交流的桥梁。孔子学院在任何一个社交媒体平台上发布信息的点赞量、评论量、回复量与转发量等数据指标都能直接体现其传播力的高低和传播效果的优劣。从目前的统计情况来看，美国孔子学院社交媒体传播的上述指标都不尽如人意，这就意味着孔子学院要关注社交媒体上网友的信息反馈，及时、有针对性地与网民进行沟通和交流，增强双向互动，增进双方感情。

五、结语

综上所述，美国孔子学院经过十几年的快速发展，在汉语国际教育、中国文化推广等方面取得了一系列丰硕的成果。随着网络技术的快速发展，在社交媒体时代，孔子学院在促进中美文化交流互鉴、加强与美国民众交流沟通、消除误解和分歧等方面还需要有新思路、新作为，从而为提升我国文化软实力、构建“人类命运共同体”做出积极的贡献。

参考文献：

[1] 周亭，温怡芳，贾文斌．“他塑”视角下涉华国际舆情的困境与应对［J］．对外传播，2018（4）．

[2] 强月新，夏忠敏．社交媒体时代中国对外传播的变革与转型［J］．编辑学刊，2018（3）．

[3] 胡智锋，刘俊．主体诉求渠道类型：四重维度论如何提高中国传媒的国际传播力［J］．新闻与传播研究，2013（4）．

[4] 张春华，温卢．重构关系：媒介融合背景下传播力提升的核心路径［J］．新闻战线，2018（7）．

[5] 朱鸿军，刘向华．“走出去”到“走进去”：对外传播新境界的新媒体作为［J］．对外传播，2017（9）．

[6] 史安斌．探析全球传播变局与外国外宣思路［J］．中国国情国力，2014（11）．

[7] 皮埃尔·布尔迪厄．关于电视［M］．许钧，译．沈阳：辽宁教育出版社，2000．

[8] 习近平．在欧美同学会成立 100 周年庆祝大会上的讲话［EB/OL］．新华网 www.xinhuanet.com

[9] 薛可．中国对外传播的几个关键点［J］．人民论坛，2017（8）．

[10] 周翔，韩为政．利用图像社交媒体提升中国国际传播力研究［J］．中州学刊，2017（3）．

[11] 奇普·希思，丹·希思. 让创意更有黏性［M］. 雷静，译. 北京：中信出版社，2007.

作者简介：

张杰，文学博士，四川大学海外教育学院讲师，研究方向为全球传播、跨文化传播等。

孔子学院在中外高校合作中的价值与实践①

张　伊
四川大学海外教育学院

摘　要：经过十余年的快速发展，孔子学院已在全球158个国家和地区建立了535所孔子学院和1134个孔子课堂。孔子学院为中外高校合作提供了重要平台，同时中外高校在孔子学院中的工作对孔子学院回归非营利性教育机构形象具有重要价值。本文以四川大学承办的5所孔子学院为例，指出在孔子学院建设中应加强中外高校校际合作、学生交流，助力高端学术交流。

关键词：孔子学院；中外高校；多元化合作与交流；非营利性教育机构角色

The Value and Practice of Confucius Institutes in the Cooperation Between Chinese and International Universities

Zhang Yi
School of Overseas Education of Sichuan University

Abstract: After more than ten years of rapid development, the Confucius Institute has established 535 Confucius Institutes and 1, 134 Confucius Classrooms in 158 countries and regions around the world. Confucius Institutes connect Chinese and international universities as a bridge, on the other hand cooperation between universities is of great support to its non-profit educational institutions' role. Taking Confucius Institutes of Sichuan University as

① 本文系四川大学2018四川大学海外教育学院中央高校基本科研业务费项目。

an example, the article points out that it is necessary to strengthen cooperation between universities, communications between students, and promote academic exchanges.

Keywords: Confucius Institutes; Chinese and International Universities; Diversified Cooperation and Exchanges; Non-profit Educational Institution

一、引言

孔子学院是中华文化走出去和中外文化交流的重要平台，是发展中国与外国的友好关系、促进世界多元文化发展、构建和谐世界的重要途径。在十几年的发展历程中，孔子学院始终致力于适应世界各国（地区）人民对汉语学习的需要，增进世界各国（地区）人民对中国语言文化的了解，加强中国与世界各国各地区的教育文化交流合作。

目前，中国已在全球158个国家和地区建立了535所孔子学院和1134个孔子课堂。2017年教育部副部长田学军在孔子学院总部调研时曾指出，孔子学院建设已经到了提质增效的关键期，要随之步入“二次创业”的新阶段。当前，孔子学院的工作重心是深入学习贯彻习近平总书记关于孔子学院建设的重要批示精神，深刻认识孔子学院发展面临的重大历史机遇，进一步增强办好孔子学院的使命感和责任感，推动孔子学院改革发展，使汉语国际教育与推广事业再上新台阶。

然而当前在少数国家，“野心”“威胁”“软实力”等针对孔子学院的负面词语不时见于当地媒体。相关研究表明，不同国家地区的媒体对孔子学院的评价与不同时期中国所处的国际地位呈负相关，一旦中国的实力对孔子学院所在国的地位构成威胁时，孔子学院就容易被解读为“中国政府宣传工具”（唐京华、孙宏伟，2016），而且将受到消极性的评价。当前，如何克服这些障碍，实现可持续发展，是孔子学院转型中首先面临的问题。笔者认为，应该强调孔子学院非营利性教育机构身份，突出高校在孔子学院建设中的角色和作用。以承办机构为主体推动、加强国内与海外承办机构（高校）间的多元化合作与交流，真正做到“国之交在于民相亲”。因此，本文将以四川大学承办的5所孔子学院的实践为例，探讨孔子学院在中外高校合作中的平台价值。

二、孔子学院是中外高校合作的重要平台

（一）孔子学院是高校国际化进程的推手

在国务院2017年印发的《关于加强和改进新形势下高校思想政治工作的意见》中首次明确提出将“国际交流合作”视为高校的又一项新使命，反映出在经济全球化背景下对大学性质和使命的新认识，也反映出当代大学使命的不断拓展。

未来，国内高校在建设世界一流大学、发扬中国优秀传统文化“走出去”、全面深化改革、创新驱动发展等政策引领下，孔子学院将肩负起汉语教学、增进多文化理解及友谊、促进国际交流与合作的多重使命，成为高校国际化进程强有力的推手。高校要以孔子学院为依托，积极开展孔子学院所在地区、学校的合作与交流，提高中外合作融合度。鼓励人文社科走出去，每年派遣相关学院名师赴孔子学院开展讲座等中华文化传播活动。

（二）孔子学院是高校对外宣传和招募世界一流人才的重要窗口

孔子学院作为合作高校在海外的“办事处”，具有极其便利的地理优势。能第一时间接触到当地学生、教师、居民，便于孔子学院发挥对外宣传和招募人才的重要作用。以孔子学院为依托，将高校最新宣传资料发放至各孔子学院，供当地学生及老师查阅。可结合当地孔子学院中国文化推广活动举行“高校日”等活动，努力宣传、推介高校，打造高校的国际地位，扩大高校的影响力。以孔子学院为依托，高校将招聘相关人才信息发放至各孔子学院，委派孔子学院中方院长和外派教师成为“广纳人才”的主要推手，挖掘所在地区符合高校人才战略的国际高端人才。

三、联系中外高校是孔子学院的工作重点

（一）强化孔子学院非营利性教育机构角色

由于不同国家在意识形态方面存在巨大差异，在文化传统方面存在不同理解，在国家利益方面亦有着不同诉求，因此孔子学院的发展态势常常随着

国际形势的变化而不断变化。在美国，孔子学院发展经过了一个快速增长期，数量的快速增长引起了外部对文化入侵的猜测，数量增加得越快其带来的负面认知、不信任感就越强。2018 年 8 月《美国 2019 财年国防授权法案》正式生效，该法案第 1091 条要求禁止国防部对已设有孔子学院的大学中文旗舰项目提供资金，但国防部准许豁免大学除外。截至目前，申请豁免的 13 所大学无一获得或将获得特批。以中外高校主导的多元化合作与交流将强化孔子学院的非营利性教育机构角色，促进“民相亲”。中外高校间高频率的交流，将带动参与交流的中外人民彼此间的理解与认识，加深友谊。因此中外高校合作对减少孔子学院的政治色彩具有重要意义。

四、四川大学承办的 5 所孔子学院概况

四川大学在构建孔子学院多元化合作平台方面做出了不少探索，积累了一定经验。以下为四川大学海外孔子学院概况。

1. 最早建立的韩国又松大学孔子学院

2006 年 11 月，孔子学院总部/国家汉办批准四川大学与韩国又松大学合作，建设又松大学孔子学院。韩国又松大学孔子学院，自 2007 年 4 月 30 日建立以来，一直秉承在韩国普及汉语，推广中华文化，以了解、交流、友好、和平为宗旨，坚持“传播中国文化，搭建韩中友谊桥梁”的理念。2010 年 12 月举办的世界孔子学院大会上，韩国又松大学孔子学院被评为全球先进孔子学院。

2. 美国亚利桑那州立大学孔子学院①

2007 年 6 月，孔子学院总部/国家汉办批准四川大学与美国亚利桑那州立大学合作，建设亚利桑那州立大学孔子学院。2007 年 10 月，亚利桑那州立大学孔子学院挂牌。截至 2019 年，亚利桑那州立大学孔子学院已在 5 个学区设 14 家孔子课堂，共招收 5500 多名当地学生，其中六家孔子课堂为小学，四家为初中，四家为高中。亚利桑那州立大学孔子学院于 2016 年被评为先进孔子学院。

---

① 美国亚利桑那州立大学已于 2019 年 5 月 31 日就“孔子学院总部与亚利桑那州理事会代表亚利桑那州立大学关于亚利桑那州立大学孔子学院建立和运行重申和修订协议”向孔子学院总部/国家汉办发布终止该合同的通知。

3. 美国犹他大学孔子学院

2007 年 10 月，经孔子学院总部批准，四川大学和美国犹他大学合作建立了美国犹他大学孔子学院。经过十年来的发展，孔院积极融入犹他大学，已经成为犹他大学的一个重要组成部分，不仅为犹他大学享有盛誉的中文专业提供学分课程，定期组织并赞助校内有关中国的活动，为学校主管部门和任何学术机构开展有关中国活动提出建议，孔院还在犹他大学全球化使命中起着至关重要的作用。

4. 美国华盛顿州孔子学院

2009 年 9 月，孔子学院总部/国家汉办批准四川大学和重庆市教委一道，与美国华盛顿大学及西雅图学区合作，成立华盛顿州孔子学院。由四川大学与华盛顿大学合作，在华盛顿州各大学开展汉语言教学和中国文化交流与推广；重庆市教委与西雅图学区合作，在中小学开展汉语言教学和中国文化交流与推广。

5. 比利时荷语布鲁塞尔自由大学孔子学院

2016 年，结合四川大学与布鲁塞尔自由大学长期合作的优势，在欧洲研究、中欧文化交流和中欧高等教育合作取得优异成绩的基础上，四川大学、中国人民大学、布鲁塞尔自由大学共建了布鲁塞尔自由大学孔子学院。该孔子学院将打造全新的研究型孔子学院，除弘扬中国文化和推广汉语言外，还将注重中国与欧洲问题研究以及加强中国与欧洲问题研究的人才培养。

五、四川大学承办的五所孔子学院在中外高校合作中的实践

（一）为高校管理层的合作提供平台

每所孔子学院都有自己的理事会，而理事会成员一般是由中外高校的副校长，相关学院院长等构成。因此，孔子学院为中外高校管理层的深入合作提供了平台。

自 2012 年起，四川大学在全国高校首创孔子学院年度经验交流会。四川大学孔子学院经验交流会是四川大学为助力“中国文化走出去”、推动孔子学院在不同文化背景下顺利运行，以及探讨如何把孔子学院建设成为四川

大学在海外的教学、科研以及国际合作多功能平台而定期举办的学术会议。会议已经连续举办7年，各孔子学院一致认为定期进行孔子学院年度联席会议对于孔子学院的统一管理、协调与可持续发展具有特殊的意义。

2017年11月四川大学与美国亚利桑那州立大学、韩国又松大学合作推出并签署了“1+1+1模式”联合培养商科硕士项目。三校通过共同制定培养计划与课程规划，为学生提供相应便利与优惠学习条件，让学生分别在三校完成培养过程。项目内学生在完成其培养计划、达到授位标准后，能够同时获得三校的商科硕士学位。该项目将从2018年在三校开始招生。

这次签署的合作项目，是四川大学与国外高校签订的第一个硕士学位三校联合培养项目，也是四川大学与美国亚利桑那州立大学、韩国又松大学共同举办孔子学院，不断增加互信、加大合作力度的结果，更是国际合作工作在研究生教育领域的新探索。三校将在该项目不断做大做实的基础上，开展更广领域、更深层面的持续合作。

（二）为中外高校学生间的交流提供支持

随着中国国力的增强，来自不同学科背景的外国学生都对中国社会和中国文化产生了浓厚的兴趣。孔子学院的各色文化项目成为不同需求、不同年龄的外国学生接触、感受、理解真实的中国建设的窗口。

据统计，2019年四川大学共接待孔子学院学生夏令营项目5个，累计接待143人。其中中学生83人，大学生60人。夏令营的活动内容分为学习部分和文化探访部分，学习部分包括汉语课、书法课、太极课、茶艺课等，而文化探访包含游览当地名胜古迹、人文景点等。除此之外，为了让学生更好地了解普通中国家庭，四川大学还积极筹备了中国家庭体验日活动，让外国学生深入、真切感受中国式家庭的生活，也为增进友谊提供了更多的机遇。同时，四川大学结合优秀校友创业案例，带领夏令营的学生走进校友企业，参观、感受充满当代中国特色的年轻企业也成为夏令营活动中受欢迎的部分。

截至目前，四川大学接待孔子学院教育官员访问团项目3个，累计接待35人。这一交流活动旨在加深当地中小学教育官员对中国语言、文化、教育和社会情况的了解，特别是对巴蜀文化的体悟与感受，有效推动当地政府和教育机构设立与发展汉语和中国文化课程。与学生团不同的是，官员团的访问内容还包括调研各具特色的公立或私立中小学，与中国教育管理者和教育者交流沟通，共同探讨开放融合的教学方法。活动还推动了中外中小学建立长期交流，为今后合作创造了可能。

在学习参访的过程中，学生和教育官员收获了知识与欢乐，切身感悟到中华传统文化的深厚底蕴和巴蜀文化灿烂的独特魅力，对中国的风土人情留下了极为深刻的印象。这类来华交流项目极大地促进了“民心相通”。

（三）为高端学术的传播提供助力

经过十余年的发展，孔子学院已经不局限于单纯的汉语培训，而是发展成为一个综合的文化传播媒介。近年来，在“提质增效”的大背景下，孔子学院将高端学术交流作为当前以及今后的发展重点，孔子学院起到了为中外高校的学术交流合作搭建桥梁的作用。

四川大学刚成立的中华文化研究院作为中华文化研究的专业机构，将为孔子学院从语言教学转变为学术交流注入新的动力。2019 年 7 月通过第七届孔子学院经验交流会的学术平台，中华文化研究院与韩国又松大学孔子学院举行了“李白诗全集韩译项目”的第一次会议。李白是中国历史上，同时也是世界历史上最伟大的诗人之一，他与杜甫是唐代诗歌两座高峰，是中国古代诗歌王国中两颗最为灿烂的巨星。将李白诗歌翻译介绍到韩国，对于中华文化走出去意义重大。本次“李白诗全集韩译项目”将作为中韩“以诗译诗”的开创性项目，是以中华优秀传统诗歌学术研究为基础的代表性合作项目。两校希望借助本次项目的合作模式，推动今后诸如杜甫、苏轼等中国古代名家诗作系列韩译和研究工作。

同时，四川大学中华文化研究院还同参与本次孔子学院经验交流会的韩国延世大学中国研究院建立合作关系：四川大学与延世大学共同合作，推动中韩巴蜀文化研究领域、古籍整理领域的学术研讨和交流、中韩名著互译等，推动中华优秀传统文化精髓三国文化在韩国的传播，未来将把《三国志集注》韩译工作作为突破口。

参考文献：

唐京华，孙宏伟. 美国孔子学院发展的困境及其消解——基于政治文化分析视角 [J]. 理论观察，2016（11）。

作者简介：

张伊，管理学硕士，四川大学海外教育学院职员，研究方向孔子学院管理研究。

古代汉语

宋代部分新生名量词的写意功能浅析[①]

游　黎
四川大学海外教育学院

摘　要：汉语量词在语言运用中承载着度量、摹状和写意的功能。其中，写意功能产生时间最晚，在语言研究中还未得到充分重视。本文通过对宋代部分新生名量词产生过程的分析，揭示了其在语言中的写意功能，指出汉语量词的写意功能主要是为适应文学形式发展的需要而产生的。写意功能的出现，使得汉语量词的产生机制更加灵活、生动，是汉语量词系统极大丰富的重要原因之一。

关键词：宋代；名量词；功能；写意

An Elementary Analysis of the Freehand Function of Partial New Quantifiers in the Song Dynasty

You Li
School of Overseas Education, Sichuan University

Abstract: Chinese quantifiers carry the functions of measurement, description and freehand in the use of language. Among them, the freehand function emerged the latest, and has not been fully paid attention to in the study of the language. Through the analysis of the process of the production of some new words in the Song Dynasty, this paper reveals its freehand function in the language, and points out that the freehand function of Chinese

① 本文受四川大学中央高校基本科研业务费项目资助，项目编号：2018-soe14。

quantifiers is mainly adapted to the needs of the development of literary forms. The emergence of freehand function makes the generation mechanism of Chinese quantifiers more flexible and vivid, which is one of the important reasons for the abundance of the Chinese quantifiers system.

Keywords: Song Dynasty; Quantifier; Function; Freehand

发达的量词系统是汉语的特点之一，也是汉语区别于其他语言的重要标志。量词之所以在汉语中占有重要的地位，主要是由于其在语言运用中承载了一些特殊的功能。在汉语量词系统发展的早期阶段，汉语名量词主要有度量和摹状两种功能。

所谓“度量”，是指量词对名物的多少、大小、重量、长短等进行指称与说明的功能。这是汉语名量词最早、最基本的功能，也是汉语名量词产生的原始动因。一般来说，承载度量功能的名量词主要有两类：一是度量衡量词，二是借用名量词。前者如斤、两、里、尺、寸等，这是汉语中产生最早的一类名量词；后者如“一碗饭”中的“碗”，“一身汗”中的“身”等，是临时借用名词为量词，故称为“借用名量词”。度量衡名量词与借用名量词的运用，使得人们对其所称量的名物的多少、大小、重量、长短等指标有更清楚的认识。

所谓“摹状”，是指量词对名物的形状、形态、性质等进行描摹的功能。汉语量词的摹状功能虽然产生的时间较其度量功能略晚，但却是名量词在汉语中最常见的功能。汉语名量词一般是由名词虚化而来的（也有少部分名量词是由动词虚化而来），在名词向名量词虚化的过程中，该名词所具有的意义与特征往往也会转移到名量词身上，也就使得名量词可以用于与某一类具有共同特征的名词搭配，因此产生了摹状功能。例如名量词“条”是由名词“条”虚化而来，名词“条”的本义是树木的枝条，而“枝条”具有［+细长］的语义特征，因此在外形上具备“细长”特点的名词，如“路”“绳子”“裙子”等，往往也就可以被“条”称量，而语言的使用者在看到“一条路”这样的用法时，也自然会感受到路“细长”的形状特点。再如看到“一面镜子”，会感受到镜子“平面”的形状，看到“一张床”，会感受到床“平铺”的外在形态，这都是名量词的摹状功能在起作用。

度量与摹状是汉语名量词最主要的两个功能，也是汉语名量词产生的重要动因。其中，汉语名量词的摹状功能尤其发达，这也是造成汉语名量词特别丰富的重要原因。不过，在汉语量词系统的发展过程中，除了度量与摹状之外，汉语的名量词还衍生出了一个新的功能，即写意功能。从目前对汉语量词的研究成果来看，学界对这一功能的研究还不够充分。下文将通过对宋代部分新生名量词的产生原因进行分析，来说明汉语名量词的“写意”这一特殊功能。

名量词的“写意”功能是指部分名量词具有创造意象的功能。这类名量词在使用中往往已经不具备度量和摹状功能，或者度量和摹状功能已不明显。它们之所以被运用于语言中，主要是由于对它们的使用能够创造一定的意向，产生一定的画面感和意境。

从汉语发展的历史来看，汉语名量词的“写意”功能大约出现于唐宋时期。这主要是因为唐宋时期是汉语诗词等文学形式蓬勃发展和高度成熟的重要时期，而诗词等文学形式的发展与成熟，对汉语语言形式的发展也提出了相应的要求。例如这一时期诗词创作在语言运用上有着明显的求新、求美的要求，也有着很高的追求简洁与意境的要求。因此，这一时期的诗词创作者在对语言字词的选择上也出现了两点变化：一是创作者们开始较主动地选择、创造更加新颖的字词，而尽量避免常用的甚至已经落于俗套的词句；二是创作者追求用更简洁的字词来创造更深远、更美的意境。这种变化，也体现在了宋代量词的运用上，其中，宋代一些新生量词的产生，就是这种变化的具体表现。

【犁】

在宋代的诗词作品中，常常可以见到以“犁”量“雨”的名量词用法，例如：

例（1）麦颖未黄乾，桑实半红湿。恰得一犁雨，田事正火急。（徐积《和张文潜晚春四首》）

例（2）山边夜半一犁雨，田父高歌待收获。（张耒《有感》）

例（3）久旱得雨方一犁，山南种豆犹其时。（《漫塘集》卷四）

例（4）人间辛苦是三农。要得一犁水足、望年丰。（王炎《南柯子·山冥云阴重》）

例（5）杜宇伤春去，蝴蝶喜风清。一犁梅雨，前村布谷正催耕。（葛长庚《水调歌头·杜宇伤春去》）

例（6）十里好山供客醉，一犁春雨劝农归。（虞俦《石照劝农晚归有

雨》）

例（7）郊园旱久只多蹊，昨夜欣沾雨一犁。（朱熹《次秀野躬耕桑陌旧园之韵二首》）

例（8）一犁好雨秧初种，几道寒泉药旋浇放。（连文凤《春日田园杂兴》）

这种用法很容易使人产生疑问："犁"与"雨"到底有什么关系？为什么"雨"可以用"犁"作为量词呢？

"犁"本义为耕田的农具，而农耕离不开春雨，如果春雨的雨量充沛，即俗谓下了一场"透雨"，则对农耕最为有利。王安中《初寮集》卷八中"壬申之旦，膏雨飘洒，鸣溜涓续，尽三日止。滰滋下达及一犁"描写了春雨降临，下浸深及"一犁"的场景。此处"一犁"当然还不是量词，但由此发展，"犁"在宋代成为量词，主要就是用于称量雨，表示雨量相当于一犁入土的深度，"一犁雨"略似于"一场透雨"。

然而"犁"的功能绝不仅限于说明春雨数量的度量功能。分析以上宋代用例可见，以犁量雨的用法在使用时有限定的语境，即农耕场景，因为这种用法本身就是在人们注意到雨量与农耕的关系后产生的。"犁"与"雨"本来并没有直接联系或者相似的特征，它们只有在农耕时才会产生相关性。"犁"本身与农耕有关，当它又被用来称量"雨"时，就自然地成了将"农耕"与"雨"联系起来的介质。

可以说，"一犁雨"这样的用法创造出了一种农耕的场面和意境，相比于以往其他量词的"度量"和"摹状"功能，其所表达的效果也更加生动形象了。"犁"这个介质的出现，将"雨"和"农耕"两个事物联系了起来，读之似乎农夫于春雨中欣喜耕作的场面已跃然纸上。俞成《萤雪丛说》"诗随景物下语"条："至若骚人，于渔父则曰'一蓑烟雨'，于农夫则曰'一犁春雨'，于舟子则曰'一篙春水'，皆曲尽形容之妙也。"王水照（1998）对此分析说："'一犁雨'，比之'一场透雨'之类，已衍生出与耕作有关的意义，更平添一种欣喜、庆幸的气氛。量词的活用和妙用，不仅扩大了诗歌意象的涵义，而且也使诗充满动感和活力。"（王水照，1988）这个分析很有道理，"一犁雨"的用法创造出了农耕的场景、意象和气氛，使人产生自然的联想，说明其已经不局限于"度量"和"摹状"，而是已经具备了"写意"的功能了。

【剪】

《汉语大字典》《汉语量词词典》等辞书均未收录“剪”的量词用法。而《汉语大词典》则认为“剪”有量词用法，其适用范围是“用于花枝”，如“一剪梅”等。根据我们的调查，“剪”在宋代确实已经发展为量词，其称量范围也不仅限于“花枝”。

我们调查发现，“剪”在宋代可以用于称量女子的“眼波”，例如：

例（9）一剪晴波娇欲溜。绿怨红愁，长为春风瘦。（刘天迪《凤栖梧·舞酒妓》）

例（10）一剪艳波横，两点愁山重。（石孝友《卜算子·人自蕊宫来》）

“晴波”“艳波”即“秋波”“秋水”，指女子之眼波。眼波之所以可以用“一剪”称量，大概是来源于唐代李贺的《唐儿歌》诗句：“骨重神寒天庙器，一双瞳人剪秋水。”李贺将女子眼睛的眨动形象地比喻为“双瞳剪水”，因此宋代就将女子的眼波称为“一剪”了。近代汉语中，这种用法一直延续，例如：

例（11）年才及笄，而丰韵天成，横波一剪。（捧花生《秦淮画舫录》“杨枝”）

例（12）白皙而颀，而秋波一剪，盈盈欲语，尤可疗饥。（西溪山人《吴门画舫录》“李倚玉”）

用“剪”来称量眼波，不但符合诗词创作中的对量词选择的“求新”原则，而且也可以从中看出“剪”所承载的写意功能。“一剪眼波”的用法中，“剪”作为名量词的度量和摹状功能基本上已经完全见不到了，但是，一个“剪”字，却生动地描写出了女子眼睛眨动如“双瞳剪水”的形象，女子双目灵动活泼的意味自然地出现在了读者面前，创造出了美好、恰当的意象。

【笛】

“笛”本为乐器，宋代时发展为量词，用于称量“风”，例如：

例（13）画图展处千山雪，渔艇归时一笛风。（黄公度《和宋永兄爱日楼见寄八首其一》）

例（14）千百栖乌，两三过雁，时有婆娑一笛风。（李曾伯《沁园春（自和即事）》）

例（15）夏日山居好，清溪一笛风。（舒岳祥《夏日山居好》）

例（16）五更缥缈千山月，万里凄凉一笛风（王安石《松江》）

例（17）半篙寒碧秋垂钓，一笛疏风夜倚楼。（李若水《题观城驿壁》）

例（18）半林残照人烟晚，一笛秋风雁影寒。（李若水《偶成》）

例（19）一笛秋风急，千岩晚照多。（李若水《次韵高子文村居》）

“笛”的量词用法各类辞书均未载，但从以上例子来看，“笛”在宋代确实已经发展为量词了。“笛”之所以可以用于称量“风”，首先是由于二者在特征上具有相似性。“风”会“吹动”，“笛”也需要“吹”。此外，“风”在吹动时往往会发出类似于笛声的声音。“一笛风”的用法既无法说明风量，也无法具体描摹出风的形貌，但这种用法却通过“吹动”这一特征将“风”和“笛”这两个原本完全无关的名物联系在了一起，甚至还形象地写出了风声，使人读之若有疾风呼啸而过于眼前之感，起到了很好的衬托意境的作用。

【梳】

“梳”本义即“梳子”，各类辞书皆未载其量词用法。其实在宋代“梳”是可以作为量词使用的，主要是用于量“月”，例如：

例（20）密遮池面荷千盖，斜插云头月一梳。（《野谷诗稿》卷六）

例（21）一梳凉月插空碧，楼头暮角催归驺。（《野谷诗稿》卷三）

例（22）群村风下鸦千点，麦陇天垂月一梳。（俞成《萤雪丛说·诗人警句》）

例（23）携去一梳水月，巧楼犹醉笙箫。（张镃《木兰花慢·七夕》）

例（24）世事虽难料，吾生固有涯。殷懃一梳月，十里伴还家。（陆游《游山》）

“梳”之所以可以量“月”，当是取梳子如月牙半弯之形，这是其“摹状”功能的体现。但同时，如果我们将“一梳月”与同样具有摹状功能的“一弯月”进行比较，就可以发现，“一梳月”除了摹状功能以外，同时也兼备了写意功能。因为“梳发”的动作而常常使人产生头发“光滑平顺”之联想，因此“梳”用于量月也增加了文辞的美感，使人产生月光光滑、平顺的想象，而这种想象是“一弯月”所不能产生的。仔细体味“斜插云头月一梳”“一梳凉月插空碧”等句，一个“插”字的运用，以梳子插于秀发之中的形貌来比喻月亮悬于空中之景，则不但月弯之形若在眼前，而且月亮的平滑光洁之貌也跃然纸上。

【杼】

“杼”本义为织布的梭子。《汉语大字典》《汉语大词典》等皆未收录其量词用法。但我们在宋代诗词中发现了“杼”作为量词的用例：

例（25）数点烟鬟青滴，一杼霞绡红湿。（周密《闻鹊喜·吴山观涛》）

例（26）海烟沈处倒残霞，一杼鲛绡和泪织。（吴文英《玉楼春·和吴见山韵》）

例（27）向醉中织就，天孙云锦，一杼新诗。（吴文英《木兰花慢·饯赵山台》）

例（25）、例（26）中“霞绡”“鲛绡”都是指轻薄的织物。由于“杼”本义为织布的梭子，因此被引申用于称量织物。例（27）“一杼新诗”是用其比喻义，“一杼”称量的其实是“云锦”，亦是用于称量织物。

值得注意的是，如果将“杼”与织物的其他量词如“片”“张”等比较就会发现，与其他量词不同，“杼”与织物的性状之间其实并无直接的联系，它仅仅是织物生产过程中使用的一种工具。换句话说，作为量词的“杼”，既不具备计量的功能（我们无法确定“一杼织物”的量），也不具备摹状的功能（“杼”与“织物”在外形上没有任何相似的特征）。“杼”能够发展成为量词，主要还是因为文学创作中诗人（词人）对用词求新、求美的追求以及创造意象的需要。实际上，当“霞绡”等织物被“杼”称量时，创作者就已经创造出了织物与织机同时出现的画面，令人产生更加生动与深刻的联想。

【痕】

“痕”本义为“伤疤”，引申为“痕迹”。在宋朝时发展为量词，其意义与“道” “条”类似，而其中隐含“浅、淡”之感，最常见的是用于量“月”，例如：

例（28）雨浥梨花粉泪香，一痕淡月照修廊。（艾可翁《春夜》）

例（29）数点霁霞山又晚，一痕凉月酒初消。（赵汝茪《梦江南·帘不卷》）

例（30）疏影黄昏，香满东风月一痕。（辛弃疾《丑奴儿·年年索尽梅花笑》）

例（31）半窗寂寞猿三咽，满户萧骚月一痕。（白玉蟾《春日饮酒》）

例（32）花外数声风定。烟际一痕月净。（黄铸《秋蕊香令·花外数声

风定》）

例（33）风前有恨梅千点，溪上无人月一痕。（吴可《小醉》）

例（34）一痕月色挂帘栊，梅影斜斜小院中。（周纯《瑞鹧鸪·一痕月色挂帘栊》）

以上“痕”量“月”，生动地刻画月光“淡而凉”之感。除“月”之外，其他一些形象轻淡而富有美感的事物，也可以用“痕”量：

例（35）寒窗月晴，寒梢露明。一痕归影灯青，又分携短亭。（王梦应《醉太平（送人入湘）》）

例（36）厌厌两点眉峰，一痕酒晕，正人在、温柔乡里。（向希尹《祝英台近·帘栊》）

例（37）算如今，也厌娉婷，带了一痕残雪。（王沂孙《疏影·咏梅影》）

例（38）误点一痕残泪粉，怕人知。（许棐《山花子·挼柳揉花旋染衣》）

例（39）篱菊褪黄秋兴懒，瓦沟财试一痕霜。（高翥《秋兴》）

例（40）一痕朝日界晴窗，森肃清寒昨夜霜。（赵孟坚《初冬客中见小春海棠》）

例（41）平芜天远，一痕黄抹秋霁。（王梦应《念奴娇·欲霜更雨》）

例（35）至例（41）中“痕”分别量“归影”“酒晕”“残雪”“残泪”“秋霜”“朝日”“色彩”等，突出了以上事物的“轻、淡”之状，同时带来美感。

进一步来说，一些抽象的事物也可以用“痕”来量：

例（42）一缕情深朱户掩，两痕愁起青山远。（吴文英《倦寻芳（林钟羽花翁遇旧欢吴门老妓李怜，邀分韵同赋此词）》）

例（43）新归重省别来愁，黛眉头，半痕秋。（吴文英《江神子·送翁五峰自鹤江还）》）

例（44）云外月，画出一痕清绝。（韩淲《谒金门·带湖新月》）

例（42）“两痕愁”、例（43）“秋”亦“愁”义（《广雅·释诂四》：“秋，愁也。”）以“痕”量“愁”，其淡淡哀伤之感更加灵动。例（44）“痕”量“清绝”，实际也是在量“月”，突出表现了月光的凄清绝美。

从上面的例句可以看出，“痕”作为量词在语言中有一定的摹状功能，但更多的是写意功能，是为了满足使用者对文学创作的美感和意境的追求。在宋代以前，已有“枚”“轮”“钩”“团”“条”“弯”“带”等量词可以用于称量“月”。从计量功能来看，“月”早已不需要其他的新兴量词称量；从摹状的功能来看，“月”似乎也不再需要其他的量词，因为以上“轮”“钩”“团”“条”“弯”“带”等量词基本已经涵盖了月亮的各种形状。但是事实上，宋代仍然产生了不少用于量“月”的新量词，“痕”即其中之一。这就是语言使用者“求新”“求美”的需要。从这些量词在语言使用中的实际作用来看，其写意的功用大于其计量、摹状的功用。

“痕”的这种称量事物并突出其“轻淡”感的用法一直延续到近现代汉语中，例如：

例（45）聚叶泼成千点墨，攒花染出几痕霜。（《红楼梦》第三十八回）

例（46）蓝蓝的天空，电杆之间连着几痕细线，多么像五线谱啊，停着的燕子成了音符，谱出一支正待演奏的春天的赞歌。（郑振铎《燕子》）

今日中学语文老师常常会问学生能否将郑振铎《燕子》中的“几痕细线”替换为“几根细线”或“几条细线”，答案当然是否定的。这就是因为“痕”作为量词所具有的似有似无、若隐若现之美感是其他几个量词不具备的。这是“痕”作为量词的写意功能的具体体现。

除了以上部分新生的专职名量词已经具备很明显的写意功能以外，宋代名量词写意功能发展的另一个表现是对借用名量词的选择更加灵活。宋代以前的临时量词的作用往往在于度量中心词的数量多少，因此最常见的是由器物类名词临时借用为量词。例如“一瓶水”是以“瓶”来度量“水”的数量，“酒一杯”是以“杯”来说明“酒”的数量。由于宋以前的临时量词有着非常明显的度量词的特征和作用，承担着名量词度量的功能。然而，随着宋代诗、词、曲等文学形式的蓬勃发展，作为文学载体的语言就面临着求新、求变的要求，因此这一时期的临时量词有了很大的发展和变化。为了实现诗词创造意象、增强美感的要求，一些唐宋以前还不能作为借用名量词的名词开始作为借用名量词出现了。例如，宋代临时量词对名词的借用不再限于容器类量词，而是更加灵活、多样，例如：

例（48）半蜗茅屋归吹影，数螺苔石压波光。（蒋捷《昼锦堂（荷花）》）

此例中“蜗”“螺”本来都是软体动物的名称，并不是承载中心词的器物，但由于蜗牛壳狭小，螺壳则有回旋重叠之貌，因此作者分别将其借用来称量茅屋和苔石。这种巧妙的借用不但给人耳目一新之感，而且非常生动。我们看到“半蜗茅屋”“数螺苔石”这样的诗句，则茅屋的逼仄狭小和苔石的回旋重叠之状已在眼前。

上例中的临时量词“蜗”有窄小的语义特征，如“蜗居”；“螺”有“回旋重叠”的语义特征，如“螺髻”。因此“蜗”和“螺”在语义特征上与中心词“茅屋”“苔石”仍然有一定的联系，它们还可以看作承担了一定的摹状功能。而以下各例中临时量词与中心词之间在词义上没有联系，在作用上失去了度量、摹状的功能，而更侧重于描写和写意的功能，例如：

例（49）从此绿窗深处，有一梢秋月。（高登《好事近（黄义卿画带霜竹）》）

例（50）白苹洲上，浩歌一棹春水。（张炎《湘月（赋云溪）》）

例（51）只欠芦花夜宿，金溪上、一苇秋风。（葛郯《满庭霜·述怀》）

例（52）一竿风月，一蓑烟雨，家在钓台西住。（陆游《鹊桥仙·一竿风月》）

例（53）忍落梅，万点苔根，化作一窗离思。（王梦应《疏影》）

以上例句中的量词，不像其他由名词发展而来的量词那样在特征上与中心词有关联（如“一轮月”“一弯月”“一眉月”等结构中，作为量词的“轮”“弯”“眉”在外形特征上都与“月”有相似之处，因此它们可以被用来称量特定形状的“月”），也像其他借用来的量词那样可以度量中心词的数量（如“一瓶水”“一盆水”“一碗水”等结构中，“瓶”“盆”“碗”都是承载“水”的容器，因此它们可以被借用来度量水的多少）。它们与中心词实际上是两个完全独立的没有联系的名词。它们被借用为量词的目的是使描写的事物更加生动、更加具有画面感。如例（49）中“一梢秋月”，“梢”与“月”本是两个独立的景物，二者在语义特征上没有联系，但将“梢”放入量词的位置之后，则生动地描绘出一轮月亮挂于树梢的画面。例（50）的“一棹春水”、例（51）的“一苇秋风”、例（52）的“一蓑烟雨”都是如此。例（53）中心词“离思”是抽象名词，以“窗”称量，描绘出了作者眼望窗外景色而心中充满思念的画面。

可见，宋代临时量词的作用不再限于度量和摹状，而是常用于描写画面和意境，这是受到文学创作形式的影响而产生的结果。这样的发展使得量词对名词的借用更加灵活，使得描写的画面更加生动形象，也使得新生量词的蓬勃出现成为可能。

以上我们对宋代部分专职名量词和借用名量词的产生原因进行了分析，从中可以看出，诗词等文学形式的蓬勃发展和日趋成熟，导致语言形式产生相应的发展与变化。在诗词等文学形式的创作过程中，创造意象与画面感是非常重要的，因此相应地，汉语的语言形式也就必须承担起创造意象与画面感的功能，因此一部分具有写意功能的量词也就应运而生了。这是除度量功能与摹状功能之外，汉语量词的又一个重要的功能和产生动因。除汉藏语系外的其他语言中的量词，往往只是承担着度量的功能，少部分量词有一定的摹状功能，但是却很少有量词系统能够承担写意功能。而汉语量词不但广泛地承载着度量、摹状功能，同时也承载着写意功能，正是因为承载着如此多重的功能，汉语量词系统具有非常强烈的产生动因和很高的能产性，这也正是汉语量词系统如此丰富的原因。因此，要了解汉语量词系统的发展历史，对其写意功能进行细致的分析是非常必要的。

参考文献：

[1] 白冰. 宋元时期个体量词的变化和发展［J］. 山西高等学校社会科学学报，2001（7）.

[2] 邵敬敏. 汉语语法的立体研究［M］. 北京：商务印书馆，2007.

[3] 王水照. “一蓑雨”和“一犁雨”——量词的妙用［J］. 文史知识，1998（11）.

[4] 游黎. 唐五代量词研究［M］. 成都：四川大学出版社，2018.

[5] 宗守云. 汉语量词的认知研究［M］. 北京：世界图书出版公司，2012.

作者简介：

游黎，文学博士，四川大学海外教育学院副教授，主要研究方向为汉语词汇史和对外汉语教学研究。

现代汉语

宋代音乐雅衰俗兴的原因浅析

杨晓琳
四川大学艺术教育中心

摘　要：宋代是我国古代音乐发展的一大转折期。此时，音乐的发展中出现了市民音乐影响宫廷音乐，并逐渐成为音乐主流的趋势。本文认为这一趋势的出现有四大直接原因：乐律音高标准的拟定、雅乐教习机构的缺失、“和雇”乐人的出现以及乐教思想的改变。

关键词：雅乐；市民音乐；乐教思想；宋代

A Brief Analysis of the Reasons for the Rise of Civic Music and the Fall of Court Music in Song Dynasty

Yang Xiaolin
Art Education Center of Sichuan University

Abstract: The Song Dynasty was a turning point in the development of ancient Chinese music. At this time, the development trend of music is Civic Music influencing Court Music, and gradually becoming the mainstream of music. The article shows that there are four direct reasons for the emergence of this trend: the formulation of high standards of music, the lack of Court Music institutions, the emergence of “hegu” musicians and the change of music teaching thought.

Keywords: Court Music; Civic Music; Music Teaching Thought; Song Dynasty

一、雅乐的起源与发展

雅即是正。雅乐，就是典雅纯正的音乐，专指古代的宫廷音乐，是祭祀天地、朝会礼仪等大型典礼时所用的音乐。我国的雅乐体系在西周初年形成，与法律、礼仪等共同构成了贵族统治的支柱。西周设置有专门的乐舞机构，命名为“大司乐”。机构中有大乐正、小乐正[①]掌管音乐教习、创作与演出。其时，大司乐创作和改编了一大批乐舞。至此以西周六代乐舞为主体的雅乐体系建立，礼乐制度趋于完备（张永鑫，1992）。这一体系以祭祀为主要功能，以歌功颂德为基本内容。换言之，雅乐最重要的价值是政治教化，而非艺术欣赏。

孔子继承了西周雅乐的传统，提出了“兴于诗、立于礼、成于乐”（钱穆，2011）的教育思想，把音乐上升为人格培养中的一种道德规范，并把乐教实实在在地纳入自己的教育内容与教学手段。董仲舒直接承袭了孔子的观点，充分肯定了音乐教育的目的就是要改变民风民俗。很明显，正统雅乐的创作与教育是掌握在统治阶级手中的，是在“民”之上的，最终的目的和功用是教化民众、肃清民风。从西周到秦朝，我国古代音乐的流动与扩散都是由宫廷到民间的单线进程。

秦汉乐府的建立标志着民间俗乐开始登上历史舞台，并开始和雅乐并存。随着隋唐时期教坊的设立以及九部乐、十部乐的发展，民间音乐开始进入宫廷，成为除雅乐之外，宫廷宴飨时的主要用乐。但这一时期，雅乐仍然处于主导地位，宫廷音乐家会对市民音乐进行大幅度的改编，使其符合统治阶级的意志与喜好。但到了宋代，雅乐的主导地位发生了根本性的转变，音乐创作逐渐由统治阶级下移到市民阶层，音乐的功用也逐渐从教化变为娱乐。这一变化是如何形成的呢？本文将从四个方面探讨宋代音乐雅衰俗兴的原因。

① “小乐正”“大乐正”均为周朝官名。

二、宋代音乐雅衰俗兴的原因

（一）乐律音高标准的拟定

北宋时期，雅乐黄钟律音高标准曾被进行了多达六次的调整，《宋史·乐志》记载“有宋之乐，自建隆讫崇宁，凡六改作”。这样多次调整准音高的一大原因是为了避免“郑声乱雅”。当时，雅乐已经有了受到市民音乐影响的苗头。为了避免让“靡乱”的市民音乐扰乱正统的雅乐，宫廷音乐家们不断调整标准音高，以使雅乐与市民音乐完全区别开来。虽然本意如此，但由于当时宫廷音乐家们多不具备系统的音乐知识，有的还怀有向统治者谄媚的目的，因而在制定音律时采用了很多错误的做法，最后事与愿违，反而使雅乐向市民音乐靠拢了。

具体来讲，宫廷音乐家们先后采用了四种方法来标注黄钟[①]音高：第一种叫“累黍成尺”法。这是一种非常古老原始的方法，在宋代已经显得不切实际；第二种是以古尺制度为根据制定的，却无法适应演奏的实际需要；第三种是以人的声音为根据定律，但被当时的很多人批评为不合古制；第四种是按照当时皇帝的指节长度定律，最后形成了著名的“大晟乐”。论及这四种方法，第一种和第二种是全盘复古，缺乏对音乐规律的认识，因此无法指导现实的音乐演奏；第四种以某人指节长度定律更是荒谬之极，必不可能持久；只有第二种做法具有一定的实践价值，因此也成为在宋朝通行时间比较长的音高标准。但是这一标准却与宫廷音乐家们希望恢复雅乐正统的初衷背道而驰。例如，主张以人声定律的音乐家杨傑就要求标准音高应接近当时的教坊乐律，而教坊乐律实际上代表的是市民音乐的音高标准。另一位音乐家刘昺的做法更是“将当时的教坊律黄钟作为夹钟，从而推得的民间的黄钟音高标准”（杨荫浏，1981）。这样一来，最后定出的雅乐标准音就表现出和市民音乐合流的趋势。

除此之外，在定律过程中，宫廷音乐家们所体现出的一些不符合音乐规律的操作方法也从侧面说明了音乐主流必然从宫廷走向民间。

---

① “黄钟”即古乐中的标准音。古乐十二律中，以这一音作为一切音律之基本。“黄钟”其名起源于周代。

（二）雅乐教习机构的缺失

从整体来看，宋代的宫廷音乐教育没有一个常设的教习机构，是一种游击战式的教法，有需求的时候临时开设，既不完善，也很不系统。这更加剧了雅乐的衰落。没有常设机构，那么在行郊享之礼时就只能临时设置教习机构。乐工也多由州府临时聚来，其演奏的音乐效果可想而知。同时，对乐官和乐工的考核机制也多为临时设计。虽然可能也起到了一定的监督效果，但是乐官和乐工的音乐水平真正能达到何种程度，就不得而知了。

大晟府是宋徽宗在崇宁四年设置的一个著名的雅乐机构，但仅仅存在了20多年，而且后来的功能也逐渐俗乐化，出现与教授俗乐的教坊合流的趋势。这样的音乐教习行为造成的最直接影响是，士大夫和雅乐的距离越来越远。此时的知识分子阶层已经开始和音乐之间产生心理上的距离，耻于习乐舞，耻于与乐工为伍。例如大观三年（1107年），徽宗曾以学校用乐不雅为由，下诏书说：今学校所用，不过春秋释奠，如赐宴辟雍，乃用郑、卫之音，杂以俳优之戏，非所以示多士。其自今用雅乐。于是要求根据周代的雅乐制度，教习国子生乐舞。但由于此时音乐教育从官学分离已久，加上知识分子与乐工已经是两个上下分明的社会阶层，因此这一诏令遭到了大部分知识分子的反对。徽宗只能再次下诏说：然士子肄业上庠，颇闻耻于乐舞与乐工为伍、坐作、进退。盖今古异时，致于古虽有其迹，施于今未适其宜。其罢习二舞，愿习雅乐者听。

可见，由于缺乏固定的教习机构，雅乐的传承受到很大的影响，吸引力也在逐渐降低。

（三）“和雇”乐人的出现

和雇是一种官府出钱雇用技工、民匠从事劳役制作的制度。和雇制度最早可以见于初唐时期，开始时尚算两相情愿的公平交易，后来在施行过程中逐渐演变为官府强取民物的手段。和雇制度在音乐活动中的应用最早可见于南宋初年的《东京梦华录》（1103年）：“八月秋……市学先生。预敛诸生钱作社会，以致雇请、祗应、白席、歌唱之人。”（孟元老，1998）经过一段时间的发展，据《武林旧事》记载，乾道、淳熙年间（1165～1189年）的宫廷教坊乐部有了被称为“守阙衙前”的乐人，主要职能就在于一旦招募补充宫廷乐工（周密，1998）。

可见，自金军南下，北宋朝庭灭亡，教习音乐的教坊宣告解散，与宫廷音乐相关的事务主要由教乐承担，具体的宴乐演出就转由“衙前乐”[1] 和民间音乐人等承担起来。正是由于演出的音乐人来源渠道多样，集中教习时间又过于短暂，演出的风格自然非常多样化。来自不同地区、拥有不同背景的乐人得以将自己的音乐所长带入宫廷。特别是到了南宋后期，来自“衙前乐”的乐人逐渐减少，直接“和雇”的乐人则越来越多，大量原生态的市民音乐涌入宫廷，雅乐的舞台逐渐被市民音乐占据了。南宋理宗端平三年（1236 年）的笔记《朝野类要》中就提道：绍兴末，台臣王十朋上章省罢之后，有名伶达伎皆留充德寿宫，使臣自余多隶临安府衙前乐。今虽有教坊之名，隶属修内司教乐所，然遇大宴等，每差衙前乐权充之不足，则又和雇市人。近年，衙前乐已无教坊旧人。多是市井歧路之辈，欲责其知音晓乐，恐难必也（赵昇，1986）。

（四）乐教思想的改变

正如上文所述，宋代的官学并无乐学一科，导致知识分子和雅乐的距离越来越远，再加上市民音乐大量进入宫廷，使得本就岌岌可危的雅颂乐教更加走向没落。因而便涌现出了一批雅颂乐教的倡导者，如张载、范仲淹、胡瑗、朱熹。张载认为乐教是为了培养道德情操，音乐能够移人性，因而要提倡雅颂，摒弃郑卫之音。朱熹则认为，三代之时，礼乐用于朝廷而下达于闾巷，学者讽诵其言以求其志。永其声，执其器，舞蹈其节以涵养其心，则声乐之所助于诗者为多（朱熹，1996）。诗教和乐教是相辅相成的，更好的乐教能更好地明“志”。他们都从乐教对人的道德情感培养着手，试图在官学体系中重建雅颂乐教。这一方案的具体实施者有范仲淹与胡瑗。范仲淹延请胡瑗做苏州郡学的主讲，由此胡瑗确立起了他的“苏湖教法”。在雅颂乐教的倡导过程中，胡瑗没有把乐教当作一项孤立的任务来完成，而是把它贯穿于其他教育与日常生活，相当于给学生营造了一种良好的氛围，在耳濡目染中自觉完成雅颂的熏陶。

但是这些努力似乎都收效甚微。范仲淹在倡导雅颂乐教的过程中已经发现了这一任务的艰巨性，宋代的音乐太过俗化，雅音流逝殆尽，而自己提倡雅颂乐教，目的也只是教化百姓。他最终认清了现状，认为不必尊古而卑

---

[1] “衙前乐”指宋代州府衙门所置的乐队。

今。因而宋代乐教的特点便是披着雅颂乐教的“外套”，而实际运作着来自市民音乐的内容。

三、结论

在商品经济繁荣的大背景下，宋代市民音乐得到了长足发展。而宫廷音乐虽然有回归雅乐正统的强烈愿望，但是由于忽略了音乐本身艺术规律和音乐教育的重要性，因此不断衰落。从此，音乐的主要活动场所由宫廷转移到地方，市民阶层成为音乐活动的主体，反过来影响了宫廷音乐，从而推动着我国古代音乐向前发展。

参考文献：

[1] 张永鑫．汉乐府研究［M］．南京：江苏古籍出版社，1992.

[2] 钱穆．论语新解［M］．北京：九州出版社，2011.

[3] 宋史：卷一二六［M］//乐一．北京：中华书局，1977.

[4] 杨荫浏．中国古代音乐史稿［M］．上册．北京：人民音乐出版社，1981.

[5] 宋史：卷一二八［M］//乐三．北京：中华书局，1977.

[6] 宋史：卷一二九［M］//乐四．北京：中华书局，1977.

[7] 孟元老．东京梦华录（外四种）：卷八［M］//秋社．周峰，点校．北京：文化艺术出版社.

[8] 周密．武林旧事：卷四［M］//乾淳教坊乐部，东京梦华录（外四种）．周峰，点校．北京：文化艺术出版社，1998.

[9] 赵昇．朝野类要：卷一“教坊”［M］//影印文渊阁四库全书．台北：台湾商务印书馆，1986.

[10] 朱熹．答陈体仁［M］//朱熹集．郭齐、尹波，点校．成都：四川教育出版社，1996.

作者简介：

杨晓琳，四川大学艺术中心主任、副教授，研究方向为艺术教育。

互动交际视角下“A+着呢”结构的语用功能探析

王 燕
四川大学海外教育学院

摘 要：本文从互动视角对“A+着呢”在不同的会话序列中浮现出的语用功能进行了考察，总结出该结构在回应话轮体现出“反驳、纠偏”的语用功能，表示与对方看法不一致；在发起话轮中是肯定某种性质或状态，用以提醒对方注意，常常带有夸张的意味；在言语互动性较弱的独白中则更强调对“A”的性状描述，在很大程度上失去了前两者的语用功能。

关键词：互动交际视角；着呢；话轮；语用功能

An Analysis of Pragmatic Functions of “A+ zhe’ ne” Structure from the Perspective of Interactive Communication

Wang Yan

School of Overseas Education, Sichuan University

Abstract: From the perspective of interaction, this paper investigates the pragmatic functions of “A + *zhe'ne*” emerging in different conversation sequences, and summarizes that this structure in the response wheel reflects the pragmatic functions of “refuting and correcting deviation”, indicating that it is inconsistent with the other party's views. In the initiation of the round is a certain nature or state of affirmation, to remind the attention of the other party, often with exaggerated meaning; In monologues with weak verbal interaction, more emphasis is placed on the description of A's character, which largely loses the pragmatic functions of the first two.

Keywords: Interactional Perspective; *zhe'ne*; Turn-Taking; Pragmatic Function

一、引言

《汉语教程》（第三版）第二册中的课后语法点将“着呢”解释为“用在形容词或某些心理动词后表示程度，相当于‘很’”。例如：

例（1）a 时间还早着呢。（时间还很早。）

b 今天外边冷着呢。（今天外边很冷。）

c ——你的肚子疼吗？

——疼着呢。（肚子很疼。）

《现代汉语八百词》把“着呢”的意义概括为“用在形容词或类似形容词的短语后，表示肯定某种性质或状态，略有夸张意味，多用于口语”。并且“着呢”前形容词有句法限制，不能再受程度副词和否定副词的修饰，也不能再带程度的补语。由此可见，“A+着呢”在实际的语言运用中已经构成了相对固定化的格式，不能将形容词和“着呢”的语义进行简单相加从而推测整体语义，另外仅仅从语义上把“着呢”解释为“很”也没有将其用法解释清楚。《现代汉语八百词》把“着呢”的语法意义概括为对性质或状态的肯定与夸张，也无法解释为何在很多情境下“太A了”“真A”“多么A啊”等体现说话人主观态度的感叹句式并不能和“A+着呢”互换。

综上分析，“A+着呢”的意义和功能的探讨还需要进一步深入，既然《现代汉语八百词》已经指出该格式多用于口语，那么就要突破形式和语义，从语用入手将其放在会话语境中，考察在不同语境中体现出的互动功能。

二、“A+着呢”在回应话轮中的交互性功能

最早从更大的话语环境中考察“A+着呢”格式的是赵元任（1968），

将“着（着）（的）呐”[①] 看成“复合小品词”，意为“很、非常”，表示对某一性状的断言，是用于驳回可能的“非 A”的断言，说明某物不仅具有 A 的属性，而且正处于 A 的状态，例如：

例（2）——他不快活吧？

——不，他快活着呐！（引自 Chao 1968：810）

对于例（2），吕叔湘（1979：365）解释为：“你说他不快活吗？你错了，他不但是快活，而且是非常非常快活。”与之前局限于单句层面研究“A+着呢”的构成成分或所在的句子不同，赵元任对“着呢”的分析是基于对话的例子，涉及交际双方互动的因素——“驳回”，体现了两者之间的话语交互。

下面就沿着赵元任所采用的观察思路，从互动交际的视角对“着呢”做进一步分析。首先考察“A+着呢”出现在回应话轮的情况：

例（3）志国：尤主编您是说这出国手续不好办？

尤主编：也倒不是，没什么不好办的，世上无难事，只要肯登攀……啊，反正这个退了休以后也没有什么事儿干，慢慢办吧……

和平：我离退休还早着呢，我三十岁我还……（电视剧《我爱我家》）

例（4）老徐说：“早恋是很危险的。”周小英说：“危险的事多着呢，说不定在马路上走着，好端端，就被汽车压死了。”（叶兆言《不娶我你后悔一辈子》）

例（5）亚平爸两只手按着腹部，无限感慨地说：“上一胎无论男女，现在都该看到了。我是怕，这胎再好，我都等不着啊！”“放心！你的日子长着呢！”亚平妈边宽慰边抚着亚平爸背。（六六《双面胶》）

例（6）鲁豫：可我看你还是把该感谢的人都谢了啊？

梁家辉：其实该感谢的人多着呢，如果要拿名单出来的话那节目肯定又要往后挪一个小时了。（电视访谈《鲁豫有约》）

例（7）我老劝父亲：爸，您岁数也大了，人家机关早上八点半上班，您干吗七点多就去？父亲说，我事情多着呢。（来源于 CCL 语料库）

上述 5 个例子中，说话人都采用了“A+着呢”形式，表明了与对方的

① 赵元任认为，“着呢”的变体形式有“着着呐”“着的呐”“着着哩”“着的哩”。其中“呐”是“呢”的音变形式，而“哩”在现代汉语中被“呢”取代。参看魏玉龙 2009。

看法不一致。例（3）中，尤主编建议志国、和平夫妇可以选择退休后慢慢办理护照，预设他们俩已经到了退休的年龄，和平用“我离退休还早着呢”来纠正尤主编的认识，提醒对方自己现在远没有到退休的时候。例（4）中周小英采用“A+着呢”反驳老徐的观点，淡化早恋的危险性，并将普通的交通事故与之相提并论。例（5）中亚平妈为了宽慰身体不好的亚平爸，用“你的日子长着呢”来消除丈夫的担心。例（6）中梁家辉在回应鲁豫的观点时，表明实际的情况是应该感谢的人并没有都感谢完，转折副词“其实”也体现了话语前后的转折关系，即梁家辉并不赞同对方的看法。例（7）中儿子劝父亲多休息，不要那么早就起床上班，采用了反问形式表明自己的立场，父亲随即用“A+着呢”做出自我评价，提醒对方是因为工作很忙，需要早到单位去处理。

由此可以看出，当“A+着呢”用于回应对方话语时，往往会与对方话语中的某种观点、看法形成对照，用来提醒对方注意谈论对象具有A的性质，体现了对对方认识的纠正。正是由于“A+着呢”在交际互动中这一负面评价功能，也让其在回应话轮中常常和否定句、反问句连用，或者出现在带有面子威胁的话语中，具体参看下面的例子：

例（8）“这些东西质量怎么样，比外边贵吗？”记者又问。这位服务员忙不迭地否定：“不会不会，比外面便宜多了，买的人多着呢。”（来源于CCL语料库）

例（9）售票员颇有些理直气壮地说：“超载了与你何干？你不愿坐就下去吧！”另一位旅客实在看不下去了：“谁说超载了与旅客没关系，关系大着呢！”一句话说得售票员无言以对，但还是超载了3个人。（来源于CCL语料库）

例（10）一阵呻吟，又一阵呻吟。他牙疼了。小芹看着也怪心疼的，就说：“这么疼，要么去看看，要么想吃什么给做什么。”他抡圆手臂给他一个大嘴巴：“去！你一边去！我这疼得烦着呢！”小芹捂着火辣辣的脸，难言的痛楚变成两串苦涩的泪珠，扑簌簌地滚下来……（来源于CCL语料库）

三、“A+着呢”在发起话轮中的交互性功能

“A+着呢”在会话中也可以处于发起话轮，也就是《现代汉语八百词》

中所解释的用来“肯定某种性质或状态”，提醒对方注意，往往是与新信息的告知与警示等相关。具体参看以下例子：

例（11）陈大妈：老傅，我把您的伴儿给带来了。

傅老：我的伴儿？

陈大妈：就是跟您一块儿唱二重唱的。来来来，进来……这位啊，就是吴颖同志，早先在中学啊，教过音乐课，唱起歌来可霍亮着呢，比那帕瓦罗蒂都不在以下。

傅老：原来是吴颖老师啊，久仰久仰。（电视剧《我爱我家》）

例（12）朱老忠说：“兄弟！我不怕你心里难受，告诉你说吧！关东三省地方大着呢，你知道他在哪一省？就是知道他在那个省，你知道他在哪个县？哪个屯？”

严志和猛地抬起头来，问：“真的？象你这一说，我那老人……”（梁斌《红旗谱》）

例（13）接着，他走到沙发跟前，随便地挨着安德莱耶维奇坐下，说：“深夜来访，请您原谅。不过，这是我的工作。有人说，我们天使逍遥自在，终日吃喝玩乐，其实那是胡言乱语。实际上，他对我任意欺压，刻薄着呢。”安德莱耶维奇一下子没弄懂，问：“这个‘他’是谁呀？”天使压低声音回答：“我告诉你吧，是上帝！”（来源于CCL语料库）

例（11）中陈大妈给傅老介绍一位二重唱新搭档，也就是吴颖，但是傅老之前并不认识她，处于默认的缺省状态。陈大妈用“唱起歌来可霍亮着呢”来进行评价，重点强调这一显著特点，提醒傅老注意。例（12）中面对严志和对东北缺少基本地理认识的情况下，朱老忠提醒他“关东三省地方大着呢”，因为这一特点，所以基本上不可能找到严志和的那位亲人。例（13）中天使告诉安德莱耶维奇真实的上帝形象，对听话人来说是一个新信息，同时也是一种警示，不要相信心中以为的那个上帝。

通过对上述例子我们还可以看出，在说话人使用“A+着呢”发起的话轮中，都是挑选的最为显著的性状特征进行表述的，暗示着听话人可能并没有注意到或者完全不知道所说的这个显著性状。同时说话人为了强调“A”的显著性，在互动过程中，也常常会采用一些语言形式来体现夸张的语用效果，比如例（11）中的比较句“比那帕瓦罗蒂都不在以下”，例（12）中从省到县到屯层层递进的反问句，例（13）中前后对比强调，利用副词“其实、实际上”来完成语力逆转。因此所谓的“略有夸张的意味”主要是来自“着呢”的语用浮现意义，是通过它本身的互动功能提醒对方注意所表述的A性状。此时，“着呢”就失去了在回应话轮中具有的反驳、纠偏性评价功能，也不带有对说话人的负面态度。这点在互动性较弱的口语独白中体现得更明显，说话人为了提醒听话人注意所表述的性状，在使用“A+着呢”做出评价时，会利用对方给予的充分时间做进一步的详述。具体参看以下例子：

例（14）咳，我们那工作累着呢，我那道机最累，因为合这个包儿的大片儿。紧张，我们都有定额。另外，你在那里面再管点事儿，更多耗点儿时间。（1982年北京话调查资料）

例（15）先前的时候我一到这儿的时候吧，就是咱们这个牛街是烂着呢，没有马路，就是坑坑洼洼都不平，那个走路呢都走不了，就得挑着走。（1982年北京话调查资料）

例（16）困着呢，小孩儿谁都解那儿过，那儿特别困，那儿见觉没够啊，那时候为什么没够啊？他不觉他不够睡，你像一般的这个工人呢，都是干十二点，也没有夜餐费钱。（1982年北京话调查资料）

四、结论

本文讨论的“A+着呢”格式在真实的话语交际中主要用于体现言语的互动性，在对话的回应话轮中主要浮现的语用功能是反驳、纠偏的负面评价，认为对方的认识不正确或者不充分；在对话的发起话轮中，主要是为了凸显A的性状，浮现出夸张的语用效果；在互动性较弱的口语独白中则侧重在“A+着呢”这一较为主观的评价之后，再做进一步详述，失去了反驳、纠偏的语用功能，不具有负面评价性，夸张的意味也比较弱，更强调是对A这一性状的描述。

通过对“A+着呢”的考察，我们认为在对外汉语教学中不仅要注重语言形式，也要强调语言功能，对于本文开头所提的例（1）“时间还早着呢!”不能从单个句子层面解释为“时间还很早”。而是应该联系上下文（见例17）进行理解，田芳采用的“早着呢”格式是对张东催促的反驳，在这个语境中，如果把“还早着呢”换成“还很早”，是存在语用功能差别的，后者只是描述了一个现实情况，并不具有强烈的言语互动性，在真实的话语交际中被采用的可能性也较低。例如：

例（17）张东：别捡了，快走吧，要上课了。

田芳：着什么急？还早着呢！

张东：你看看表，几点了？（来源于《汉语教程》第三版第二册上：126）

参考文献：

［1］方梅．负面评价表达的规约化［J］．中国语文，2017（2）．

［2］方梅，乐耀．规约化与立场表达［M］．北京：北京大学出版社，2017．

［3］方梅，李先银，谢新阳．互动语言学与互动视角的汉语研究［J］．语言教学与研究，2018（3）．

［4］胡承佼．“A着呢”语串的构成差异及其演化历程［J］．安徽师范大学学报（人文社会科学版），2012（5）．

［5］李文浩．作为典型构式的非典型“X着呢”及其固化分析［J］．汉语学习，2013（2）．

［6］李文山．句末助词“着呢”补谈［J］．语言教学与研究，2007（5）．

［7］吕叔湘．汉语语法分析问题［M］．北京：商务印书馆，1979．

［8］完权．汉语（交互）主观性表达的句法位置［J］．汉语学习，2017（3）．

［9］王彦杰．“着呢”句式中形容词性成分的使用情况考察［J］．世界汉语教学，2010（2）．

［10］魏玉龙．语气助词“着呢”的演变历程［J］．现代语文，2009，（2）．

［11］翟燕．“着哩”的语法化［J］．语言科学，2005（6）．

［12］Cho，YuenRen．A Grammar of Spoken Chinese［M］．Berkeley and Los Angles：University of California Press，1968．

作者简介：

王燕，四川大学海外教育学院讲师，研究方向为对外汉语教学法及汉语语法研究。

中医学词汇与普通词汇的互构与衍生*

吕 彦 李 庆

成都中医药大学外语学院

摘 要：投射是中医学词汇和普通词汇互构及衍生的重要途径之一。作为一门历史悠久的学科，中医学是一个从整体角度研究人与疾病、人与社会、人与环境关系的综合型领域，其具有独特的思维方式和理论体系，也融入了中国的哲学思想。这些理念与我们日常认知交互影响，从而丰富了汉语词汇，同时也产生了大量跟中医学相关的词汇和语言。但在跨文化交流时，这类词语和语言可能会成为交流中的障碍。因此为更好地推进中西交流，我们需从源头上厘清这类词语产生的原因和类型。

关键词：投射；中医词汇；互构；衍生

The Study of Inter-Construction and Derivation of TCM Vocabulary and Common Vocabulary

Lü Yan Li Qing

School of Foreign Languages, Chengdu University of TCM

Abstract: Mapping is an important methods for inter-construction and lexical derivation of TCM vocabulary/Daily life vocabulary. As an ancient subjects, TCM formed the unique systematology and holism through historically and chronica study the relationship between

* 本课题为2017年成都中医药大学校项目“认知理论下中医汉语国际教学词汇及策略研究”成果，项目编号：RWQN1720。

human with diseases, with societies, with surroundings, which also reflects the Chinese philosophy. Those conceptions, interacting with our daily cognition, spurs on diversifying the Chinese vocabulary as well as generating a bunch of words which involve to TCM. On the contrary, those words involves to TCM will hinder the intercultural communication go smoothly. Thus, we have to clarify the generative mechanisms of those words from the source for promoting the exchange between China and the west.

Keywords: Mapping; TCM Vocabulary; Inter-construction; Lexical Derivation

一、引言

人类认知世界是一个能动过程，在此过程中受到各种主体因素的影响，或需要依靠辅助手段认知新的事物和领域。同时为了阐释世界，人们也在不断地改进对人与世界关系和人自身的认知。医学是人类为了生存与疾病斗争而形成的领域。在该领域中，人们对大自然及人自身的认知不停地进化，知识结构及容量也逐级地细化和丰富，在此过程中，逐渐诞生了一系列与医学相关的新词汇。中医学是自中国远古伊始，古人为了抵御疾病而形成的领域，在中医学形成过程中，古人依靠业已成型的概念化知识体系对新事物新领域进行认识并命名，使得医学知识得以传承并形成系统化学科。由于中医学还涉及人文哲学领域，因此中医学领域的某些专用词汇和日常生活词汇或文哲词汇[①]交汇互生的情况时常发生，从而出现了“普通词汇－中医专用词汇－普通词汇”“普通词汇－中医专用词汇”及“中医专用词汇－普通词汇”等三种模式。在这个模式系统中，词汇的词义、义项或者义素发生了改变或进行了重组，进而发生了语义衍生，如“脾气”“胆怯”“胆识”等词语的形成，以及“生气”等语义在日常生活中发生的演变。

由于中医学是中国特有的学科，也涉及人文哲学领域，与欧美国家认知世界的方式有极大的差异，因此从中医学演化而来的普通词汇，欧美留学生在学习过程中受阻程度较高。在教学实践中，我们发现，留学生学习这类词

① 在本文中，为了有别于“医学专用词汇”，我们将日常生活词汇和文哲词汇统称为“普通词汇”。

语并不难，但他们普遍反映记忆难度较大，导致语用的频率较低，或在语用的同时采用回避或替代的方式使用，如“胆小”“胆怯”留学生常使用“不勇敢”来代替。观察到该现象后，我们搜集到更多跟中医术语有关联的词语、短语和俗语，如词语类：胆识、胆量、大胆、肝火、肺腑、心血、心腹、脾胃等；成语类：肝胆相照、忠肝义胆、肺腑之言等；俗语类：怒从心头起、恶向胆边生等。从所搜集到的词语，我们可以观察到，其大致可分三类：第一类是直接来自中医术语，比如“脾气”“脾胃”等，不过其内涵和外延范围更广；第二类是其语素来自中医术语，如“胆”“肝”“肺”等，这些语素和新的语素组合在一起，形成了普通词汇，如“胆怯”“心肝”，其词义取其医学特征但有别于术语；第三类则是语义演化，如“生气”，其词义已逐渐脱离医学特征。这些词语、短语和俗语的核心语义语素均来自中医术语，但其语义泛化程度高于术语，因此这类词的语义在形成过程中既涉及人文哲学类又涉及中医学，糅合了两个领域的概念化形成过程。

但就目前关于中医词汇方面的研究主要集中考察中医词汇形成的方式，如赵阳（2009）在《〈内经〉修辞格及英译实例分析》中从修辞学角度分析了《黄帝内经》语言中的隐喻，归纳了三种隐喻方式：借喻、暗喻和明喻，并列举文本材料进行了翻译分析。李照国（2012）在《门外译谈》中也特地写到了《黄帝内经》的修辞特点与翻译技巧。贾春华（2009）《中医学：一种基于隐喻认知的语言》，运用概念隐喻的理论，论述了隐喻在中医语言中的普遍存在。贾春华（2010）《中医理论思辨录》则指出，隐喻认知是中医理论体系建构的主要工具，中医学是一种基于身体经验感知而形成的理论。

前人的研究主要集中在直接采用认知语言学中隐喻等假设理论解释中医词汇形成的原因，但未对其形成的模式作具体描述，同时对中医专有词汇渐渡到日常生活中的过程也鲜有关注，因此本文将集中在此领域进行研究。

二、中医词汇和普通词汇的互构与衍生

20 世纪后期，美国语言学家莱克夫和约翰逊在《我们赖以生存的隐喻》中从认知的角度提出了语言中的隐喻假设，认为隐喻是人类认识世界并构建概念的重要机制之一，人类对新生事物及其领域的认知和概念化系统的形成依赖于隐喻机制。其后，随着认知心理学和语言学的发展，人们发现无论是隐喻还是转喻，实现这两种机制的途径都是“投射”。投射是人们在认知新

的事物时，将已概念化的事物特征投射到即将认知的新生事物上，过程较为复杂，且尚在研究当中，其模式大致为相似特征的投射、部分到整体的投射、已形成的可触知性的相关参数之间的相互投射等，从而达到认知新事物的目的（泰尔米，2017）。投射所依凭的是人类对世界的感知，根据泰尔米（2017）《认知语义学》一书中的观点，大致有可触知程度、清晰度、强度、位置（方位/空间）、可识别性/特性、内容/结构、确定性等参数作为投射的基本量化标准。

中医理论体系是在古代中国“观象取物”和“援物比类”的哲学思想中形成的，《易传·系辞下》中记载：“古者包牺氏之王天下，仰则观象于天，俯则观法于地，观鸟兽之文与地之宜，近取诸身，远取诸物，于是始作八卦，以通神明之德，以类万物之情。”而《黄帝内经》中对“比类”也有明确记载，如《素问·疏五过论》：“善为脉者，必以比类、奇恒，从容知之。”再如《素问·示从容论》：“夫圣人之治病，循法守度，援物比类，化之冥冥。”对“天象”“地法”“鸟兽之文与地之宜”等自然、社会客观事物的感性观察与理性类比，帮助古代中国人创造了中医独特的理论框架与语言体系。

由此根据现代语言学理论，中医领域中词汇的形成是一种基于已有的概念化投射的模式。比如“心者，君主之官，神明出焉”（《素问·灵兰秘典论》），即“心是君主”，即“君主”是国家的最高统治者，处在社会阶层中最核心的位置，是国家意志的主宰，具有［＋核心意志］的特征，而中医学也认为“心”这个脏器在身体器官中处于核心地位，如“心主神明，脏腑百骸，惟所是从”，其特征与“君主”的［＋核心意志］具有相似性。因此相似域的投射让“心”获得更显著的语义，使阅读者能够认识到“心”在人体中的地位和功能，继而，在文学作品和日常生活中也得以沿用，衍生出更多的词汇，如“心血”“心肝”等，这类词汇都有共同的语义特征［＋核心］。

古人以自身感受为参照尺度，将身体空间、事物特性、自然气候等不同领域的体验性经验投射到中医的各种抽象概念中，为中医学理论框架和语言体系的形成提供了客观的参考理据。同时，在中国古代的文学作品中，又常常使用中医专有词汇所具有的特有属性来凸显所描述事物的特性或重要性，这样中医专用词汇又慢慢渗入日常生活。中医专用词汇和普通词汇的互构和衍生都涉及投射机制，模式有三类：功能投射、空间投射和性质投射。

1. 功能投射

功能投射强调的是性质和整体结构的图示映射，它通过可触知的具体实物的性质和功能，将其实物的抽象特性投射到所需的或相似的中医概念空间，同时获得新的语义，进入文学或生活词汇，如前文“心”例。

2. 空间投射

空间投射指依据空间方位组建的概念投射，即上下、前后、内外、深浅、中心边缘等一系列空间方位概念较早被人类感知，当一些新的抽象概念，如情绪、性质、关系、身体状况等医学概念出现时，人们将其方位特性投射到抽象的医学概念上，从而产生了用方位组合的词语表达抽象概念的语言现象。中医学中的“外感内伤”“表证里证”“上焦下焦”等概念，就是人们根据身体的经验感受与外界环境的空间关系所概括出的方位投射。同时“内伤”“外伤”等词进入日常生活。

3. 性质投射

性质投射指根据人类与物理世界的接触，将实物的性质投射到需要表达的抽象概念上。将离散、有形的实体投射到抽象、模糊的感觉、思想、观念和状态等领域，将抽象的概念具化，使其能被识别和量化。如将“金木水火土”等实物相互克制和转化的规律投射到五脏之间相辅相成的运作关系上，以及人的体质方面的描述，从而让这些实物获得新的语义。在文学作品中，又将使用这些实物去对人物进行描述。如“体质”一词，《黄帝内经・灵枢》以木材比类：“匠人磨斧斤砺刀削，斫材木。木之阴阳，尚有坚脆，坚者不入。脆者皮弛，至其交节。而缺斤斧焉。夫一木之中，坚脆不同，坚者则刚，脆者易伤，况其材木之不同，皮厚薄，汁之多少，而各异耶。”其将匠人斫木时木材的差异投射到人之“体质”差异当中，就是性质投射。

三、普通词汇构建中医专用词汇

认知的普遍规律是从具体实物抽象到概念化层面，然后再利用概念化后的实物描述需要认知的新事物，如《周易》“近取诸身，远取诸物”。但在某些专业领域中，如中医学，则需要使用已有词汇的特点来描述新的抽象概念，从而才能继续了解新的事物。而这些已有词汇大都来自生活中人们对实物或环境的主观感受和对其特点形成的某种固有认知，这就是常用词汇构建中医专用词汇的过程。其主要类型有四种。

第一，物体[①] A——人们对 A 的感受和认知凝结成 A 的某个凸显的语义特征［+特性 A’］——使用 A 替代 A’——中医专有领域借助 A 形成“（）A”或“A（）”结构。

比如，“气”在《说文解字注》中：云气也，气本云气。引申为凡气之称。《汉字字源》中认为“最早的字形是三条横线，表示空中的气流，后来为了与三区别，字形逐渐发生了变化”。因此，早期的“气”之意，更接近于“气流”之意，有［+流动］的特性。《庄子·齐物论》：“大块噫气，其名为风。”在古代，源于古人对人体生命现象的观察，古人通过对呼吸时气的观察，对活动时蒸腾热气的观察，动植物气味传递的观察，逐渐产生了对气朴素而直观的认识，于是演绎出人体之内存在着能上下流动的细微物质，因此，使用文哲领域中的“气”描述中医学中“气”的基本概念。进而慢慢衍生出“气”的具体概念，形成了如“气化”“元气”“谷气”“清气”“人气”“正气”“邪气”“营气”“卫气”“中气”等中医专有词汇。

第二，物体 A 的某种特性 A’——使用 A 替代 A’——使用 A 描述中医学中的某个抽象概念，将抽象概念具化，并以此命名，此情况多用于脉象当中。

“春弦”“夏洪”“秋毛”“冬石”是脉象术语，其中“弦”“洪”“毛”“石”采用具体的词汇来说明脉象情况。《难经·十五难》中“春脉弦者，肝东方木也，万物始生，未有枝叶，故其脉之来，濡弱而长，故曰弦”，其意大致为春天的脉象好比自然界中的树木，枝叶处萌生阶段，虽弱小但呈生长之态，柔和、从容且有力。“夏洪”来自《素问·四时刺逆从论》，“夏者经满气溢，入孙络受血，皮肤充实”，“孙络”是人体最细小的络脉，从“夏气在孙络”中可知夏季的脉象应洪大有力，满溢直达最细小的络脉。“秋毛”出自《素问·四气调神大论》，书中认为：秋季阳气渐衰，阴气渐长，草木逐渐枯萎，河水由春夏的满溢湍急变为缓流。《素问·阴阳离合论》认为秋天阳气收敛，汗孔由开放转为收缩，故阳气也由表到里收引。“毛”是“细小”之意。《难经·十五难》中云：“秋脉毛者，肺西方金也，万物所终，草木华叶，皆秋而落，其枝独在，若毫毛也，故其脉之来，轻虚以浮，故曰毛。”“冬石”出自《素问·玉机真脏论》，书中有“冬脉者，肾也。北方水液，万物之所以合藏也。故其气来沉以搏，故曰营”，认为冬季脉象表现为

① 这里的“物体”包括现实世界中的一切，物体、位置、环境、季节等。

沉以搏的石脉。其中“弦”“洪”“毛”“石”取其［+萌生 +缓和］［+大 +有力］［+细小］［+稳健 +沉下］的特征，而“春”“夏”“秋”“冬”则是表时间，进而构成中医专有脉象术语。

第三，用现实世界中某些事物的空间移动特性投射到药材性质概念域上，并特此命名，多用于药剂命名。

如“小青龙汤”，小青龙汤为中医解表剂，解表散寒、温肺化饮，主治外寒里饮证，在临床上有着广泛的应用。“龙”属“震卦”，其属性“刚也”“健也”，属“阳”性范畴，在中国人的认知系统中，龙属于神类范畴，有控制和权力的象征，同时与水有关。张仲景《伤寒杂病论》中借助“龙”这一概念域，将“龙”［+升发 +控制 +主导］语义特征投射到该药剂主导调节人体水液代谢的功能域上，以便于他人理解。就算不知道“小青龙”方的具体功效是什么，也可以根据“龙”与水液运行有关的文化概念而推导出其大致功效。同理还有升浮之药：薄荷、苏叶、金银花、菊花、旋覆花；沉降之药：代赭石、龙骨、牡蛎、紫贝齿。

第四，从哲学含义到中医专有词汇。

在中医理论基础方面，如“神”，《说文解字注》中有“天神，引出万物者也”，《周易·系辞》中有“阴阳不测之谓神”。在古代哲学范畴中“神”是指宇宙的主宰及规律，是有关宇宙万物发生发展变化的认识；而在中医概念体系中“神”是有关人体生命的认识，包括意识、思维、情志等活动，与古代哲学“神”的概念在内涵和生成来源上是有严格区别的，但中医借助哲学范畴中的“神”［+主宰 +不可接触］的特征来描述医学中“神”，以便大众理解。《类证治裁·内景综要》：“一身所宝，惟精气神。神生于气，气生于精，精化气，气化神。故精者身之本，气者神之主，形者神之宅。”中医学认为，精是生命本源，气是生命维系的动力，神是生命活动的主宰。同理还有“命门”一词，其在中医学中始见于《灵枢·根结》篇，专指“目”，秦汉以后才把它作为藏象学说中的一个概念，指督脉命门穴，在五脏学说中指“肾脏”。

四、中医专有词汇再构生活词汇

随着社会的发展，精细化交流对词汇描述功能要求逐级提升，现有词汇已不能满足语用需求，因此人们便从生活各个领域借助词汇用以表达，以求信息传递的精准。借助的渠道多样，有跨语言的外来词，也有跨领域的词汇。其中，中医专有词汇向生活词汇的渐渡，是其方式之一。在这个渐渡过程中，中医专有词汇失去医学的专业词汇含义，保留其普遍语义特征，该特征便投射到日常生活中需表达的抽象概念中。该过程将中医学中某种功能和特性投射到生活中抽象的性质特征，以便于描述，例如：

例（1）自其异者视之，肝胆楚越也。（庄子《庄子》）

例（2）吾为子起歌都护，酒阑插剑肝胆露。（杜甫《魏将军歌》）

例（1）和例（2）中，都利用了“肝”与“胆”在人体中的“表里”位置和“互助”功能，将“位置和功能”的具体概念投射到“关系”域中，使肝胆具有了表示临近互助关系的含义。明朝时，《东汉秘史》中出现了“肝胆相照”一词：“铁本与萧王首谋兴汉，剿服寇兵，结荣枯之计，誓生死之盟，意气情孚，肝胆相照。”人们在“肝胆”的基础之上又增加了“相照”来凸显其位置紧密关系和功能互助关系，[+位置临近 +功能互助]等表征让“关系紧密”的含义逐渐渗入“肝胆”这一组合，使其从医学领域逐渐进入到生活领域。中医语言通过投射机制，将医学中带有某种特性功能的词语投射到生活中相关联的领域，表达其抽象含义构建生活词汇，如“胆识”“胆怯”“脾气”“虚”等。在对外汉语教学中，避开中医文化背景的单纯译介是不合理的，只有回归认知的源头，研究词汇的形成过程，才能有效地进行对外汉语教学，起到促进文化传播的作用。

但中医专有词汇渐渡到普通词汇有别于前两类相似性的投射。这部分的投射方式更为复杂，是医学特征和人们普遍认知的相似域投射①，其类型有三种。

1. 从[+空间][+运化功能]到“关系紧密度”“程度重要性”

例（3）自其异者视之，肝胆楚越也。（庄子《庄子·内篇·德充符》）

例（4）铁本与萧王首谋兴汉，剿服寇兵，结荣枯之计，誓生死之盟，意气情孚，肝胆相照。（谢诏《东汉秘史》第四十回）

例（5）丞相金銮直谏君，忠肝义胆孰能群。（许仲琳《封神演义》第二回）

① 因为该部分的投射涉及人们的普遍认知，因此并非所有的医学词汇都能渐渡到日常生活形成人们所能理解的普通词汇。具有何种特征的中医词汇能渐渡，不在本文的研究范围。

经语料查阅，“肝胆”一词最早出现在战国时期，“肝胆楚越”意思是楚越是春秋时两个诸侯国，虽然土体相连，但关系不好。这里庄子借用了中医学中对肝胆的认知，肝与胆互为表里，胆为肝府，将“位置和功能”的具体概念投射到“关系”的抽象概念中，使肝胆具有了表示临近关系的含义。明朝时，人们在“肝胆”的基础之上增加了“相照”去凸显关系的亲密度。此外，《素问》中：“肝主谋虑、胆主决断。”胆决才能肝谋，肝胆在人体运作需求中具有相互配合的功能。正如《类经・藏象类》所说：“肝胆相济，勇敢乃成。”于是，《三国演义》中将智慧与忠诚的抽象概念转置到了“忠肝义胆”一词之中，使“肝胆”的语义得到扩大，并因文学作品的流传，逐渐概念化并成为固定的用法。

同样的还有“脾胃”。脾位于腹中，在横膈之下，与胃相邻。《素问・太阴阳明论》中有“脾与胃以膜相连”，脾的主要功能是运化和存储血液，食物经胃初步消化后，从胃到小肠的过程中，必须经脾气促进和激发，进一步被消化和分解，这一过程在《内经》上被称为“脾主为胃行其津液”。如脾气的运化作用减退，必然会影响到食物的消化和水谷精微物的吸收，从而出现腹胀、便溏、食欲不振等病况。

例（6）即以永隆二年二月九日合葬於京城南洪固乡界韦曲之礼也。孤子□等痛伤脾胃，切甚心肠，惧陵谷有迁，式旌不朽。（陆心源《唐文拾遗》）

例（7）如饭必用吃，衣必用著，脾胃壮者吃得来多，弱者吃得来少。（黎靖德《朱子语类》卷五十六）

例（8）又如脾胃伤弱，不能饮食之人，却硬要将饭将肉塞入他口，不问他吃得与吃不得。（黎靖德《朱子语类》卷一百二十四）

例（9）回归寓中多吃了几杯生酒，坏了脾胃，破腹起来。（冯梦龙《警世通言・老门生三世报恩》）

2. 从［+形态］［+运化功能 +储存功能］到“用途”“程度重要性”

最早在东汉出现“肺腑”一词时，是用来形容帝王的宗室近亲“刘豫州，使君之肺腑，可与交通”（《三国志・蜀志・刘璋传》），而后又逐渐演变出亲近的含义。到了明朝，小说中出现了“肺腑之言”一词，意为发自内心的话。《素问・经脉别论》中有“肺朝百脉”一语，现在一般解释为“百脉朝会于肺”，意思是全身的血液都通过百脉流经于肺，经肺呼吸，进行气体交换。《灵枢·九针论》中，有“肺者，五脏六腑之盖也”。肺司呼吸，主一身之气的生成和运行，又能宣发卫气于体表，用以保护其他内脏免受外邪侵袭，因此也称为“脏之长”。而“腑”在中医中指“六腑”，为“胆”“胃”“大肠”“小肠”“膀胱”“三焦”，它们的生理机能是“传化物”和“传化水谷”，也就是传导和代谢运化的功能，与“五脏”[②] 相对，其形状特点都是中空有腔的器官，有一定容积，所以能够受盛水谷。“肺腑”一词，“肺”取其能［＋交换 ＋传化］的特点，“腑”取其能［＋储存 ＋传化］的特点，而“肺”在某种程度上也是“脏之长”。因此，用“肺”投射到整个“五脏”的概念系统，形成“肺腑”合用的方式表达“脏腑”之间的关系。例如：

例（10）今大司马卫将军高安侯董贤，累世无功于汉朝，又无肺腑之连……（荀悦《前汉记·前汉孝哀皇帝纪》卷二十九）

例（11）蝉曰：“容妾伸肺腑之言”。（罗贯中《三国演义》第八回）

3. 从［＋调节功能］到“主体的情绪或意识”

“肝火”和“脾气”最早出现时，都是指人体对血液的某种运化能力。由于后来文学作品中表达的需要，人们利用对肝脾的作用的认知，将肝脾在身体中的具体功能转置到了表达情绪方式的抽象概念上。中医认为，“肝”是贮藏血液的主要器官，能够根据人体的活动情况调节全身血量，主疏泄、调达。人的精神状态与情绪表现除了由心主宰以外，就依赖于肝的作用。“肝”在五行中属“木”，木过之则生火，因而衍生出“肝火”。“肝火”旺意味着肝气失于调达，因而表现出躁怒。“脾”则有统摄血液的作用，即维持血液在脉管内的正常运行，而不致渗溢到脉外。脾气旺盛，脉管致密，就能控制血液按照脉道正常运行，使其不致流溢脉外，反之。因此，“肝火”逐渐被用来表示“怒气”，“脾气/性”被用以表示性格。例如：

例（12）所以知潘满如病者，臣意切其脉，深小弱，其卒然合合也，是脾气也。（司马迁《史记·扁鹊仓公列传》第四十五）

例（13）肝火胜了的人，那性气日甚一日的乖方。真是千人唾骂，骨肉畔离。（西周生《醒世姻缘传》第三九回）

例（14）也别论远近亲戚，什么穷啊富的，只要深知那姑娘的脾性儿好

② 中医学中脏有五个，即心、肺、脾、肝、肾，但在经络学中，心包有单独的经络，也属于脏，所以也可以说“六脏”。

模样儿周正的就好。（曹雪芹《红楼梦》第八十五回）

例（15）王如一等来，二十四日才到，我发脾气说他太迟了，叫他回去，发路费九百六十文，家里不必加钱给他，作为对懒惰的人的惩戒。（曾国藩《曾国藩家书·为政（下卷）》第七十五章）

例（16）独携大胆出秦门，金粟堆边哭陵树。（李贺《吕将军歌》）

例（17）“这厮大胆做得好事！”把那任一郎吓了一跳，告道：“有事便好好说。”（冯梦龙《醒世恒言》第十三卷）

例（18）公明真胆识兼优者也！（罗贯中《三国演义》第七十六回）

例（19）陆公初莅此地，即廉知枉，毅然开释，此非有十二分才智，二十分胆识，安能如此？（冯梦龙《醒世恒言》卷二十九）

同理还有“大胆”，其最早出现在唐代的诗歌中，用来形容人的勇敢和无畏，后在元朝时的小说中大量应用，明朝时又出现了“胆识”的说法。通过将中医学中“胆者，中正之官，决断出焉”的医学特征投射到生活中需要表达“勇敢”的概念域中，并添加其他相关语素组合成为新的词语“大胆”“胆量”“胆识”“胆怯”等，为我们的生活提供了更多的语言表达词汇。

五、小结

中医学是我国独有的一门学科，其中既有自然科学知识，又有人文社科知识，还有古代哲学思想的融入，而人文社科和古代哲学思想建构了中医学认识人体生理疾病和疾病防治的理论框架与方法体系，因此，中医学和文学中的概念时常发生交互现象。由于文学家在创作中有意识地创造意象，许多诗词歌赋中都出现了中医学的语言词汇，这些词汇以文学作品为载体，逐渐融入社会的不同阶层，成为我们日常生活中使用的词汇。于是，中医语言和其中蕴含的哲学思想再次通过投射机制对生活语言进行了丰富和再现，为我们提供了更多样化的语言表达手段。同时，语言差异的背后是文化的差异，文化差异的本质是对客观世界的认知不同。因此，在跨文化交流和教学中，面对涉及中医学领域的词汇，我们不能回避，要正视差异，注重差异，主动回归认知的源头；同时，研究中医专有词汇和普通词汇之间交汇互构的过程和模式，有助于准确把握这类词汇内在的中医学特征和中医文化特征，这样才能有效地进行教学，促进文化的交流和传播。

参考文献：

[1] 赵阳，施蕴中.《内经》修辞格及英译实例分析 [J]. 山西中医学院学报，2009 (5).
[2] 李照国. 门外译谈 [M]. 苏州：苏州大学出版社，2012.
[3] 贾春华. 中医学：一种基于隐喻认知的语言 [J]. 亚太传统医学，2009 (1).
[4] 贾春华. 中医理论思辨录 [J]. 北京中医药大学学报，2010 (7).
[5] 乔治·莱考夫，马克· 约翰逊. 我们赖以生存的隐喻 [M]. 何文忠，译. 浙江：浙江大学出版社，1980.
[6] 伦纳德·泰尔米. 认知语义学 [M]. 李福印，译. 北京：北京大学出版社，2018.
[7] 黄帝内经·素问 [M]. 北京：人民卫生出版社，2012.
[8] 孙广仁. 中医基础理论讲稿 [M]. 北京：人民卫生出版社，2016.

作者简介：

吕彦，文学博士，成都中医药大学外语学院讲师，主要研究方向为语法学/对外汉语教学；李庆，文学学士，成都中医药大学外语学院讲师，主要研究方向为古代汉语。

“又……又……”结构的韵律模式研究[③]

胡 翼

四川大学海外教育学院

摘　要：现代汉语中的“又……又……”组合在语言交际中的用例十分广泛，与其搭配的成分既可以是词，也可以是短语，在搭配形容词成分时，其音节数量呈现出一定的规律性，即前面成分的音节数量要不多于后面成分的音节数量，组合形式才合法。我们认为这一规律是语义与句法之外的韵律规则在起作用，具体而言，是汉语的普通重音规则在制约其组合形式，而这一分析为汉语语法研究提供了新的视角，一定程度上丰富了汉语研究的理论，具有一定的理论价值。

关键字：韵律；音步；并列连词；理论意义

A Study on the Rhythm Pattern of a Modern Chinese Combination“又……又……”

Hu Yi

School of Overseas Education，Sichuan University

Abstract：In modern Chinese，the combination“又……又……”has a wide range of use cases in language communication，and the collocation elements can be either words or phrases. In collocation of adjective components，the number of syllables shows a certain

③ “又”在现代汉语各类辞书中均作副词理解，但是由于“又……又……”经常连用，在用法上具有整体性，但其并非一个独立的词，因此，文中我们将“又……又……”暂称为副词组合。

regularity. That is, the number of syllables of the preceding component is not more than the number of syllables of the following component, the combination form is legal. We believe that this rule is a function of rhythm rules beyond semantics and syntax. In particular, that the ordinary stress rules of Chinese are restricting their combination forms, and this analysis provides a new perspective for the study of Chinese grammar. To some extent, it enriches the theory of Chinese study and has certain theoretical value.

Keywords: Rhythm; Foot; Coordinating Conjunction; Theoretical Significance

一、引言

韵律句法学是以韵律学为基础，针对一门以汉语为基础而建立起的新兴学科，其所主张的“韵律制约句法”的理念在西方语言学理论中还没有得到广泛的认同，而在现代汉语中，韵律制约句法的语言现象比比皆是，如现代汉语中，“又……又……”的使用频率非常高，它们在句中可以连接两个词，也可以连接两个短语，被连接的两个成分是并列关系，在对这两个词的考察中发现，“又……又……”之间使用的形容词或形容词短语在音节上体现出一定的规律性④，即在“又”之后，形容词或者动词的音节数量需要保持一致，形成［又1又1］、［又2又2］的韵律组合模式，或［又1又］、［又1又多］⑤ 等韵律组合模式，而目前尚无学者从韵律角度探讨其用法规律与内部机制。本文从BCC语料库⑥中随机抽取298条使用“又……又……”的例句进行了考察，并希望从汉语普通重音规则的角度来分析其形成机制。

④ “又……又……”之间也有动词或动词短语成分的例句，这里我们暂不作讨论，只讨论形容词的情况。

⑤ 这里的“1”“2”表示成分的音节数量，下文同。

⑥ BCC语料库即北京语言大学BCC现代汉语语料库，总字数约150亿，包括报刊、文学、微博、科技、综合和古汉语等多领域语料，是可以全面反映当今社会语言生活的大规模语料库。

二、对“又……又……”用法的考察

在现代汉语中，我们经常会使用“又……又……”来组建句子，在汉语是母语的使用者看来，其用法并无特殊之处，因为我们的语感不会出错，母语使用者很难说出“＊又漂亮又好”之类［又2又1］组合形式的句子，但是母语非汉语的人在学习汉语的过程中，却很难感知这种“语感”，极容易说出像“＊四川的菜又好吃又辣”⑦的句子，但如果将这个句子中的形容词“辣”和“好吃”换位，将句子变为“四川的菜又辣又好吃”，句子似乎就更文从字顺了。如果不改变两个形容词的位置，将第一个形容词“好吃”换作同义词“香”，句子变为“四川的菜又香又辣”也是合法的。这里就会有疑问：同样的形容词，同样的句法结构（又＋形容词＋又＋形容词），为什么处于前后不同位置时其合法性就会恰恰相反呢？为什么将第一个双音节形容词换为同义的单音节形容词，句子也合法了呢？这里，既不是语义的问题，也不是句法的问题，而是在句法与语义层面之外，汉语的韵律规则控制着这组连词与其后成分的组配模式。

将BCC语料库中报刊语料的前4000条语料进行考察，从中一共得到298条使用“又……又……”的语料，并对其韵律组合模式做了分析，其组合模式体现出一定的规律性。

在考察的这298条使用“又……又……”的语料中，一共有五类搭配模式⑧。

［又1又1］组合模式在语料中的数量最多，占考察的例句总数的60%，共有180组，如：

例（1）戴上这顶草帽，她的脸显得又小又白。

例（2）下辈子咱也托生成城里人，也找个又白又嫩的城里女人做老婆。

例（3）月亮刚从田野后面上升，又圆又亮。

［又2又2］组合模式在语料中的数量仅次于［又1又1］模式，占所有例句的28%，共有83组，如：

---

⑦ 句子来源于留学生作文。

⑧ 我们是通过人工方式逐条检索并摘录的，所以例句不免有所遗漏，数据也许稍有偏差，但整体比例并不会受到太大影响，因此考察结果能够反映出客观的语言事实。

例（4）她得到了这么些钱，又惊奇，又兴奋。

例（5）他又嫉妒又委屈，脑袋发热了。

例（6）可是这种爱好却保持着，保持得又严峻又纯洁。

［又 1 又 2］组合模式占到例句总数的 9%，共有 28 组，如：

例（7）她的手倒真是又小又嫩，可也称得上是又瘦又平凡。

例（8）桌布上躺着那封又大又奇怪的信，里面含着生或死。

例（9）小顺儿的妈长得不难看，中等身材，圆脸，两只又大又水灵的眼睛。

［又 1 又多］的组合模式占例句总数的 2%，有 5 组，如：

例（10）可以略知事件的全貌，但文章又短又不详尽。

例（11）病人觉得卧室里又热又不方便。

例（12）全班合影里她的脸又小又不自然。

例（13）天空是不同层面的不同云朵，有些又厚又不透明。

例（14）虽说镇又小又无特色可言，但毕竟是我的镇。

在考察的所有包含“又……又……”的例句中，［又 2 又 1］组合模式是出现得最少的，298 例中仅有 2 例，只占到总体的 1%，如：

★例（15）咱家旁边有比这套又便宜又好的。

★例（16）她只是又年轻又傻，给你迷住了。

虽然在语料中存在，但是这里的两个例句是不符合汉语韵律规则的，如果将两句中前后形容词互换位置，分别变为“又好又便宜”和“又傻又年轻”，两句话说起来就更顺口了。因此，这里的两个例句属于例外情况，其整体存量也能反映这一事实。

以上是考察的 298 例包含“又……又……”连词的句子的整体情况，为了更直观地反映其语言事实，列表如下：

组合模式	数量	比例	例句
［又 1 又 1］	180	60%	他的鼻子又扁又塌。
［又 2 又 2］	83	28%	他感到又气愤又荒唐。
［又 1 又 2］	28	9%	这些声音听起来就又响又刺耳。

续表

组合模式	数量	比例	例句
[又1又多]	5	2%	病人觉得卧室里又热又不方便。
[又2又1]	2	1%	(1) 她只是又年轻又傻，给你迷住了。 (2) 咱家旁边有比这套又便宜又好的。

从上表的数据对比中，可以总结出三个规律：

第一，[又1又1]与[又2又2]组合模式应当是连词“又……又……”的典型用法，而[又2又1]模式是“非法”组合，这种组合不符合汉语的韵律规则。

第二，在所有的“合法”组合模式中，前面的成分音节数量均不少于后面的成分音节数量，即或者前后音节数量保持一致，或者前面音节数量小于后面音节数量，如“又大又圆”“又气愤又荒唐”“又响又刺耳”“又热又不方便”等，所有的这些“合法”组合都遵循这一规律。

第三，根据以上结论，再进一步推理，所有的不合法组合模式均应是前面成分音节数量大于后面成分音节数量。除了从语料库中得到的两例[又2又1]组合模式例句外，还可以根据推理“制造”出“非法”组合，如：

★例（17）可以略知事件的全貌，但文章又不详尽又短。

★例（18）病人觉得卧室里又不方便又热。

★例（19）全班合影里她的脸又不自然又小。

★例（20）天空是不同层面的不同云朵，有些又不透明又厚。

★例（21）虽说镇又无特色可言又小，但毕竟是我的镇。

以上例句均是不符合汉语韵律的句子，是将例（10）至例（14）句“又……又……”前后成分互换位置所得，互换之后句子变得非常拗口，这些例句的“非法”再一次证明了我们推论的正确。

行文至此，我们不禁追问：为什么这个连词的组合模式会呈现出这样一种规律？音节数量的不同真的能影响一个组合的合法性吗？是什么导致其后的成分在音节数量上表现出如此强的对应性？下文将试着回答这些问题。

三、对“又……又……”连词用法的机制探究

在回答“为什么”之前，可先引入一个韵律句法学的概念——普通重

音。“普通重音指的是一个句子在没有特殊语境的情况下所表现出来的重音结构。”（冯胜利，2009）普通重音是非焦点重音，即把特别强调句子中某个成分的特殊情况排除以后的重音形式。汉语中的普通重音遵循以下规则：

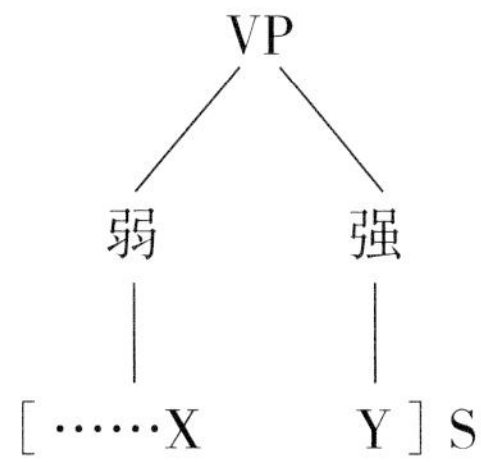

上图中的“X”和“Y”是以动词为中心构成的VP中的两个成分，“X”是句中的最后一个动词，“Y”是“X”的宾语，VP是句中最后一个动词短语，句子的普通重音要落在“Y”上，如果句中不存在“Y”或者“X”为不及物动词，则由“X”承担普通重音。[⑨]

我们知道，形容词和动词在现代汉语中均可做谓语成分，按照传统的分类，动词又有及物与不及物之分，那么，按照普通重音规则，我们就可以得出如下结论：若句子的谓语成分是由形容词充当，那么形容词就承载整个句子的普通重音，其性质相当于最后一个VP中的不及物动词。

现在，再来看上文中的组合模式：

［又1又1］模式中，“又……又……”与其搭配的成分在语料中存在两种情况。第一，一起充当整个句子的谓语成分，在这种情况下，“又A又A”自然承担整个句子的普通重音。但是，在整个谓语成分内，还需要遵循“后重”原则，即句子的普通重音应该落在后副词“又”后的成分上，如：

例（22）街上卖的那些粉纸叠又糙又厚，真不讲究。

例（23）她象木乃伊一样的干瘪，又瘦又冷，缩在火炉旁边。

以上两例中，“又糙又厚”是例（22）前一句的谓语成分，“又瘦又冷”是例（23）前一句的谓语成分，在韵律层面，“又糙”“又厚”分别组成两个双音节音步，韵律重量是相当的，因此，后副词“又”与其后的成分可以得到重音，也就满足了韵律上的“后重”，读起来就顺畅。

第二，整个组合充当定语成分，起修饰作用，这种情况下，虽然其整个

---

⑨ 具体论述请参看冯胜利（2009）：86—92。

成分充当了定语，但是在组合内部，还需要遵循“后重”原则，将重音落在后一个成分上，如：

例（24）在又热又干的天气里，它们会在地上撒尿。

例（25）他头戴镶满宝石的金冠，周身上下被一个又亮又大的黑色的斗篷裹着。

同理，在［又2又2］模式中，前后同样是双音节词，在音节重量上，前后相当，后面的双音节成分不比前面的双音节成分轻，可以顺利承载重音，因此［又2又2］组合模式也符合韵律规则，因此也是合法的。

而对于［又1又2］组合来说，其合法性就更能得到有效解释了，前面成分是单音节，后面成分是双音节，在音节重量上，前面的成分轻于后面的双音节成分，因此，后面的双音节成分可以得到重音，整个组合也就符合汉语的韵律规则，也就变成了合法形式。而［又1又2］组合模式的合法，也就可以推出，为何［又2又1］模式不合法了，因为后面成分的音节是单音节，前面成分的音节是双音节，按照普通重音规则，重音应该落在后面的成分，但是现在由于前面成分的音节重量较重，抢夺了重音，而后面成分在得不到重音的情况下，就会韵律规则排除出合法形式之外，这也就是此类组合模式在语料中的存量如此之小的重要原因。

言至于此，对于［又1又多］组合形式的合法之由，也就非常清楚了。汉语普通重音规则要求“后重”，而在我们前文考察过的所有符合韵律规则的合法组合形式中，“又……又……”的前成分音节数量至多都不多于后成分的音节数量，而［又1又多］组合形式完全能够满足其要求，因此，其形式也为韵律规则所允许。

四、结语及余论

副词组合“又……又……”与其搭配成分所表现出来的组合规律受到汉语韵律规则的支配，具体而言，是汉语的普通重音规则在支配着其具体的表现形式，而其支配作用不受语义与句法的影响，独立于这两个层面之外。现代汉语中有许多句法形式受到汉语韵律规则的影响，韵律在某些时候会大大制约句法的形式，我们所考察的“又……又……”组合所表现出来的搭配模式也是受到汉语的韵律规则影响所致，文中只讨论了“又……又……”组合与形容词及形容词短语组合所表现出来的韵律模式，对于其与动词搭配的各类形式，暂时还未作讨论，并且，除“又……又……”之外，汉语中许多关联词的搭配成分在形式上也体现出很强的音节对应性，希望在以后的研究中能够逐渐进行探索。

韵律句法学是一门新兴学科，也是以汉语为材料建立起来的新理论，虽然还未得到国际主流语言学理论的广泛认同，但是它确实已经解释了许多用传统理论无法解释的语言现象。随着理论的不断发展，一定会有越来越多的语言现象得到解释，这不仅对该学科的深入发展有帮助，对如何构建理论的思考，也有着现实意义和借鉴作用，对中国语言学理论的发展也有着深刻的意义。

参考文献：

[1] 冯胜利. 汉语的韵律、词法与句法 [M]. 北京：北京大学出版社，2009.

[2] 冯胜利. 汉语韵律句法学 [M]. 北京：商务印书馆，2013.

[3] 吕叔湘. 现代汉语八百词 [M]. 北京：商务印书馆，1999.

[4] 商务印书馆辞书中心. 古代汉语字典 [M]. 北京：商务印书馆，2014.

[5] 中国社会科学院语言研究所词典编辑室. 现代汉语词典 [M]. 第 7 版. 北京：商务印书馆，2016.

作者简介：

胡翼，四川大学海外教育学院讲师，研究方向为国际汉语教学。

动力情态助动词“能 1”场景化功能试析[⑩]

邓　波

四川大学海外教育学院

摘　要：场景化理论是认知语言学研究的一个新路径。场景化理论把传统语境研究与认知研究结合起来，对概念化主体如何在语言符号与认知场景之间建立有效联系，从而实现交际的过程做了深入分析。本文基于此理论，对汉语多义助动词“能”表达动力情态时的场景化功能以及“NP＋能 1＋VP”结构的语义建构过程进行了初步探讨。本文认为，作为场景化成分的“能 1”所代表的潜能力被具体识解为来自主语的情态力，而不是来自说话人的主观认识，因此是一种相对客观的识解。

关键词：场景化；助动词；动力情态

Research on the Grounding Function of the Dynamic Modality Auxiliary Verb “Neng 1”

Deng Bo

School of Overseas Education, Sichuan University

Abstract: Grounding theory is a new approach in cognitive linguistics. It combines traditional context research with cognitive research, and makes an in-depth analysis of how the conceptualized subject establishes an effective connection between linguistic signs and

⑩　本文系 2018 年四川大学中央高校基本科研业务费项目“生态语言学视域下网络时代的语言特点和语言文明”成果，项目编号：2018skzx－pt56。

cognitive scenes, thus realizing the communication process. Based on this theory, this paper discusses the grounding function of Chinese polysemous auxiliary verb "neng" when it expresses dynamic modality and the semantic construction process of "NP+neng 1+VP" structure. It is argued that the latent capacity represented by "neng 1", as a grounding element, is interpreted specifically as the modal force of the subject rather than the subjective knowledge of the speaker, so it is a relatively objective construal.

Keywords: Grounding; Auxiliary verb; Dynamic Modality

兰盖克（Langacker，1991）在“焦点—背景”（figure-ground）基础上，提出了“场景化”（grounding）的概念，后来又逐步将这一概念发展为认知语法场景化理论。泰勒（Taylor，2002）探讨和阐述了场景化理论的一些基本观点，之后不断有学者进一步深化场景化理论的研究。近几年，兰盖克也在不断完善和发展场景化理论。国内学者近年来也开始接触和运用场景化理论进行研究，较早介绍该理论的有完权（2009），他还将场景化理论运用到“的”字结构的研究；牛保义（2015）也将场景化理论看作认知语言学研究的一个新途径，并运用该理论研究了英语情态动词“may”的情景植入功能。

场景化理论（Grounding Theory）[11] 认为，自然语言是符号系统，同一事件常常既可以用动词描写，又可以用名词刻画，一个简单名词或动词只是凸显一种型概念（type），并不能用于交际，只有通过场景化，转化为名词短语或限定小句，表征一个该类型的实例（instance），才能在概念化主体（通常包括说话人和听话人）的心智中把作为符号的单个名词或动词跟现实的认知场景建立起联系，实现交际。场景化的实现一般需要借助一定的场景

⑪ “Grounding Theory”有不同译法：入场理论（李国宏，2013；完权，2009；吴吉东，2011）、入景理论（邢晓宇，2015）、接地理论（木村英树，2008）、情景植入理论（牛保义，2015）。本文将其译为“场景化理论”，因该理论涉及的术语“Ground”在认知语法中有两个义项（Evans，2007：97—98）：一是指与焦点（Figure）相对的“背衬”；另一个就是认知场景，包括言语事件中的所有话段、参与者及其互动、言谈时间和即时物理语境等，亦即言语场景（situation of speech，沈家煊，2001）。一般通行译为“场景”。本文取第二个义项的通行译法，不另增名目。

化成分（grounding element），英语中场景化成分通常由冠词、时态、情态动词等高度语法化的成分来充当，场景化成分可以建立型概念和认知场景中某实体的关系，并让听话人感知到这种关系，从而顺利识别出发话人语言符号表征的独特个体。因此，场景化本质上是主观性的（Brisard，2002：8），因为说话人对场景的观察视角无疑会影响其言语的编码方式和表达（Langacker，2007；李国宏，2013）。

英语场景化系统主要由两种基本时态（现在时和过去时）和五个基本情态动词（can，will，may，shall，must）构成，这些情态动词本身有某些时态上的对立，其“过去”式分别为“could，would，might，should”等。英语情态动词又常常与“have”和“be”一起被称为“助动词”（auxiliary verb）。在语义上，时态与情态具有认识价值，能明确唤起场景，并共同承担场景化功能。在语法上，时态与情态对限定小句而言带有强制性（有时时态与情态可以有零形式）。实义动词通过时态与情态的植入转为限定小句，跟名词转化为名词短语以后实现了从类型到凸显实例的情形类似，动词也从过程类型（type of process）定位（locating）为一个过程实例（instance of process），凸显特定言语事件。

一般认为汉语没有跟英语对应的“时态”（tense），但汉语有“体”（aspect），“了、着、过、在”等是常见的体标记（aspect marker），可以表示时间的进程，比如“将要开始、开始、持续、完成、完成后”等。汉语助动词与英语情态动词类似，是重要的情态成分，也与体成分一起，发挥场景化功能。下面我们将以汉语助动词“能”为例进行分析。

我们把吕叔湘（1988）给“能”分的6个义项进行了合并，表示“能力”（ability）、“客观可能性”（possibility）的“能”，我们标记为“能1”；表示“主观推测的可能性”（probability）的“能”，我们标记为“能2”。帕尔默（Palmer，1986）按照情态动词的语义类型将其分为动力（dynamic）情态（表达能力和意愿）、道义（deontic）情态（表达义务、责任和许可）和认识（epistemic）情态（表达说话者对说话内容的认识、信念和态度）。“能1”表达的是动力情态，“能2”表达的是认识情态。下面我们将分析“能”表现为动力情态时，“NP+能1+VP”的场景化模式，以及场景化成分“能1”在“NP+能1+VP”结构的语义建构过程中所发挥的场景化功能。限于篇幅，本文对认识情态“能2”的场景化功能暂不涉及。

一、"NP+能 1+VP"结构的场景化模式

动力情态"能 1"表达 NP 有能力或有条件实施某种行为，NP 可以是有生之物，也可以是无生之物。当 NP 是有生之物时，动力情态"能 1"的语义就体现为吕叔湘（1988）归纳的前两个义项：（1）表示有能力或有条件做某事；（2）表示善于做某事。这两个义项的释义共同点是都凸显"做某事"，而隐含了"做某事"的主体，即某种有生之物，这种有生之物可能是人，也可能是非人类的生物。其语义可以表述为：某生物有能力实现某个行为过程。当 NP 是无生之物时，动力情态"能 1"的语义就体现为吕叔湘（1988）归纳的第三个义项：表示有某种用途。这个释义隐含了"用途"的主体，即某个被使用之物。其语义可以表述为：某物能用来实现某个行为过程。这个"某物"进一步抽象泛化，可以指一种行为或状态。例如：

例（1）**她**能工作，能走路，能吃苦。（华中师大语料库/吴强《红日》）（主语是人）

例（2）这种永远燃烧永不熄灭的**信念的火**，能使人返老还童，变得年青！（华中师大语料库/冯德英《苦菜花》）（主语是非生命体的抽象物）

例（3）初中时，柳清听人家说，**跑步**能减肥，于是跑了三个月。（华中师大语料库/郁秀《花季雨季》）（主语是动作行为）

例（4）**有钱**能使鬼推磨。（俗语）（主语是一种状态）

上述四个例句的共性是助动词"能"所表征的潜能力都源自句子主语 NP，而充当 NP 的成分语义特征各不相同。从场景化的角度来讲，作为场景化成分的"能 1"表征一种潜在能力，这种力量不是来自说话人，而是来自主语。受到该潜在能力的驱动，VP 被概念化为非现实的过程。"能 VP"作为一个被植入场景的表达式，勾画了一个事件过程，即主语有能力实施 VP。动力情态"NP+能 1+VP"的场景化模式如图 1 所示。

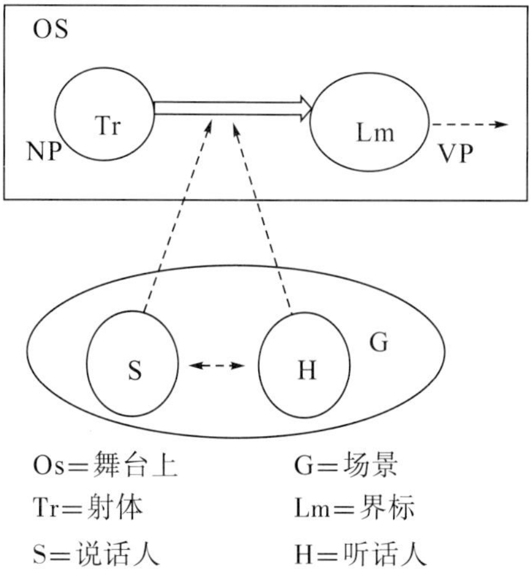

图 1 "NP+能 1+VP" 场景化模式图

图 1 中方框代表舞台上区域（OS），即交际双方关注的范围，G 所在的大椭圆形代表交际双方所处的认知场景，S 所在的圆圈代表说话人，H 所在的圆圈代表听话人，联结说话人和听话人的双向虚线箭头表示交际双方的互动，虚线单箭头表示交际双方的注意力指向"能 1"所植入的潜能力，Tr 所在的圆圈代表射体，Lm 所在的圆圈代表界标，联结射体和界标的空心实线箭头代表"能"植入的潜能力。"能"所代表的潜能力来源于位于台上的主语 NP，也是在台上被凸显的成分，目标是后面的过程 VP。也就是说，作为场景化成分的"能 1"所代表的潜能力被具体识解为来自主语的情态力，而不是来自说话人的主观认识，因此，是一种相对客观的识解。

二、"NP+能 1+VP" 结构中 VP 的语义凸显

陈昌来（2003）把汉语动词分为以下五类：动作动词［动作］［自主］、致使动词［致使］［±自主］、心理动词［心理］［±自主］、性状动词［性状］［－自主］、关系动词［关系］［－自主］。"能 1"能与哪种类型的动词组合并使之实现场景化呢？场景化以后 VP 的语义凸显有什么改变呢？下面我们结合语料进行分析。例如：

例（5）a 他们正成立草绳生产合作社，他**能**安排人。（邓友梅《那五》）
b 他们正成立草绳生产合作社，他安排人。

例（6）a 想到这里，他说了声："用不着再背我了，我**能**走。"（刘流《烈火金钢》）

b 想到这里，他说了声："用不着再背我了，我走。"

例（7）a 她总在快速的移动中，一分钟**能**走一百步。（王小波《白银时代》）

b 她总在快速的移动中，一分钟走一百步。

以上例句中，VP 的主要动词"安排""走"是动作动词，都有［动作］［自主］的语义特征，属于动作动词，句子中的"能"是表示能力的"能1"。我们对比一下用"能"和不用"能"的句子，可以看出，例（5）b"他安排人"勾画（profile）的是言者说话时已然的现实，例（5）a"他能安排人"勾画的是非现实事件的判断，即言者认为主语"他"有致使"安排人"这一事件发生的潜能力。例（6）b"我走"勾画的是言者主语的决定，是即将发生的现实，例（6）a"我能走"勾画的是言者"他"对自己有能力实施"走"这一行为过程的判断，即言者认为"我"有致使"走"这一行为发生的潜能力。例（7）b"（她）一分钟走一百步"表示言者对主语"她"在一分钟内行走距离为一百步这一现实事件的描述，例（7）a"一分钟能走一百步"表示言者认为主语"她"具有"一分钟内走一百步"的潜能力，这样的句子在主语 NP 和"能"之间往往有"一分钟"这一类表示时间期限的时间名词，勾画主语在单位时间内具有的做事效率。也就是说，前者是现实性的客观性描述，通过"能"实现场景化以后，概念化者把 VP"走一百步"概念化为非现实性的动作过程，表示说话人认为 NP"她"有能力完成"一分钟走一百步"这个动作过程。

以上 3 例中，"NP"都是"VP"的施事，下面一例稍有不同：

例（8）a 运气好，整到一只狍子，皮子**能**铺盖，肉**能**吃半拉月。（周立波《暴风骤雨》）

b 运气好，整到一只狍子，皮子铺盖，肉吃半拉月。

例（8）b 中，"能"前主语 NP"皮子""肉"都不是 VP 中主要动词"铺盖""吃"的发出者，"皮子"是实施"铺""盖"这两个动作行为的工具，"肉"是"吃"的受事，前者表示"皮子"被用来实施"铺盖"的用途，后者表示"肉"的用途是"吃半拉月"。加上"能"以后，如例（8）a 中，"皮子**能**铺盖"表示言者判断主语"皮子"具有满足"铺盖"用途的潜能力，

“肉**能**吃半拉月”表示言者判断主语“肉”满足“吃半拉月”用途的潜能力。也就是说，当NP的语义角色不是动作动词的施事而是工具或受事，则“能VP”呈现的语义是“NP”有满足某种用途的潜能力，而不是实施动作行为的潜能力。

当VP的主要动词是致使动词的时候[12]，加上“能1”的“能VP”在语义呈现上跟VP相比有什么差异呢？如例（9）、例（10）中，“加强”“丰富”都是典型的致使动词，不加“能”的时候，“这加强羞臊的效果”和“因为它丰富我的人生”没有明确的时间参照点，只能表征抽象的类型过程（type process），只有转化为实例概念，才能用于交际。它们作为类型概念，分别可以对应“这加强了羞臊的效果”“这可能会加强羞臊的效果”“因为它丰富了我的人生”“因为它有可能丰富我的人生”等具体的有交际功能的句子（实例概念），后面这些表达形式中，动词分别标记了完成体标记“了”及表示预测将来现实的认识情态标记“可能会”“有可能”等，因而动词所勾勒的内容就具有了时间情境和认识情境，处于台下场景中的听话人注意力被正确引导指向处于台上的动作过程，交际双方就可以在一定语境和心理空间下对其所指进行有效解读。也就是说，动词已经完成了场景化。

例（9）“你照我说的做就是了，”团长说，“这**能**加强羞臊的效果。”（孙犁《风云初记》）

例（10）我很喜欢挑战，因为它**能**丰富我的人生。（新华社2002年4月新闻报道）

例（9）中的“这**能**加强羞臊的效果”，“能”表达“有能力做某事”，“加强羞臊的效果”从现实转化为潜在现实，或者说，说话者通过“能”将“加强羞臊的效果”这一过程凸显为主语有能力实施的未知事件。例（10）中的“因为它能丰富我的人生”，说话人同样通过“能”植入了“有能力做某事”的情态致使力，句子的语义凸显为非现实过程，说话者将“丰富我的人生”概念化为主语“它（挑战）”有能力实施的未知潜在过程。当VP的主要动词是心理动词、性状动词、关系动词时，也可以做同样的分析。例如：

---

⑫ 根据陈昌来（2003：50），致使动词的动作行为能使其支配的事物发生某种变化，产生某种新的性质、状态、动作行为，“V+NP”能变换为“使+NP+VP”。

例（11）今天是它们特殊的日子，我们希望它们都**能**开心。（新华社2002年3月新闻报道）

例（12）假定你膀胱不**能**发炎，而财政部长却**能**血管硬化，（血压太高）他便占优势，而你立下风了。（林语堂《论政治病》）

例（13）我特别希望我的痛苦**能**有一个人来倾听。（安顿《绝对隐私》）

例（11）、例（12）、例（13）中“能开心”“能血管硬化”“能有一个人来倾听”语义均凸显为将来时间（相对于说话时间）发生的非现实过程。

三、余论

综上所述，我们认为，“能”作为场景化成分（grounding elements），其功能是将实义动词表示的类过程（type process）转化为一个场景化了的例过程（grounded process instance）。“能”给句子凸显的行为过程植入了能力、认识判断等情态力量，这种力量促使认知主体将句子所凸显的过程概念化为具有出现可能性的过程。也就是说，“能”的场景化功能体现为“能”的植入对句子凸显过程的实现可能性（likelihood）的影响，即通过“能”所表达的情态力的植入，认知主体将VP所凸显的过程概念化为可能发生的过程。“能”表达动力情态时，“NP+能1+VP”表示句子主语NP有实施VP所表征过程的潜在能力，如下例（14）；作为对比，“能”表达认识情态时，“NP+能2+VP”表示说话人判断VP所表征的动作行为有可能发生，如下例（15）：

例（14）我**能**吃苦，我不嫌寒碜。（王朔《千万别把我当人》）

例（15）孩子们都有火性，可心地都不差呀，你养了他们的小了，他们**能**不对你养老报恩吗？（李英儒《野火春风斗古城》）

例（14）中助动词“能”所表示的潜能力来自主语“我”，从场景化的角度来讲，作为场景化成分的动力情态“能1”给动词的语义凸显植入的是主语有完成动作行为过程“吃苦”的潜能力，“能1+VP”（能吃苦）作为一个被植入情境的表达是表征NP“我”有能力实施行为“吃苦”的过程。例（15）中助动词“能2”所表示的不是来自句子主语而是来自说话人主观判断的“可能”义，表示说话人主观推测VP表征的动作“对你养老报恩”具有发生的可能性。从场景化的角度来讲，作为场景化成分的“能2”给动词的语义凸显过程植入一种认识判断力，在这种认识判断力的作用下，VP 所表征的过程被概念化为非现实时间中可能出现的过程。

多义性是汉语助动词的典型特征之一。对留学生来说，多义助动词是学习的一个难点。多义助动词的不同义项之间的差异往往在语言环境中才能体现出来，场景化理论关注语言使用者、句子主语、动词之间的动态交互关系，因而能很好地解释多义助动词结构语义建构的内在规律，从而为教学实践提供有价值的参考。

参考文献：

[1] 陈昌来. 现代汉语语义平面问题研究［M］. 北京：学林出版社，2003.

[2] 李国宏. 从（交互）主观性看“不”和“没”的分工及语义表现［J］. 西安外国语大学学报，2013（4）.

[3] 吕叔湘. 现代汉语八百词［M］. 北京：商务印书馆，1988.

[4] 牛保义. 认知语法情境植入研究综述［J］. 外语学刊，2015（5）.

[5] 牛保义. 英语情态动词 may 的情境植入功能研究［J］. 外国语，2017（3）.

[6] 完权. 入场理论：认知语法的新进展［J］. 外国语，2009（6）.

[7] Brisard，F.（ed.）. *Grounding: The Epistemic Footing of Deixis and Reference* [M]. Berlin：De Gruyter Mouton，2002.

[8] Langacker，R. W. *Foundations of Cognitive Grammar: Descriptive Application*. Vol. II [M]. Stanford：Stanford University Press，1991.

[9] Langacker，R. W. *Investigations in Cognitive Grammar* [M]. Berlin：Mouton de Gruyter，2009.

[10] Palmer，F. R. *The English Verb* [M]. London：Longman，1974.

[11] Taylor，J. R. *Cognitive Grammar* [M]. London：Oxford University Press，2002.

作者简介：

邓波，文学博士，四川大学海外教育学院副教授，研究方向为对外汉语教学与研究。

“果然”的连词用法及其连词化

胡 朗

西华师范大学文学院

摘 要：“果然”是现代汉语中的一个多义（功能）词，但其是否具有连词用法一直存有争议。本文考察了“果然”的连词用法，并通过历时分析发现连词“果然”是由表强调情态的副词“果然”在假设语境吸收的作用下演变而来，同时，其演变也一定程度上受到类同引申的作用。

关键词：“果然”；连词；语境吸收；类同引申

The Formation of the Conjunction “*guoran*”

Hu Lang

The College of Literature, China West Normal University

Abstract: “*guoran*” is a polysemous word in modern Chinese, however, it has always been controversial that whether it is a conjunction. This paper explores the use of the conjunction “*guoran*”, and through diachronic analysis, it is found that the conjunction “*guoran*” is evolved from the emphasis of the modal adverb “*guoran*” through contextual absorption. At the same time, its evolution is also affected by similar extension to some extent.

Keywords: “*guoran*”; Conjunction; Contextual Absorption; Similar Extension

《现代汉语词典》（第7版）将“果然”标注为副词、连词两种词性，副词“果然”用于表示事实与所说或所料相符，连词“果然”用于假设事实与所说或所料相符。但对于其是否有连词用法多有分歧，张超、李步军（2010）等认为“果然”无连词用法，而李小平（2007）等认为“果然”是连词性的。那么，“果然”究竟有无连词表现？其连词用法又是如何来的？本文拟围绕这些问题进行探讨。

一、“果然”的连词用法

根据语料考察，连词“果然”在现代汉语中分布率极低，甚至在随机抽取的400条现代汉语语料中一条连词用法也没有。可见，汉语母语者对其连词用法的敏感度极低，李冰（2009）的考察也印证了这些表现。然而，以下语例的“未然”用法的存在仍然证明了其连词属性：

例（1）辛修甫笑道：“你果然能够把别的事情做个比例，自然更好。你只顾发议肆论，我们大家都在这里洗耳恭听就是了。”（《九尾龟》第一百七十九回）

例（2）你果然爱她，就该帮助她。（《现代汉语词典》第7版）

例（3）只有这样做，才能支持长期战争，取得全面胜利。果然这样做了，就一定可以支持长期战争，取得全面胜利。（毛泽东《论持久战》）

例（1）、例（2）、例（3）中“果然”引导的都是“未然”事件或行为，只能理解为假设，不能理解为“事实与所说或所料相符时”。例（1）和例（2）中“果然”假设的是可能会发生的事情，还带有强调的意味。例（3）的“果然”位于句首，表示假设。

在搭配上，连词“果然”则有如下表现。

第一，一般与“就”构成一个假设框架，例如：

例（4）你果然想改正错误，就应该拿出实际行动来。（《现代汉语虚词词典》：215）

第二，也可以同有关联作用的“那”共现，例如：

例（5）方先生果然能来，那真是我们的荣幸！（钱钟书《围城》）

第三，还可以同时与“那、就”共现，例如：

例（6）果然你愿意参加，那我们就太高兴了。（《现代汉语八百词》：239）

更有意思的是，下面两个用例中的“果然”虽然在形式表现上看起来一样，但表达的却是不同意义，属于不同词性：

例（7）……只有坚持统一战线和坚持战争，才能有最后胜利。果然是这样，一切困难就能够克服。（《现代汉语虚词例释》：217）

例（8）宋泉安心寒齿冷，“果然是这样，那么我就没什么好顾忌了，你们要做夫妻，到阴间去做好了，我送你们一程。”（梅贝尔《爱你情深莫问愁》）

例（7）表示的是未然，例（8）表示的是已然。例（8）乍一看，有“那么”共现，似乎就等同于“如果”了，然而通过上下文可知，这里的“果然”是一种合预期的意义，表示发现“事实与所想相符”，“那么”在这是基于上文中发现的事实而不是假设来引出下文中的决定的。

因此，“果然”的假设连词用法是确切存在的。其实，这在其他方言中也可以找到旁证，例如，福州话的“如果”类似北京话的“果然”，如“如果其，我野早就准到是伊”（马清华，2003）。

二、“果然”的连词化

“果”，《说文·木部》：“果，木实也。”其先引申为事情的结果，又进一步引申为抽象的结果，并最终虚化为副词，例如：

例（9）室之始成也善，其后果败。（《吕氏春秋·似顺论》）

例（10）骊姬果作难，杀太子而逐二公子。（《国语·晋语》）

例（11）师若果进，军必有殃。（《晏子春秋·内篇·谏篇》）

例（12）若果立之，必为季氏忧。（《春秋左传·襄公》）

虽都是副词用法，前两例中的“果”与后两例的“果”表义有明显的不同，前者表事实与预期相符，后者则是在假设连词“若”之后表强调。

除了副词用法，“果”在先秦还有假设连词用法，例如：

例（13）不行谓之临，有帅而不从，临孰甚焉？此之谓矣。果遇，必

败，彘子尸之，虽免而归，必有大咎。（《春秋左传·宣公》）

例（14）果能此道矣，虽愚必明，虽柔必强。（《礼记·中庸》）

先秦开始，“果”就与“然”构成短语“果然”，既用于表示一种认知情态，意为情况或事实“果然如此”，例如：

例（15）乃召其堂下而谯之，果然，乃诛之。（韩非《韩非子·内储说下》）

例（16）或言：“往者公卿重臣缺，而众人咸豫部署云：‘甲乙当为之。’后果然。彼何以处知，而又能与上同意乎？……”（桓谭《新论·谴非》）

“果然”也开始用于表示一种强调情态，强调说话人认为“的确如此”“真的如此”，例如：

例（17）劝公以其死也有自也，而生阳也无自也，而果然乎？（庄子《庄子·杂篇·寓言》）

例（18）又云，物无妄然，必以类感，常善以救，善亦从之，势犹影表，不虑自来，斯言果然，则类感之物，轻重必侔，影表之势，修短有度。（南朝梁 僧祐《弘明集》）

例（19）初权疑竺泄之，及服，以为果然，乃斩竺。（裴松之《三国志·陆凯传》

除此之外，表强调的短语“果然”也开始出现在了假设条件句中，常与“若”“如”等连用或共现，表示“如果真的如此”，例如：

例（20）是若果是也，则是之异乎不是也亦无辩；然若果然也，则然之异乎不然也亦无辩。（庄子《庄子·内篇·齐物论》）

例（21）如其果然，以传子孙，纵非六玺之数，要非常人所畜，孙皓之降，亦不得但送六。（裴松之《三国志·孙坚传》）

例（22）生曰：“若果然，幸一枉驾。”（《太平广记·定数五·李揆》）

魏晋南北朝时，“果然”还出现在谓语动词性成分之前，发展出副词功能，其中“然”的指代功能不再发挥作用，“果然”表示“事实与所料或所想相符”，是一种合预期确认，例如：

例（23）依他设想做去，果然在广都县的龙泉山脉部分取得食盐了。（常璩《华阳国志》卷十二）

例（24）大将军闻恪死，谓众人曰："诸葛恪多辈耳！近张敬仲县论恪，以为必见杀，今果然如此。敬仲之智为胜恪也。"（裴松之《三国志·张既传》）

唐代的副词"果然"则已经出现了强调情态用法，表说话人对自己所表达内容的真实性的肯定。例如：

例（25）妇儿男女，共为欢乐，自夸楼猡："得伊造作：'耕田人打兔，跖履人吃臛'古语分明，果然不错。"（《敦煌变文集》卷三）

例（26）和上言：不辞为说，恐无解者。法师言：道俗有一万馀人，可无有一人解者？和上言：看见不见。法师言：见是没？和上言：果然不见！（《神会禅话录》）

宋元时，副词"果然"的语义-语用语境发生了扩展，出现在了假设条件句中，表示对假定事实的强调，例如：

例（27）若文王之囿果然纵一切人往，则虽七十里之大，不过几时，亦为赤地矣，又焉得有林木鸟兽之长茂乎？（朱熹《朱子语类》卷五十一）

例（28）康叔若果然用此意而皆诛杀之，则是为君为长不能教化。（《尚书详解》卷十九）

例（29）你说什么话。若果然使不得。你肯要么。（《老乞大新释》）

在假设条件句中的此类"果然"都分布在前分句，且常与"若"连用。

在宋代，假设条件句中的"果然"则已经开始单独承担"假设"这一语义，演变为假设连词，例如：

例（30）曰："……如六祖衣钵，说移不动底，这只是胡说。果然如此，何不鸣鼓集众，白昼发去？却夜间发去做甚么？"（朱熹《朱子语类》卷四十七）

例（31）那孙子果然真个风魔，这不必说了；若是假呵，小官用些小智术，救得他出了魏国。（《马陵道》第三折）

例（32）果然行者肯来，我就与他一路来了；他若不来，你却也不要望我，我也不来了。（吴承恩《西游记》第三十回）

例（33）黛玉从没见妙玉做过诗，今见他高兴如此，忙说："果然如此，我们虽不好，亦可以带好了。"（曹雪芹《红楼梦》第七十六回）

例（34）那主人听得肯卖，不觉喜从天降，笑逐颜开，起身道："果然

肯卖，但凭分付价钱，不敢吝惜。”（抱翁老人《今古奇观》第九卷）

值得一提的是，李小平（2007）认为“果然”假设连词用法在唐代就已经出现，并举例：

例（35）果然怀恩自毙，回纥来降，羌浑诸蕃，内难外散，天实有眼，心可负乎？（独孤及《敕与吐蕃赞普书》）

然而，通过对原著上下文的查证和梳理，我们发现此“果然”其实仍是副词用法。其所在片段描述的是对“赞普”的斥责，发生在打败叛臣与赞普的结盟后，赞普派使臣来求和。其原文片段为：

自我国家有安禄山、史思明之难，朕谓言赞普必有恤邻救患之意，岂知乘我之衅，恣其侵轶，掠略河湟之人，争夺汧陇之地？又与朕叛臣仆固怀恩共扇诱回纥等诸蕃，同恶相济，犯我都邑，三年之间，三至城下。此实赞普苟窥分寸之利，自弃一家之信，不念婚姻之好，忍绝甥舅之欢，累代亲邻，一朝并弃。有目有耳者，皆为赞普羞之。夫以小国伐大国，且劳师袭远，而助叛臣，有是三者，神宜悔怒。果然怀恩自毙，回纥来降，羌浑诸蕃，内难外散，天实有眼，心可负乎？朕顷以背盟不祥，绝亲不义，宁人负我，我不负人，所以含垢数年，未忍致讨。（独孤及《敕与吐蕃赞普书》）

这段话充分表明了对赞普的气愤，“果然”后的“怀恩自毙，回纥来降，羌浑诸蕃，内难外散”已明显是事实，其后的“天实有眼”中的“实”用来表明说话人对“天有眼”这一事实的确认，并进而反问“心可负乎？”。也就是说，“果然”在此不应是一种假设，而是表示一种事实与情理“心不可负”的相符。

由上可知，副词“果然”在副词化时就虚化出两种用法，一种用来表示认识情态，一种则用来表示强调情态，当出现在假设条件句中主要是后一种用法在发挥作用。这种强调情态义在语义上极虚，主要表示的是一种语气，语义本来就极虚的“果然”在这样的语境中极易受影响，“假设”加“强调”实质还是“假设”，只是在语气上有所加重，表明了说话人在语境中对假定事实的一种肯定，也就是说，此语境中的“果然”［＋假设］特征逐渐得到了加强，而［＋强调］这一语义特征发生了弱化，在语义上表现出对语境的极强适应力，吸收了假设义，演变出假设连词用法。从历时来看，这一演化路径与副词“果”类同，可以说副词“果”和短语“果然”在假设句中的用法对副词“果然”的连词化是不无影响，后者有极大可能发生了类同引申。

三、结论

“果然”的连词用法的确是存在的，其在宋代就已经发生了从表强调的副词到表假设的连词的演变，演变路径如下图所示：

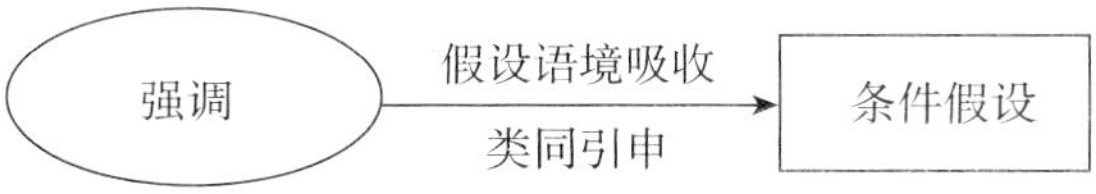

“果然”从强调类副词再虚化为假设连词，这与其极虚的语义和假设语境的互动有关，在互动中“果然”吸收了假设语义，演变出连词用法。同时，与“果”的演变路径类同，也一定程度上说明了其发生了类同引申。

其实，在假设语境中表强调的确认类词不只有“果然”，还有“的确”“确实”“真的”等，如：

例（36）如果的确如此，就非用负的方法不可。（冯友兰《中国哲学简史》）

例（37）那么如果确实你这个土地，在过去36个月时间，确实没有使用过化肥农药，那么它这个土地可以得到认证。（百家讲坛）

例（38）反之，假如真的出现能源短缺，那么我们的一切经济活动势必将陷于停顿。（《读书》）

且“真的”在语境中也浮现出一些假设用法，如：

例（39）娇娘骤然色变，忿忿地说：“事情已到这种地步，你还怕什么！人生如白驹过隙，天下如我俩如此钟情的人能有几人？即使事情败露，我当一死为快！”申纯说：“真的如此，我又有什么担忧惧怕的呢？”（曹绣君《古今情海》）

但此类用法对语境的依赖性极强，且我们暂只发现一例。也就是说，“真的”还没有真正的连词用法，但这些语例也可从侧面说明“果然”连词化的合理性。

参考文献：

[1] 北京大学中文系1955、1957级语言班. 现代汉语虚词例释［M］. 北京：商务印书馆，1982.

[2] 张斌. 现代汉语虚词词典［M］. 北京：商务印书馆，2001.

[3] 马清华. 关联成分的语法化方式［J］. 中央民族大学学报（哲学社会科学版），2003（3）.

[4] 李小平. “果然”的成词过程及用法初探［J］. 东方论坛，2007（1）.

[5] 李冰. “果然”与“果真”的用法考察及对比分析［J］. 汉语学习，2009（4）.

[6] 张超，李步军. “果然”是连词吗?［J］. 辞书研究，2010（1）.

[7] 中国社会科学院语言研究所词典编辑室. 现代汉语词典（第7版）［M］. 北京：商务印书馆，2016.

作者简介：

胡朗，四川大学文学博士，西华师范大学文学院讲师，研究方向为现代汉语词汇和语义。

"V1 着 V2"结构的句法属性

樊　洁

西华大学文学与新闻传播学院

摘　要：本文尝试对"V1 着 V2"的句法属性进行讨论，首先确定了"连动式"的基本性质是时序性，然后通过对 V1 和 V2 的时间顺序、主次关系以及事件融合等特征的分析，认为［一共时］及［±共时］"V1 着 V2"属于连动式，［+共时］"V1 着 V2"是状中式，最后发现"V1 着 V2"内部存在一个从双事件到单事件的连续统，它们在时间顺序、主次关系、事件数量、事件融合、结构特征等方面存在渐变差异。

关键词："V1 着 V2"；时序性；事件融合；连动式；状中式

Syntactic Attributes of "V1 *zhe* V2" Structure

Fan Jie

School of Literature and Journalism, Xihua University

Abstract: This paper attempts to discuss the syntactic attributes of "V1 *zhe* V2". Firstly, it determines that the basic nature of "serial verb structure" is chronological. Then, through the analysis of the chronological order, primary-secondary relationship and event fusion of V1 and V2, it is concluded that [-synchronic] "V1 *zhe* V2" and [±synchronic] "V1 *zhe* V2" belong to serial verb structures, and [+synchronic] "V1 zhe V2" belongs to adverbial-verb structure. Finally, it is found that there is a continum from double events to single events in "V1 *zhe* V2" structure, and there are gradual differences in chronological orders, primary-secondary relations, number of events, event fusion, structural characteristics and so on.

Keywords: "V1 *zhe* V2"; Chronological Order; Event Fusion; Serial Verb Structure; Adverbial-verb Structure

一、引言

前人对"V_1着 V_2"结构的句法、语义、语法化路径、动词选择限制等问题展开了许多富有见地的讨论，如赵元任（1948、1979）、丁声树（1961）、吕叔湘（1944）、朱德熙（1982）、胡树鲜（1981）、宋玉柱（1985）、邢欣（1987）、孙朝奋（1997）、孙德金（1997）、沈家煊（1999）、张伯江（2000）、戴耀晶（2001）、李向农和张军（2001）、高增霞（2003）、彭育波（2004）、陈立民（2006）、丁崇明（2009）等。"V_1着 V_2"结构的句法属性是研究中需要面对的第一个问题，目前学术界的看法还不统一，有的认为是连动式，有的认为是状中式。这种分歧一方面和对"连动式"界定的宽窄有关，另一方面和"V_1着 V_2"结构内部的复杂性，尤其与 V_1 和 V_2 的不同关系有关。因此要回答这个问题，首先要明确"连动式"的界限，其次要明确"V_1着 V_2"的特征。

本文语料都来自北京语言大学大数据与语言教育研究所（BCC）语料库，文中不再单独标注。

二、"连动式"及其结构特征

连动式（serial verbs construction）的界定要避免两种极端的倾向：一是将连动式的范围界定得太宽，只要表层形式中有动词性成分连用，都归入连动式；二是取消连动式，将其归入其他结构类型。

一方面，连动式如果界定太宽，会把许多属于其他句法结构的现象，包括一些不在同一层次仅在线性上前后出现的现象划入连动式。范围过宽的连动式则失去了在句法结构上的分类意义。另一方面，真实世界中确实存在多个动作或事件连续发生的现实现象，需要使用相应的语言形式进行反映，连动式的存在是其他句法结构无法取代的。这类现象最本质的特征就是动作事件的“时序性”，映射到语言结构中，连动式也应当具备这种特征。赵元任（1948）最早讨论连动结构时，将其称为“动词结构连用式”。张志公（1953）明确将“连动式”界定在“连续动作”的动词连用范围内。戴浩一（1985）认为连动结构是一种具有高度时序象似性的句法结构，遵循时序原则在线性序列上前后出现。高增霞（2003）认为典型的连动结构是一种句法化程度较低的多核结构。艾肯瓦尔德（Aikhenvald，2003）与此观点相似，认为语法化程度高的“连动句”和功能词的形成密不可分，也就是说典型连动结构应当是语法化程度较低的形式。张军（2014）提出典型连动结构的动词在时间上有先后。这些主张都说明“时序性”是“连动式”的基本特征。

综合前人观点，从连动式的分类意义出发，明确连动式的基本特征是时序特征。典型连动式是像“推开门走进教室坐在椅子上”这样的多核结构。但是，绝对单纯的时序性极少，更多情况下，后一动词以前一动词的结束为前提，这样的时间顺序本身就蕴涵着一种条件意味。因此，连动式在强调“时序性”的前提下，并不排斥动词之间更加丰富的语义关系，如目的、趋向等，如“来北京开会”“到山里去了”。

连动式内部存在着从典型到边缘的连续统，“时序性”特征是规定这个连续统的边界。随着“时序性”特征的逐渐减弱，连动式从典型过渡到边缘，各项语义特征也随之变化。当“时序性”特征完全消失以后就不再是连动式。可以把典型连动式的特征（主要是动词之间的关系）总结为两点：（1）时序性特征，即动词之间的时间关系具有［－共时］特征；（2）多核结构，即动词之间没有明显的主次（如限定、描写等）关系。

三、“V_1着 V_2”结构的特征

“V_1着 V_2”结构存在多个动词连用的情况，这也是很多学者将其归入连动式的形式要素。吕叔湘（1944：535－536）认为 V_1和 V_2“两个动作，或同时，或先后，但第一个动作表示第二个动作的情景（或手段等）”，“次要动作开始在主要动作之先”。其论断说明了两点：第一，V_1和 V_2的时间关系存在共时和异时两种情况，而只有异时关系的“V_1着 V_2”才能进入连动式的范畴；第二，V_1和 V_2之间存在主次关系。我们将从时间顺序和主次关系两个方面来具体考察“V_1着 V_2”结构的特点。

本文所讨论的“V1 着 V2”结构有以下限制：（1）V1 和 V2 都为肯定

的动词，不包括“V 着 AP”（吃着很香）和“V1 着不 V2”（抓着不放）；（2）不包括“V1 着 V1 着 V2”结构”（说着说着打起来了）；（3）不包括 V2 在 V1 的宾语范围内的情况（他还肩负着押解七千名俘虏的任务她梦想着成为一名编辑）。

（一）V_1和 V2 的时间关系

通过对语料的分析发现，V_1和 V_2的时间关系存在共时、异时、交叉三种情况。在随机抽取的 977 条“V_1着 V_2”语料中，“共时”有 773 条（79.1%），“交叉”27 条（19.5%），“异时”1 条（1.4%）。例如：

例（1）他缩头缩脚地蜷曲着睡，正是活该。

母亲微笑着怂恿过儿子们的创造，又微笑着收纳了这种创造。

小女孩哭着离开了。

我只需静静地坐着观看便是了。

这些夜间生活的动物……尖叫着去捕捉昆虫、瓜果为食。

直升机呼啸着离开桌面，升到空中。

这一类“V_1着 V_2”结构的两个动词是共时关系，可以描写为［+共时］。从动词的时间关系来看，例（1）的两个动词未必一定同时开始，但“V_1着 V_2”结构不关注两个动词的现实起点，只关注两个动作（或状态）在持续阶段的共时关系。V_1在语义上往往表示 V_2的伴随、情状和方式。李向农、张军（2001）提到的“交替发生”的情况（吃着谈、喝着聊），虽然“吃”和“谈”的动作片段不能同时发生，但是这两个事件是同时进行的，因此不做单独讨论，一并计入［+共时］类型。

这也是“V_1着 V_2”结构中数量最多、频率最高的一类。形式上以最简式居多，即 V_1后面无宾语，V_2前面无状语，V_1和 V_2在语码上的距离最近。也有一些带简单宾语的情况，但数量不占优势。例如：

例（2）推着冲车井栏往城墙上压过去。

摇着装满丝绸的大船进入大运河。

赶着四轮大马车进了城。

揪着他的衣领拎小鸡似的举了起来。

例（2）的“V_1着 V_2”结构的两个动词既有前后发生的异时关系，也有伴随并行的同时关系，可以描写为［±共时］。V_1先于 V_2发生，持续到

V_2并与之相伴随。如图 1 所示（横实线表示动作事件的实际发生，虚线表示未发生，T1 表示 V_1的起点，T2 表示 V_2的起点）：

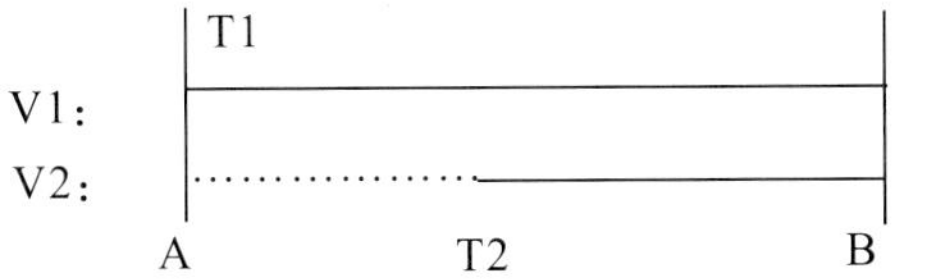

图 1　［±共时］“V_1着 V_2”结构的时间关系

图 2 的关注焦点在直线 AB 之间，包括了异时和共时两个阶段，使整个“V_1着 V_2”结构的理解也出现了两种可能：当关注焦点集中在 V_1和 V_2所表两个事件的起点时（T1—T2），两个动词呈现出前后相继的时序性特征，如“揪着他的衣领拎小鸡似的举了起来”；当焦点集中在 V_2事件开始后，V_1和 V_2的共时意味加强，意同“揪着衣领举起来”。这一类“V_1着 V_2”结构的特点是，两个动词中间加入 V_1的宾语和 V_2的状语，动词的距离拉大，“V_1着 V_2”不是最简形式。例如：

例（3）鱼留着晚上吃。

第三个停着以后用。

舍不得用，只是放着以后欣赏而已。

这类结构可以描写为［－共时］。V_1和 V_2表示两个在时间上前后相继的事件，V_1发生时，V_2还是未然事件，当 V_2发生时，V_1所表事件自然结束。V_1和 V_2在时间上前后相继，没有交叉，是三类之中“时序性”特征最突出的“V_1着 V_2”。这一类“V_1着 V_2”有几个特点：V_1和 V_2往往有目的关系；V_1往往是有“留置”含义的动词；V_1和 V_2之间多有一个表示未来的时间词，如“晚上”“以后”等。

这三组“V_1着 V_2”结构在 V_1和 V_2的相对时间关系上呈现出一种渐变的连续性：［＋共时］—［±共时］—［－共时］。V_1和 V_2的相对时间关系如图 2 所示：

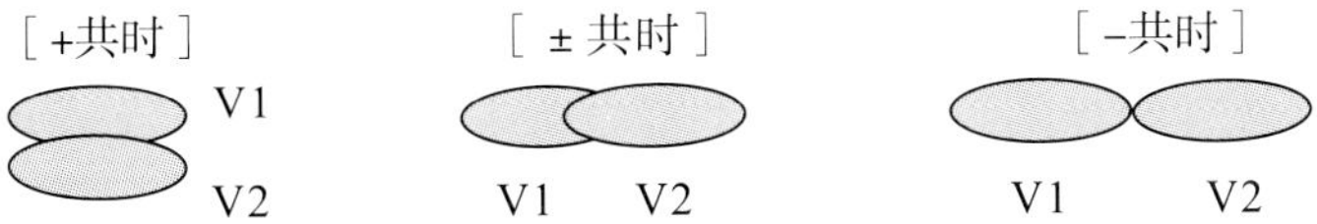

图 2　“V_1着 V_2”结构的时间顺序

符合连动句“时序性特征”的是“异时”［－共时］类和“交叉”［±共时］类。从事件的角度说，带有［－共时］特征的“V_1着V_2”结构的语言编码顺序与事件发生顺序一致，符合时间象似性原则，体现为一种线性的事件组合关系，是典型的连动结构（Aikhenvald：2006）。同时也应看到，“异时”和“交叉”两种“V_1着V_2”结构所体现的事件融合度不同，后者的融合度高于前者，印证了在连动式内部，融合度越高的连动句越边缘，融合度越低的连动句越典型（高增霞，2003）。

（二）［＋共时］“V_1着V_2”的主次关系

［＋共时］“V_1着V_2”是单核结构，两个事件之间存在主次关系，下面主要从认知编码和事件融合两个方面进行论证。

1. 认知和编码的证据

从认知角度讲，两个事件同时发生，必有一个是结构的核心，另一个则退到次要位置。因为在同一时间，人只能对一个对象开启注意力视窗，产生“前景”（figure）和“背景”（background）的分化。其中动态的、非均质的、边界清晰的对象易于前景化，静态的、均质的、具有延展性的对象易于背景化。［＋共时］“V_1着V_2”中两个动词同时发生，其中只有一个能够成为注意焦点，因此该结构只能是单核结构。同时，由于“着”表示进行或持续，使“V_1着”具有“状态”（state）的体特征（非完成、持续性、均质性），更易成为背景；V_2往往是行为动词，动态性明显，更易成为前景。因此从认知上来说，［＋共时］“V_1着V_2”结构中，“V_1着”是背景，V_2是前景。

语言编码方式与认知特点相吻合，前景编码为结构的核心，背景编码为从属成分。汉语的语言编码顺序，往往是修饰限定性成分居于中心成分之前。在［＋共时］“V_1着V_2”结构中，“V_1着”居于V_2之前，表示V_2发生时的背景信息，如伴随、情状、方式等，对V_2起限定或描写作用，可以回答“怎样V”的问题。

2. 事件融合现象

所谓事件融合，是指在多动词结构中，V_1和V_2所表事件在特定结构中融合为一个事件的现象。事件融合的程度和动词的主次关系密切相关，我们发现，往往是处于次要地位的动词逐渐融入处于主要地位的动词所表事件之中，而不是相反。根据詹卫东（2013）的操作方法，我们以“动词的独立性”来判断它们在结构中的融合度和主次关系。

[+共时]“V_1着 V_2”结构内部有事件融合的现象，且存在程度差异。随着 V_1的独立性降低，依附性增强，逐渐融入以 V_2为核心的事件中，整个“V_1着 V_2”结构的主次关系更加明显。根据融合程度的高低，将[+共时]“V_1着 V_2”结构分为 3 个小类进行说明。

(1) V_1和 V_2融合度低——V_1表伴随义

例（4）站着写/蹲着吃/坐着聊天/躺着喘粗气/哭着拜堂/呼啸着扑下山坡/开着门睡觉/埋着头走路/听着音乐做饭……

例（4）的“V_1着 V_2”结构是双事件单核结构，这一类是[+共时]“V_1着 V_2”结构中数量最多、频率最高的一类，在语料中占比 87%。两个动词独立性都比较强，是可以各自分立的两个动作，不以对方的发生为条件，因此看作双事件。同时，V_1和 V_2所表达的事件之间存在比较明显的主次关系，V_2描述主信息；V_1描述 V_2的伴随性背景信息，因此看作单核结构。

但是这一类的单核性不典型，如果在“V_1着”和 V_2之间加入语音停顿，结构就出现了异时性特征，如“站着，写/蹲着，吃/坐着，聊天/躺着，喘粗气”等。V_1和 V_2两个动词本身有可能是两个起点不同的动作事件，只是“V_1着 V_2”这个结构在编码时只关注共时的部分（如图 1 a，b，c 所示），并且区分出主次关系。这种主次关系是结构赋予的，而不是动作本身的关系。因此可见 V_1和 V2 的语义关系比较松散，事件融合度较低，是非典型的单核结构。

(2) V_1和 V_2融合度居中——V_1表情状义

例（5）硬撑着唱/支吾着说/引申着讲/偷着嘲笑/凑合着过/尝试着聆听……

例（5）的“V_1着 V_2”结构是单事件单核结构，这在[+共时]“V_1着 V_2”语料中占比 7.8%。V_1多表示心理或身体的内在状态，不能构成一个独立的动作行为，必须依附于 V_2的动作行为才能得以体现，V_1的独立性明显比前一类要低，对 V_2的依附性更强，V_1不能构成一个独立的事件。因此我们认为这一类是单事件结构。同时，V_1对 V_2的描写限制从外在转向内在，可比较“站着说”和“支吾着说”两个例子，“站”是对“说”的外在伴随情况的描写，“支吾”则是对“说”的内在情状的描写；“站”的动作行为可以独立于“说”单独成立，“支吾”则无法脱离“说”而单独成立。V_1和V_2的语义关系比上一小类更加紧密，两个动词之间的融合度更高，单核性质更突出。因此这一类“V_1着V_2”结构是比较典型的单事件单核结构。

（3）V_1和V_2融合度高（单事件/单核）——V_1表方式义

例（6）盯着看/跳着走/唱着说/跑着离开/摸索着寻找……

例（6）的“V_1着V_2”结构也是单事件单核结构，因为V_1和V_2的关系比较受限，所以数量和频率较前两者为低，在［+共时］“V_1着V_2”语料中占5.2%。这一类“V_1着V_2”结构中，虽然V_1和V_2都是行为动词，但它们并不表示两个各自独立的动作行为。两个动词描述的是同一动作，不同点是侧重的方面。例如“盯着看”，“盯”是动作的方式，“看”是动作的目的，“盯”就是“看”，“看”就是“盯”。例（6）中相当一部分是位移事件中的方式动词（manner verb）和路径动词（path verb）。由于事实上只发生了一个动作，只有一个事件，自然只能看作单核结构。这是三个小类里事件融合度最高的一类。

［+共时］“V_1着V_2”结构的上述三个小类，V_1从伴随、情状、方式的角度对V2进行限定和描写。处于从属地位的V_1事件逐渐融入处于主要地位的V2所表事件中，由双事件向单事件发展，由不太典型的多核结构向典型单核结构发展，主次关系分明。综上，从认知编码和事件融合两个方面来说，［+共时］“V_1着V_2”结构是状中结构。

其中，表示“情状”和“方式”的两个小类，事件融合度高，是比较典型的单事件单核结构，主次关系非常分明，但是它们的数量和频率不占优势；而数量最多、频率最高的是表“伴随”意义的第一小类（站着写/蹲着吃/坐着聊天……），并不是最典型的单核结构，处于多核结构过渡到单核结构的前端。

四、余论

通过上述两方面的论证，［－共时］和［±共时］“V_1着V_2”结构符合时序性和多核性特征，属于连动结构。［+共时］“V_1着V_2”具有共时性和单核性特征，属于状中结构，其形式、意义和语用都有愈加凝固的趋势。

同时，各种类型之间界限不是截然分明的，它们在形式和意义上都有密切的联系。从典型的连动式到最典型的状中式之间，“V_1着V_2”内部存在一个从［－共时］到［＋共时］、从双事件到单事件、从多核到单核的连续统，“V_1着V_2”结构的内部连续统如表1所示：

表1 “V_1着V_2”结构的内部连续统

时序性	主次关系	事件数量	事件融合度	V_1-V_2之间	句法属性	
鸡腿留着晚上吃	［－共时］	多核	双事件	不融合	能插入成分	连动
划着大船进入运河	［±共时］	～多核	双事件	不融合	能插入成分	连动
听着音乐做饭	［＋共时］	～单核	双事件	融合度低	插入的多是V1宾语	状中
凑合着过	［＋共时］	单核	单事件	融合度中	不能插入成分	状中
唱着说	［＋共时］	单核	单事件	融合度高	不能插入成分	状中

注：～表示非典型。

从表1可见，从连动式到状中式，“V_1着V_2”结构内部是一个渐变的连续统，是从异时到共时，从多核到单核，从双事件到单事件，从事件不融合到事件逐渐融合，从形式自由到形式逐渐凝固的连续统。

影响“V_1着V_2”句法属性最重要的因素有两个：一是两个动词之间的相对时间关系；二是动词所表事件的主次关系。动词词义、事件类型、结构特点、语码距离都会对这两个因素产生影响，这个方面值得我们进一步深入探讨。

参考文献：

［1］陈立民．时间的两种切分方式和“着”的语法意义［J］．语言教学与研究，2006（6）：9－18.

［2］戴浩一．时间顺序和汉语的语序［J］．国外语言学，1988（1）：10－20.

［3］戴耀晶．“VP_1＋着＋VP_2”结构的语义分析［J］．中国语言学报，2001（10）.

［4］丁崇明．现代汉语语法教程［M］．北京：北京大学出版社，2009.

［5］丁声树．现代汉语语法讲话［M］．北京：商务印书馆，1961.

［6］高增霞．现代汉语连动式的语法化视角［D］．北京：中国社会科学院，2003.

［7］胡树鲜．“着”的表情状方式的作用［J］．四平师院学报，2009（3）：87－93.

［8］李向农，张军．“V着V”结构的意义关系及结构中的“V”的语义特征分析［J］．华中师范大学学报，2001（3）：109－115.

［9］吕叔湘．中国文法要略［M］．北京：商务印书馆，1944.

［10］彭育波．“V1着V2”结构多角度研究［D］．上海：华东师范大学，2004.

[11] 沈家煊. 语法研究的分析和综合 [J]. 外语教学与研究，1999 (2)：1-8.
[12] 宋玉柱. 助词“着”的两种用法 [J]. 南开学报，1985 (1)：75-79，13.
[13] 孙朝奋. 再论助词“着”的用法及其来源 [J]. 中国语文，1997 (2)：139-146.
[14] 孙德金. 现代汉语动词做状语考察 [J]. 语言教学与研究，1997 (3)：116-129.
[15] 邢欣. 简述连动式的结构特点及分析 [J]. 新疆大学学报，1987 (1)：116-122.
[16] 詹卫东. 复合事件的语义结构与现代汉语述结式的成立条件分析 [J]. 对外汉语研究，2013 (1).
[17] 张伯江. 汉语连动式的及物性解释 [C] //语法研究和探索（九）. 北京：商务印书馆，2000.
[18] 张军. 现代汉语动词作状语的主要形式及动因分析 [J]. 华中师范大学学报，2014 (5)：100-108.
[19] 张志公. 汉语语法常识 [M]. 北京：中国青年出版社，1953.
[20] 赵元任. 北京口语语法 [M]. 李荣编，译. 北京：开明书店，1952.
[21] 赵元任. 汉语口语语法 [M]. 吕叔湘，译. 北京：商务印书馆，1979.
[22] 朱德熙. 语法讲义 [M]. 北京：商务印书馆，1982.
[23] Aikhenvald，Alexandra Y. Serial Verb Constructions in Typological Perspective. Serial Verb Constructions: a cross-linguistic typology [J]. *Folia Linguistica*，2006.

作者简介：

樊洁，语言学及应用语言学博士，西华大学文学与新闻学院讲师，主要研究方向为现代汉语语法、语义研究。